The 7 Secrets of Successful Parents

RANDY ROLFE

Foreword by Robert E. Kay, M.D.

CB

CONTEMPORARY BOOKS

Library of Congress Cataloging-in-Publication Data

Rolfe, Randy
    The 7 secrets of successful parents / Randy Rolfe.
        p.   cm.
    Includes bibliographical references and index.
    ISBN 0-8092-3156-5
    1. Parenting.   2. Child rearing.   3. Parent and child.
I. Title.   II. Title: seven secrets of successful parents.
HQ769.R637   1997
649'.1—dc20
                                                    96-31883
                                                    CIP

Interior design by Scott Rattray

I dedicate this book with all my love

to my husband,

to our children,

and to my parents.

Contents

Foreword

ROBERT E. KAY, M.D.

Those of us who spend a great deal of time watching television come to believe that the world is full of crime and violence. For parents it's an especially frightening prospect, and it's even more intimidating to kids. *The 7 Secrets of Successful Parents* goes a long way to liberating families from this kind of chronic worry, insecurity, and fear by empowering you the parent to create a more secure, nurturing, and accepting environment in which your children can grow into strong, good, mature, contributing, and convivial citizens.

It's true that the teenage murder rate in the inner city currently is getting worse. But adult criminality seems to be showing a slight decline. It's interesting to note that in the animal kingdom battles over territory usually end with the loser slinking away to fight again another day. But in 2 percent of the conflicts, signals to release the opponent get crossed, and one of the animals ends up dead. Meanwhile, all the wars in the history of humankind are estimated to have killed off roughly 2.1 percent of the population. According to history, then, we cannot expect to eliminate violence in our children's lifetime, but by the same token, it thankfully seems to have some limits.

Of course we have to continue to be concerned, because there are too many guns in private hands, and we know we can do better to help families who suffer malnutrition, devastated neighborhoods, joblessness, and lack of basic resources.

However, most people outside of the poverty areas living in fairly stable areas may expect never to personally encounter significant violence. As parents we can acknowledge, with Randy Rolfe in *The 7 Secrets of Successful Parents,* that despite our capacity for feeling threatened, frustrated, and angry we are fundamentally social creatures, programmed at birth by our genes to survive and reproduce, with each other's help—a very good example of cooperative behavior!

We are, of course, from the beginning a mass of needs: for safety, security, affection, comfort, pleasure, control over what happens to us, and good relationships with other people. But these needs are usually met by the parent or parent-surrogate, with varying degrees of success. And while it's true that no more than 20 percent of us appear to have achieved our full emotional and intellectual potential, it's also true that no more than 1 or 2 percent become criminals (even though some 12 percent of us have a significant psychiatric disability).

So in one sense we're not doing too badly, but in another sense, there is plenty of room for improvement. And this is where *The 7 Secrets of Successful Parents* comes in: to show us how to do it.

In my many years of practice as a psychiatrist working with children, adolescents, and families, I have seen that a child's growth is inevitable—if parents water the plant. But it also takes anywhere from 20 to 30 years before the brain is fully developed, and there is even reason to believe that we may continue to mature through age 60 or 70. So the good news is that no matter what age a child has reached, both the child and the parent are still growing and things can get better, as so beautifully illustrated in *The 7 Secrets of Successful Parents.*

We must also accept the fact that, despite the best of intentions, immature brains are going to produce spasms of immature behavior and thinking for a long time. Parents must expect the unexpected.

Also, we cannot control all the influences in our children's lives. This is especially true in a culture like ours, where children may be separated from their parents for many hours a day even in the first years. In addition, we give kids no meaningful work or role in society to help them mature, and they spend most of their time cared for by adults whose sole function is to manage children—not to parent them, love them, or share the spectrum of their lives with them.

Moreover, most kids are sent by age five to some form of school where passivity, obedience, physical inactivity, coercion, assessment, and judgments are the order of the day. Eighty percent of first-graders have a high self-esteem; no more than 5 percent of high school seniors still feel the same way. Ninety-nine percent of kindergartners enthusiastically play games; by 12th grade, we have 10 percent participants and 90 percent spectators. Though the child actually spends a mere 10 percent of his or her life inside a school building memorizing, regurgitating, and forgetting little hunks of disconnected subject matter, this figure hardly speaks to the full negative impact that the school system can have on most parent-child relationships. In *The 7 Secrets of Successful Parents,* Randy shows how to recognize and minimize these effects in each family, although as a society we need to do more to address the systemic problems.

In the meantime, here are a few observations about parenting today that may reflect some important truths and also stimulate some questions for which you can find the answers that best suit you and your family as you turn the pages of *The 7 Secrets of Successful Parents.*

• Respecting school, parents should get out of the school business and teach responsibility by giving the responsibility of school to the child—which is where it belongs. We needn't ask about homework or even grades unless the child asks our help or feedback, nor should we speak to the teacher unless the child asks us to. Few kids wish to fail if left to themselves, so 95 percent will respond eventually to this approach and perform satisfactorily in school. This one change alone can significantly reduce family stress and improve parenting success.

• Children should be treated like distinguished visitors from a foreign land, who are unfamiliar with our language and customs. The perfect parent is the one who does the correct thing 51 percent of the time. Make every mistake in the book, but try not to make the same ones over and over again.

• If kids look reasonably comfortable and happy most of the time to an observant interactive parent on the scene, then development is proceeding normally even if their behavior is at times distinctly unpleasant. Always try to put yourself in your child's place and ask, How would I like to be treated if I were small, immature, and dependent?

• Parents might do well to think of themselves as benevolent despots who are fundamentally in charge of the household and who can therefore give the kids plenty of room to maneuver. Children's freedom to swing their arms ends where our nose begins. Setting limits is relatively easy once a parent grasps the fundamentals—that is, we can let our boundaries be known, then counsel, hold, sit on, or grab our kids by the scruff of the neck and move them on out if they cross the boundaries we've defined. We just need to recognize when and how to do it.

• Or, in a pinch we can simply scream at the ceiling: "Your despicable behavior is causing me significant aggravation!" This response at least teaches some vocabulary, as well as getting across the important message that we are very unhappy with their behavior but are not going to take it out on them with threats of any kind. The idea is that there is nothing we can do about what has already happened except just feel as we feel for a moment. What we want from the perpetrators is to get them thinking about what they are going to do differently in a similar situation in the future. You can even have your own little tantrum, getting down on the floor and showing your child how to have a really good one. If you have the courage to be silly and let your child laugh with you at you, you both become human again, and you can quickly detoxify any situation!

• Getting kids to do things for you when you request it is an art that *The 7 Secrets of Successful Parents* can help any parent become more successful in. For instance, a great strategy is simply to say, "Let's go; let's do it together," or "Sure, I'll be glad to do that for you when you've done what I asked you to do a half-hour ago." But even this kindly coaxing is going too far if we are making a fetish out of eating a certain way or having them clean up their rooms, which moves into their territory and rightly meets with resistance.

• Basically, never take a hard line if you can't stick to it. That is, if it's not a life-and-death situation, a parent can't make a child do anything if he or she absolutely refuses, unless we make all sorts of threats and run the risk of ruining the relationship in the process. So choose your absolutes wisely and adjust them regularly. Every rule needs a sunshine provision.

• No child should be allowed more than one or two hours per day in front of a television, video game, or computer screen. Kids shouldn't have a television or computer in their own room either, especially in the early years, and one per family is best.

• Parents should be seen and not heard, except for perhaps an occasional "Hey, kids, please hate each other more quietly," or "I know this is going to make you angry at me, but xyz just has to be done," or to relate to their children simply as wonderful young people. Real, ongoing childhood anger is a reaction to threat, deprivation, or unsatisfied needs and must be distinguished from transient blowups of the immature, maturing brain.

Spanking with the bare hand on the clothed backside may, rarely, be necessary, but only if it's the only way to get a message across quickly in a dangerous situation like crossing the street.

• In many respects, as *The 7 Secrets of Successful Parents* illustrates, your child is the real expert on how to parent. Kids will tell you by their requests and reactions how they need to be raised from minute to minute. Your job is to read their reactions, listen, and think, while remembering that showing respect and kindness may be just as important and sometimes a lot easier than feeling unmitigated love.

• Once children are outside the front door, they are on their own, literally and figuratively. The saving grace is that their survival instinct is very powerful, which means that very few well-treated kids will let themselves get into major difficulties.

• But they will experiment. Expect every sort of deviant behavior at least once, short of real violence. And, please recognize the difference between experimental pot/alcohol/cigarette use and real addiction.

Finally, within our society's maelstrom of kindness, caring, support, community, coercion, threat, uncertainty, change, unpredictability, and growing awareness of the limits of technology for solving our human problems—within this maelstrom in which we must raise our kids—know that there are voices of sanity and reason that tell us how it should be done. Randy's is one of those voices.

She has the right idea, the willingness to put it into practice, and the determination to set it down here so that you will have the knowledge, the confidence, and the tools to become an ever more successful parent. I heartily recommend *The 7 Secrets of Successful Parents* to you. You'll want to refer to it again and again.

Acknowledgments

It can't be easy to be the child of a parenting–book author, but my son and daughter have made it look easy. They make me proud and happy and fill my days with delight. The faith and love of my husband is likewise a continuous joy, as is his willingness to try new approaches and help me learn what I need to know. I also thank my parents for their loving example.

My thanks to my clients and other mothers and fathers I have worked with, who always inspire me; to the many parents who helped by reading drafts of this book; to my editor, Kara Leverte, and Contemporary Books for their quality work; and to my agent, Ruth Wreschner, who has stuck by me since the start.

I thank also the many women and men who by their example and wise words have paved the way before me. I hope you will enjoy meeting them in these pages.

Lastly, thanks to you, my reader, for dedicating so much of your energy and love to being a more successful parent. May the world show its gratitude to you.

Every child born into the world is a new thought of God, an ever fresh and radiant possibility.

KATE DOUGLAS WIGGIN

In every child who is born, under no matter what circumstances, and of no matter what parents, the potentiality of the human race is born again; and in him, too, once more, and of each of us, our terrific responsibility toward human life; toward the utmost idea of goodness, of the horror of terror, and of God.

JAMES AGEE

All happy families resemble each other; each unhappy family is unhappy in its own way.

LEO TOLSTOY

A happy family is but an earlier heaven.

SIR JOHN BOWRING

Introduction

Success as a parent is the greatest investment you can make in your future, and it's your most creative act. It can bring you the greatest joy in your life and also your greatest challenges. You will become a more successful parent as soon as you begin to hear and absorb the seven secrets I want to tell you in this book. That's quite an assertion. But give me a few minutes of your time, and I think you will begin to agree.

As a loving parent who wants the best for your child, enough to read a book about how to do even better than you are already doing, you probably want most to know that what you contribute to your child's life will bring out the best in your son or your daughter. The seven secrets are all you require to do this successfully. They work because they show you how to make love real. Your child will respond to your parental love the way you want, once you learn how to make your love real in your child's life.

In this introduction, I will give you the background you need to grasp fully the power of these secrets. Then you can look forward to delving more deeply into the meanings, uses, skills, implications, and benefits of each of the seven secrets.

As you hear about each secret, I will describe case histories from the lives of some of the hundreds of mothers and fathers I have worked with as a family counselor and workshop leader. Only names and a few particulars have been changed to protect the privacy of the families—a value I hold very dear, as you may notice when we discuss the privacy issue in child rearing.

I will also be telling you true stories from my own life and from the lives of parents I have known over the years as friends, relatives, colleagues, and readers.

And I will be sharing with you engaging research from numerous disciplines that all touch on the human family and its successes and failures. I will also try to apply some good old common sense, a quality that can get shortchanged in our overly technical, multiopinionated world.

And finally, I will count on you to contribute your own wealth of observation, practice, and experience—as a parent, as a former child, and as a person—to your adventure here, discovering the seven secrets.

Some Important Thoughts

Between the case histories, true stories, research, good sense, and your own experience, I hope you will come to agree with these important points about the seven secrets:

- No matter what your situation you can be quite a successful parent, starting now and in the future.

- The place to start for motivating yourself to success is with a clear understanding of your own personal goals for parenting, staying as independent as possible of impositions by others or unfinished business from your own past.

- Successful parents are made, not born, so each parent is born with the power to be more successful.

- The seven secrets of successful parents are your ticket to that success because they identify the core attitudes and thoughts that motivate parents to success.

- You and your child can be the best and only judges of your success, though others will notice it.

- The seven secrets make sense, are easy to learn, and are impossible to forget once you make their acquaintance.

The seven secrets have brought success to thousands of parents across the nation and around the world. They have done it for me and my two children, and they can do it for you.

I did not invent them, but only uncovered them—through research, observation, interviews, and practice on my own kids—over the past 20 years. Imagine if the wisdom of thousands of parents were condensed into a book just for you. This is what I have tried to do.

My Personal Payoff

Here's why I want to share these great secrets with you:

First, I want you to benefit from the wonderful gift these secrets have been for me and for the thousands of other successful parents who helped me discover and develop them.

Second, since I know your parenting will now be successful, in the future both your children and mine will have a better world to live in, because they will now become healthier, happier people.

Third, I love the feeling I get when all I have learned in the past now benefits other people, saves them trouble and pain, and brings them real happiness. I love the light that goes on in a parent's face when she experiences her power to create success with her child. So write me and share that light with me after you have read this book!

Parents' Hopes Are Universal

All the parents I meet are sincere in their deep caring, concern, and love for their children. They are all trying their best.

You may have met parents whose behavior you found offensive and uncaring, but even these are most likely acting out of ignorance about themselves and their children. They act out sad scenarios of emotional stress that hurt them and their children unintentionally.

I know there exist parents who don't care about their children, but even in those cases, I can't help thinking that it is only out of desperation, helplessness, and hopelessness that they have shut down their passion for their kids.

Even mothers who are addicted to drugs and have lost their children to foster homes—I have met many on *Geraldo, Sally Jessy Raphael, Gordon Elliott,* and other shows—even these mothers wish desperately that it could have been otherwise. Basic parental love seems virtually universal. It can be a reliable beginning on which to build more successful parenting.

There is nothing sadder than a parent who because of poverty, addiction or other disease, or war or other violence is blocked from being a successful parent. But even in those cases, the depth of parental love cannot be denied, if only the parent is allowed to look into her heart, to learn about herself and her child, and to get support of the kind the seven secrets can give.

The thing that saddens me most when I am out among parents is that there is so little knowledge available to help them translate this universal parental love into successful parenting. I hope this book will make it so that the seven secrets are no longer secrets but are known to every parent.

The Lucky Ones

At the other extreme from these sad conditions are the parents like you who make up the vast majority I encounter in counseling and workshops around the country. Like them, you probably learn everything you can about parenting. You put your valuable resources of mind, body, spirit, and environment to its service. And you are willing to take time to read a book from a woman you probably have never met, who just might be able to help you be an even more successful parent than you already are!

My thanks and applause to you. I know you will enjoy this adventure I'm going to take you on, into yourself, around and around your dear child, and up into the clouds with both of you. I think it will exhilarate you and propel you into new joys of parenting. And as an extra bonus, I know that as you get more engrossed in the seven secrets, your example will inevitably rub off on those around you. Even parents who won't or can't read will eventually benefit from what you're hearing now.

From Parent to Parent

I know you are reading this book because of your dedication to being a successful parent. The reward will be that you will soon learn how these seven secrets of successful parents can immediately begin to improve your parenting success.

You will see the special benefits of reading each secret in a conversational form, even though each one is profound and could constitute an entire book in itself. I have tried to get to the meat of each feast of insight that the secrets offer, so that you can put them to work quickly and effectively. I hope you will agree I have done so.

I will present the seven secrets to you exactly the way successful parents say them in a conversation, often without knowing they are the real secrets behind the parents' success. By hearing the secrets in the words of everyday language that a friendly parent would use to share a secret, you can more easily and quickly put each secret to work for yourself.

Knowing You Are a Successful Parent

Once the seven secrets have become your secrets, your increased success can be just the beginning. As you start to put the power of these secrets to work for you, you can imagine yourself enjoying these other benefits:

- You not only are a successful parent, but you know it.

- You have a happy child, and you feel happy about your child.

- You feel good about your relationship with your child, and you sense your bright new outlook on your family's future.

- You have all the parenting strategies you need for this stage of your child's life, and you have confidence it will be the same for future stages.

- You have—or know how to get—all the support you need to feel great about your parenting.

- And you welcome all the extra support that comes to you, now that you are successful.

Once all these benefits are yours and the seven secrets become second nature, you can enjoy reading this book again and again. Coming back to it for a refresher will make you appreciate yourself in new ways you may not have thought of, and you may feel a companionship with the other successful parents you have met in these pages. And in rereading, you'll have taken a moment or two just to pat yourself on the back! Who can't use an occasional moment like that?

Now I'd like to have you hear a bit about my own parenting story and how I was initiated into the truth and power of the seven secrets of successful parenting.

My Parenting Adventure

Eighteen years ago I gave birth to a son, and two years later I gave birth to a daughter. They are the crabmeat cocktail and Dutch apple pie of the feast of experiences that has made up my life. The alpha and omega. My deepest connection with the creative power of the universe. How glorious it has been!

It's been the most demanding project of my life—even though I have had my share of demanding projects, including my delightful and ever growing marriage of more than 20 years, a legal career before switching to family counseling, the untimely death of my father, financial strains, health concerns, and all the other stuff you know all too well, I'm sure.

Parenting has also been the most stimulating experience of my life and certainly the most worthwhile. When I decided to spend time at home with each of my newborns, friends said I wouldn't be able to stand it; my intellect would go to mush. But it was the most intellectually stimulating enterprise of my life. Something new every day, and new ways of looking at the world through my child's eyes, and so much to learn about health, language, and being a mother! But I'm getting ahead of my story.

Preppie Preparations

Both of us from suburban backgrounds and what I like to call "overeducated," both with law degrees, my husband and I commuted into Philadelphia to ply our trade. We were in no rush to become parents because we wanted to get to know each other as a new family, and we each, I think, secretly knew we had some growing up to do. I wanted to feel fully baked before I put another generation in the oven!

However, we saw the commuter life gobbling us up and going nowhere, and we sought out other lifestyles. We spent a summer in France. We visited my great-uncle and -aunt, Scott and Helen Nearing (then 90 and 70), homesteading on the rocky coast of Maine. And we read about different lifestyles and how children fit into the picture of family and community. Plus I had traveled extensively with my parents who, lucky for me, wanted to see the world and wanted to take their children with them. In each spot, we talked about culturally distinctive family traditions and also noted the universals, and there were many.

With all this background, though we didn't know it then, we were formulating a distinctly new, holistic approach to being parents. We wanted to put family first, to use the power of positive thought, to respond directly to the good in each child, and to draw on the weight of human history and the spiritual connection to enrich our parenting.

Back to the Woods—and the Traditional Family

When we were finally ready for kids, we chose to leave the suburban life, where cultural pressures devalued the real demands of parenting and favored staying in the fast lane. We bought an old farmhouse on the edge of the Adirondack Mountains.

I'll never forget being up on the 40 percent pitch roof (necessary to shed all the snowfall), hammering on roof shingles, with my son protruding from my belly under a big sweatshirt! I was safely tied to a tree and was determined to stay active through my pregnancy. It was great!

In the rural farm community of upstate New York, family was the center of community life, and our new family thrived in the supportive atmosphere. People I hardly knew stopped by with gifts for the new baby when they saw diapers flapping in the wind. (There's nothing like sun-dried diapers and sheets for comfort and fragrance!)

A special bonus was our acquaintance with two expert native healers of the Iroquois nation on the St. Lawrence River, between the United States and Canada. They became our fast friends, midwifed our babies, served as our healers, and shared with us their spiritual heritage. They told us about the sacred wisdom of the Great Spirit and the injunction to plan seven generations ahead. Their influence stretched our European-American consciousness and continues to enlighten our thinking about what it is to be a parent.

Then the Reality

Like so many of our contemporaries, my husband and I had taken great care to consider when, why, and how we were going to be parents. But when I actually became a mother the experience bewildered me, with both joys and challenges. I was surprised by my lack of preparation in spite of my 20 years of education.

We talked endlessly about each detail, we read, we talked to friends, we tried to tap into cultural wisdom and our own experience as kids, we watched and listened to our children as they made their needs known to us, and we tried always to keep an open mind and trust the process, with God's good grace.

All our attention and efforts paid off. We have had a wonderful experience. We have enjoyed each age and learned constantly as all of us grew some each year in mind and spirit—and body in the kids' case!

The Value of Sharing

It didn't take long after my babies' births for me to discover the value of sharing my experiences with other parents. Soon I discovered people were seeking me out for guidance because of our success. Without knowing it, during my semiretirement from law, I was beginning my new, lifetime career helping families.

Meanwhile, sudden and severe recession in our rural county forced us to leave our rustic home. Even the farmers who had grown up on their farms could hardly afford to stay, and they watched as their children left. We returned to Philadelphia, trying always to live somewhere between suburbia and country and trying to apply all we had learned as our children grew.

Both my husband and I made choices in our careers that allowed us to keep family first. We struggled to develop our own businesses so that we would have flexibility and control over our time. We made adjustments in other areas of our lives to suit our family-centered living. We faced all the issues of schooling, nutrition, relatives, health, entertainment, moving, communication, friends, sports, rules, sitters, and more and came up with creative solutions that benefited our family. With each choice, adjustment, and issue we faced, our commitment to the seven secrets became stronger because these crucial ideas made our way clear and guided us to success.

I tried returning to law practice and taught law school for a time, but I discovered my heart was elsewhere, in helping to create healthy families. I wrote and published a book on parenting,

You Can Postpone Anything but Love, and I began a family counseling practice. Then I wrote another parenting book, and another with my husband.

Our son is now grown and beginning college, and our daughter is beginning to drive, one year of high school to go. We find ourselves proud and happy parents, watching fondly as our children go out to find their own way with confidence, skill, and wisdom—things we helped bring into their lives by applying the seven secrets.

Everything I have seen in clinical practice and in my travels all over the country and overseas has reinforced my faith in and commitment to the seven secrets. For me and many others, they epitomize the wisdom of the human family.

Now I am doing my best to pass on the seven secrets to you with this book. I hope you will make full use of them so that your life as a parent will be richer, more worry free, and ever more successful.

Before taking you straight to the secrets, I want to take a quick look with you at some special aspects of parenting today.

The Great Parenting Experiment

Parents born in the second half of this century are as large and literate a group of parents as the United States has ever known. Like many of these parents, you probably ask lots of questions and expect real answers. You are eager to hear what experts have to say about everything, and then you like to make up your own mind. You want fresh new ways of looking at old methods. You want knowledge of how to make families really work. You take what your parents gave you and try to break new ground. And you are committed to making a better world.

What better way than by being a successful parent?

On the Move

Along with this personal penchant for fresh and real advice, social and economic pressures have made parents seek out more help and support than ever. After World War II we became a mobile society. Children moved away from parents as never before, setting up families far away because of jobs or college. Extended families that had once offered ready guidance about child rearing were no longer there to offer help and support.

Without that homegrown family support, parenting that used to be a private family thing has entered the arena of public discussion. We wanted more help from our community and society to replace the close-knit extended family. I'm sure you have noticed how politicians have discovered the greater demands of parents for a more supportive community and country.

Strapped for Cash

On the economic front, today's parents have to fit parenting into ever more efficient time slots. For two-parent families, if you want your kids to grow up with the same standard of living that you had, you need to have two incomes today, where just one could do fine for your parents. And most parents are still wedded to the American ideal that their child's quality of life should be better, and certainly not worse, than theirs.

For single-parent families, you must squeeze parenting into fewer hours than if you had a partner to share the chores and income demands. And the demands are double for emotional support for your child.

With the increasing number of blended families, there are also larger numbers of unrelated children under one roof, and more complicated relationships, further adding to the demands on parents today.

For these reasons, parents want more than ever to do things right the first time—and quickly. They demand shortcuts to everything, including successful parenting. I hope you will soon agree that the seven secrets can be your shortcut.

The Fear Factor

There's still another reason parents want more advice and support than ever. It's the steady stream of scary stories from media, teachers, other parents, clergy, doctors, your own kids, and more. Just when time and resources are decreasing, dangers are increasing. The "sex, drugs, and rock and roll" that scared our parents seem like the good old days. No wonder we want help!

Life magazine put this list of childhood dangers on its July 1995 cover with the title "How Can We Keep Our Children Safe? Sex Abuse, Abduction, Television, Accidents, Neglect, Violence, Drugs, Vulgarity and Alienation." They didn't even mention AIDS, depression, learning disorders, sexual identity crises, parenticide, virtual reality, runaways, children divorcing parents, shopping addiction, malnutrition, eating disorders, sports competitiveness, exhaustion, aftermath of divorce, environmental allergies, increasing use of nicotine and alcohol, and even contaminated hamburgers! It's darned scary.

However, once you have the seven secrets in your pocket, you can become free of fear that your child will become one more statistic. In fact, together we can even change the statistics!

Creating Congruence of Love and Action

Whenever you bring your deepest love and your moment-to-moment decisions and actions into harmony, you feel and become successful, according to leading experts on motivation and management, including author Stephen Covey, corporate consultant Charles Hobbs, and others. They teach that the greatest success and satisfaction in life—at home and at work—come to you when your moment-to-moment choices are in complete agreement with your highest motivating principles.

As you apply the seven secrets to your parenting, you will discover that your satisfaction will grow each day, because this is what the seven secrets do. They bring your everyday words and actions into complete agreement with your core parental love.

The seven secrets move you from your deep parental love to successful parenting, one moment and one choice at a time. As you may know from experience, each choice you make as a parent can mean the difference between a bad day and a good day, a hurt child and a happy one, a perturbed parent or a peaceful one.

Imagine, then, if you would, that a friend is swapping parenting stories with you in your living room and the deepest secrets of her parental heart burst out for your benefit. As you absorb what you hear, these seemingly simple secrets will go to work in your life immediately, to ring in sweet success.

How to Use This Book

As you hear about each secret in the chapters to come and imagine how what you hear can apply in your own situation, you may wonder about the specific age, stage, and other developmental circumstances of your child. Parenting is a gradual process of change, and things you say and do one year may need modification the next year, or even month to month. Often situations call for radical rethinking or readjustment of attitudes and solutions that have worked fine before.

These times can be scary and frustrating, and we often don't come up with the ideal response to each situation. But with parenting, you virtually always get a second chance with a similar situation. Luckily the relationship of parent and child is so close and vital that no matter how poorly we have responded to a situation, opportunities will present themselves soon again for us to do a better job.

With each secret, I will sketch for you specific ways in which that secret applies across the years, so that you can feel more confident in using the secrets at each distinct age. Likewise, I will be giving you examples of parenting situations sometimes involving a son and sometimes a daughter, from the point of view now of a mother and now of a father, so that you can best imagine how the examples might apply to your family. (For this reason too, I have chosen to alternate the pronouns "him" and "her," and "she" and "he," from one situation to another when speaking generally about a child or a parent.)

Always keep in mind that no generalities in this book or anywhere else can substitute for your own keen observation and intuition about your child. Each child develops at his own pace, with tremendous variation even between siblings. Each parent must feel her own way, led by the child himself, who is the one and only final arbiter of his needs.

Making Love Real

To end this introduction, I'd like to share a letter from a reader of one of my previous books. As I learned from the letter, my correspondent is both a parent and a psychologist. She writes: "No one else I've read or heard of has so well 'operationalized' love for me as you have—and our whole family has benefited. I appreciate your ability to use your brilliance to such nonmental and graceful ends. Thank you for the work you've done with yourself."

Operationalize is a big word, but it just means making love real in everyday life. Since that book, I have tried to condense even further the essence of parenting, and you have in your hands the result.

Clare Boothe Luce said, "Love is a verb."

When you begin to use the seven secrets, you may get excited about parenting like you never have before. You will have the pleasure of seeing yourself begin to operationalize love—to actualize it, effectuate it, proclaim it, communicate it, reveal it, unfold it, display it, manifest it, fulfill it, and make it real, in everything that goes on between you and your child. Parents tell me they develop a new feeling of awareness and control about their lives with their children.

Please keep reading to see exactly how the seven secrets can turn even the most frustrated and confused parent into a parent full of confidence and joy—and that may be you.

You can feel you have concrete tools to help you in any situation that arises with your child—whether you're feeling tense or calm, in charge or on the sidelines, tired or gung ho, prepared or unprepared, supported or hanging out on a limb. Imagine how wonderful you can feel, knowing that whatever comes up in your family's life you will know exactly how to do your part to create the best outcome and how to foster the most agreeable process along the way to help your family grow in freedom, strength, and joy.

Every child comes with the message that God is not yet discouraged of man.

RABINDRANATH TAGORE

The men of old wanting to clarify and diffuse throughout the empire that light which comes from looking straight into the heart and then acting, first set up good government in their own states; wanting good government in their own states, they first established order in their families; wanting good order in their families, they first rectified their hearts.

MENG-TZU

Cruel blows of fate call for extreme kindness in the family circle.

DODIE SMITH
(PSEUDONYM C. L. ANTHONY)

No, I don't understand my husband's theory of relativity, but I know my husband and I know he can be trusted.

ELSA EINSTEIN

"I would never give up on my child."

❖ Faith ❖

In a recent interview, the head of the school district of the city of Philadelphia said that today's city schools fail so often because they lack faith in their children. Superintendent David Hornbeck affirmed that when an adult has faith in a child, two things happen. First, the adult becomes more optimistic, so that his words and actions toward the child point in a more positive direction. Second, this new attitude from the adult empowers the child to learn and grow with more courage and enthusiasm. Hornbeck asserted that the schools will succeed as soon as they really believe that "every child can succeed."

This is the kind of faith you need to have in your own child in order to bring out her best. "I would never give up on my child" is the embodiment of that faith. It's the first and most important secret of successful parents. Parental faith supports a can-do attitude. It enables you to carry on, knowing that things will work out, that your child will be all right, that you are all right as a parent, and that the whole universe is on your side, helping you raise a healthy, happy child. And this is true no matter what it looks like on the outside, or on any given day.

Faith Fundamentals

So that you can get the most out of the examples, case histories, and practical tips in this chapter, please take a moment to absorb these fundamental ideas about how your faith in your child enables you to become a more successful parent:

- You deserve to have faith in your parenting. You are naturally inclined to do your best at parenting and to want the best for your child, and you can depend on that.

- Your child deserves your faith. Your child naturally depends upon you, believes in you, wants to please you if at all possible, and seeks to be happy, healthy, and independent. You can depend on these.

- Your faith need not fear any challenge. When problems arise, you may need to rethink old assumptions, change old attitudes, make new choices, say different things, take fresh action, or alter old habits. But, you never need to abandon faith in your child or to withhold your love.

- Faith attaches to the person, not the problem. If you're careful to distinguish between behavior of your child, which you may not like, and the person of your child, which forever has your faith, you will find that unshakable faith in the person is your ticket to more agreeable behavior.

- Your child always tends to respond eventually to your faith. Your child will meet you halfway in any new efforts you make, as soon as he recognizes them to be genuine.

- Faith puts your past behind you and welcomes the future. With some effort daily, your faith can liberate you from self-defeating feelings from the past and worries about the future, so each day you feel more confident and successful.

A Test of Parental Faith

"I would never give up on my child" means you would always believe your child meant well, had goodness in her heart, did the best she knew how, and would be true to herself as best she could, no matter what the evidence showed.

I have seen this kind of faith pay off many times.

First, an example from the annals of Hollywood. Hollywood is famous for dysfunctional families. But, in at least one celebrity family, parenting seems to be a success. Donna Lawrence is the mother of Joey, a teen star on the sitcom *Blossom*. When that show ended after a long run, heartthrob Joey and his two brothers became the stars of another sitcom, entitled *Brothers*.

A favorite of teenagers, Joey is also a favorite of their parents. Why? Because of his sensible attitude and clean living—despite wealth, fame, and adoring fans. His mother is outspoken about how she has avoided parenting pitfalls. Recently an interviewer challenged her obvious faith in her son. What would Donna do, the interviewer asked, if Joey said he wanted to go out with a particular Hollywood starlet of rowdy reputation?

Donna said simply, "He wouldn't say it." She had complete faith that she knew her son and that he wouldn't do something so out of character. Then just to drive home her point, she added that if he did say it, then, "I would have to believe that every single thing that's been written about her is untrue."

That's the kind of faith I hope you want to have in your child. If some event seems to contradict your faith, then you must rethink everything rather than give up on your child.

In my own family, faith saved us all from a dark night getting even darker. I had been married just a year when my mother called at 4:30 A.M. and told me this story.

At three o'clock that morning, my father had answered the phone. A police officer asked if he had a red car registered to his name. It was his, yes, but his son had it with him away at college. The officer said that unfortunately there had been an accident, the car was wrapped around a telephone pole, and the young man driving was dead. They had called the registered owner because the driver wasn't carrying any identification.

My parents panicked, but then my father said, "Wait, let's review this. It's not like our son to be out at 2:30 in the morning." They talked about it and realized they had no idea how late he stayed out now that he was at college. Crying resumed.

But wait, my father thought, he would never be out without his wallet. Never. They took hope. They called his room.

My brother answered, sleep in his voice. Imagine his surprise when both parents swooned on the phone and treated him as if they feared they would never see him again! Later he told me it took a while to piece the story together between his sleepy confusion and their hysterical excitement. It turned out his car had been parked outside his window, but sure enough when he looked out it was gone. It had been stolen and the thief had killed himself in the crash, after a high-speed chase with the police.

For my parents it had been such an incredible roller-coaster ride; they wanted to retell it to me just to get some perspective on it. Here were two parents whose faith in their child saved them from giving up, even when the evidence was enough for the police to suspect the worst had happened to their son.

One of my clients, Midge, had a parallel experience. She had dropped her 10-year-old son, Jeff, off at his friend Pete's and planned to pick him up at 4:00 P.M. When she called at 3:30 to say she would be a little late, Pete's grandmother was in tears. She explained that she had sent the boys to town to get a haircut for Pete and had just received a call from him saying hysterically, "We're in New Jersey and can't get home," and were cut off.

Midge was frightened. She had been working hard trying to keep faith in Jeff in spite of his tendency to go always a little beyond what she authorized and to forget to tell her exactly where he was going. But she said to herself, "This is a big step, worse than anything he's ever done. I can't believe it." She hung on to that hope while she and Pete's mother tried to sort out the grandmother's story and find the boys.

Eventually they found them walking home from the barbershop. It turned out that the call from New Jersey had been a wrong number! Perhaps the frightened boy hung up when he didn't recognize the voice of the grandmother. They will never know. But Midge felt wonderful about her faith, and so did her son.

In another case, Jill returned home to find her husband, Gene, calling all over the neighborhood. Their child was supposed to have arrived home on the bus just 10 minutes before his father but could not be found. They called the police, who assumed he had run away. But Jill and Gene had faith in their son, traced all his connections from school to home, and finally found him asleep in the bus at the home of the bus driver.

These true stories show the kind of faith successful parents exhibit in their children. What happens when faith is lost?

A Loss of Faith

My client Mary was staring down at her neat green skirt and wringing her hands. She had been trying some new communication techniques with her daughter, Erin, who was "11, going on 25."

"What if I never get this?" she worried. "It's so hard to remember to be patient when she's pressing my panic buttons. What if it's already too late? What if Erin never listens to me? What if she has already given up on me?"

The problem was that Mary had already given up on Erin. You may be able to read between her lines. She was afraid that she could never establish a good relationship with Erin because she had made too many mistakes already as a mother. She waffled between resentment, hopelessness, and self-pity.

Erin sensed her mother's lack of faith and was nasty and short with her without even knowing why, except that she thought her mother didn't really care about her, only about controlling her.

Deep down, Mary feared that Erin couldn't heal, that the damage was permanent, that she didn't deserve Erin's forgiveness even if Erin could give it, and that she could never forgive herself. Mary had settled for control, but after a certain age even that is impossible. So her frustration was acute.

Mary was wrong to suppose that she had so much power in Erin's life that she could permanently mess her daughter up and leave no room for things to get better. If given half a chance, a child will heal and forgive. She will meet you halfway. It's up to the parent to give her the chance. Mary's job was to let go of any assumption that her past actions could limit Erin's potential. She needed to forgive herself for past mistakes.

Mary felt tempted to struggle with self-blame and make excuses for why she hadn't been a better parent. And she had to fight a habit of collecting explanations to excuse her mistakes or delude herself that they weren't as bad as they were.

But she worked hard to stay in the present and bolster her belief in Erin's internal strength and vitality and in her own ability to change gradually for the better. Success came more quickly than she expected, once she let go of her circular thinking and focused her thoughts on her faith in her child.

Many parents have told me it must be too late to take a positive, optimistic, faithful attitude. Their children were too old, they feared. With some, their children were only six or seven years old. With others, a child of 20-something had broken off relations. Each case has shown that it is never too late. Patience and expressions of faith always reach the child. It's in the genes.

Daily habits are the hardest thing in the world to break. Any physician will tell you it is easier to get dozens of sick patients to take prescription medications regularly than to get one patient to change her lifestyle so that she will stay well. So go easy on yourself when you decide you want to make changes. It will take time. But it will happen.

Faith in the Person, Not the Behavior

"I would never give up on my child" is really the basic proposition of unconditional love. You can keep your faith in your child because you set no conditions on it. You continue to love your child as a person, even when you must set limits on the unwanted behaviors of your child the actor.

My client Dave did not understand how he could keep faith in his son Sam when he knew Sam was "heading for juvenile hall." Sam had taken to going into Dave's wallet, which Dave kept on his dresser. Sam would pull out a few dollars to buy candy, which he would then give out at school to win friends and be more popular.

Dave feared that if he couldn't force his son to respect his possessions, he would lose faith in him altogether and abandon him to a future of delinquency. Dave confused faith and trust.

Having Dave lose trust was a natural consequence of Sam's stealing. Any child would expect it. Faith doesn't mean you must trust untrustworthy behavior. In fact, if you know your faith will not waver, you may find it easier to be firm about behavior. You know it will be worth it, because you have faith in the lovable kid underneath all the nonsense.

In contrast, the child will not expect you to lose your faith, your unconditional love. Every child that's born has the right to expect that he has a champion in this world, someone who is unconditionally devoted to his welfare. In fact, a child may subconsciously test the strength of your faith and love by acting untrustworthy, especially if they have been in doubt. Tough love is what you need when trust and faith are at odds. Draw lines and boundaries where you must, but don't lose faith.

Dave needed to admit he could not trust his child right now, while holding on to his faith in Sam. Once he got some practice, it got easier. He affirmed as often as he could how much he loved and believed in his son. He initiated discussions about how important it was to him that he be able to trust Sam with his things.

With all the little indignities Dave was accustomed to imposing on Sam, it took some time to demonstrate he had faith again. It helped Dave to notice Sam's social motives for buying the candy. Sam wanted to be liked by people but was just going about it wrong. Eventually Dave also had to look honestly at himself. He had to own up to the fact that his own example of respecting others' things hadn't been so good.

Dave started to see that Sam's disrespect for his father's possessions wasn't a result of not knowing what was right and wrong or of not caring. Sam's behavior stemmed from mixed feelings about himself and his father and had taken this particular form because Dave himself didn't model appropriate behavior.

Dave realized that, in the past, he had thought nothing of barging in on Sam in his room and accosting him about his homework, or taking Sam's bike and locking it up if he didn't like the way he had mowed the lawn, or taking away Sam's favorite CD if he didn't like the way Sam spoke to his mother. Dave found he had to change a lot in order to create a safe environment and set an example of mutual respect. As Dave set a better example and trusted Sam's desire to be good, Sam caught on quickly and the stealing stopped. With more emotional support at home, even the drive to be popular at school was not so tempting.

Even better, Dave's relationship with Sam got on an altogether better footing. Dave reached a point when he could hardly remember feeling uncomfortable about saying, "I would never give up on my child."

Faith in Your Child's Own Timing

When my daughter first entered kindergarten her teacher told me she was doing very well, except for one little thing. She was shy about joining in with group activities. I explained that it was my approach to have faith in her ability to decide for herself when she was ready to participate. If we had faith in her personal sense of timing and her own developing intuition about her personal capacities and limits (as long as the particular situation was a safe one), then she would find her own best stride in each situation.

The teacher respected my approach and, before long my daughter was happily participating in group activities, with neither pushing nor coddling, but instead with faith in her ability to respond in her own good time to a fun and safe social situation.

You may have observed that accidents happen when we are either forcing ourselves to rush into something before we are ready, or when we are pressing on with an activity beyond our limits of concentration or endurance. So it is with our children.

I believe that one reason my own children have had very few mishaps in their childhoods has been my and my husband's willingness as parents to show faith in their ability, both innate and developed, to know when to start an activity and when to stop.

A child can rush into something against her better instincts in response to pressure from a parent, teacher, peer, or other role model. She may want to prove herself, to meet others' expectations or demands, or to test limits someone else has imposed. But in contrast, if you allow your child to develop her own sense of her capacities and limits so she will know when it is best for her to start or finish—always with guiding tips from parents, of course—accidents will be few.

So if you wish your child to begin an activity, whether it be a small one like putting away today's toys, or a big one like taking up dance or karate lessons, don't insist it be done right away. Allow a little time for her to assess, adjust, get in the mood, set aside her preoccupations, get an impression, or get herself psyched. Likewise, when she thinks it's time to stop, honor that inclination. Have faith that if more needs to be done, she'll see the need and proceed with it later.

The Many Spheres of Faith

The secret of faith can apply to many different spheres of your child's life. Your faith in yourself and your child, and in the positive power of your relationship together, will benefit you whether you are operating in the emotional, social, or physical spheres. You may easily see how a parent's faith can pave the way for smooth progress in the emotional and social spheres, as in the previous examples. But what can it do in the physical sphere?

Much is being done to explore the mind-body connection today, and the limits of faith in physical healing are far from clear. An experience I had with my son has certainly left my mind open to its potential. One summer when the family was on a camping trip, my 16-year-old son was teaching himself to whittle with a little pocket knife and a stick from the woods. Suddenly I heard him say, "Mom!" with a deep tone I couldn't remember ever hearing before. I ran to where he was sitting. He said slowly, "I cut off the top of my little finger." Later he told me he tried hard to say it in a way so that I wouldn't freak.

I certainly thought of doing just that, but the situation seemed too serious to afford me that luxury. I remembered instantly a book I had read about working with the body in a crisis. I kept calm, affirming my faith in the wisdom of his young body, as long as it didn't go into panic mode.

I quickly had him sit down, because he was becoming faint. He had cut off the top three-eighths of an inch of his finger, through to the nail. I asked him to realign the tip perfectly and to hold it gently and firmly in place, while thinking good thoughts about the power of his tissues to reconnect. Then we talked quietly about the healing powers of his finger, and of his whole body and mind, and about his ability to make the finger whole again without any permanent damage. As he listened in a kind of joint meditation, I said every positive, affirming thing I could think of. When it seemed time to do something else, we discovered two hours had passed.

We made a little tentlike hat perched on a splint to attach to his finger, so that it could get lots of air but could not be accidentally touched or bumped. We drenched it in vitamin E oil to help healing and prevent infection. Then he slept a couple of hours and rose to join his campsite friends.

There was no inflammation and little pain. Each day we shared some positive thoughts. In a week he could find no sign of the cut. In a month he had full sensation in his fingertip. His friends thought it was a miracle. I saw with my own eyes that a faithful attitude can do such things.

When physical (or any other kind of) trauma does happen, it may be more than a parent can handle without help. One of the positive thoughts my son and I shared that day was that if either of us or his father thought his finger needed medical attention, we would go to the hospital right away. In that case, we just never reached that point. But a parent needs to have faith in her own sense of when to get help, just as in all other things.

Like your faith in your child's sense of timing and personal limits, so too you must have faith in your own sense of timing and your own personal limits. Another parent might have taken her son to the emergency room right away, or another child might have wanted it, or another father might have insisted, and that would have been the right thing for that family. If you cultivate this faith and apply it to any situation after gathering the essential information, you are then most likely to succeed, and least likely to be pulled off track by inappropriate, though well-meaning, expectations or advice.

Faith Never Gives Up

Here's one more story about faith in your child's power and right to be well and happy and in your own power and right to parent. While I watched their six-year-old daughter, Ellen, play cheerfully nearby, Alice and Ben told me the story of her younger years.

Ellen had cried her first two years of life. Alice had talked to every expert she knew, or that anyone else knew. Her marriage was falling apart because doctors suggested she was just a hysterical mother and the child was reacting to that. Ben was confused and angry. Alice cried herself to sleep worrying about her daughter's pain and distress. She saw psychiatrists, counselors, allergists, pediatricians, neurologists, and more.

At last someone suggested she see a research physician at a local teaching hospital. She told him the whole story and sat in tears. He opened his drawer and pulled out a typed sheet of paper headed "The Chocolate and Milk Tension-Fatigue Syndrome." He mentioned it was based on new research. She almost kissed him and zoomed home ecstatic to try the cure.

Chocolate milk was the only thing that had ever consoled her daughter. Now she knew it was all an allergic reaction that had begun as an untreated allergy to the cow's milk she had drunk while breastfeeding. Ellen's horrible mood swings disappeared within days after Alice took her off all products containing either sugar, cow's milk, caffeine, or chocolate. Within three weeks, her daughter was acting like any other child her age.

Alice was surely a mother who could have given up—on her child, on herself, on her husband, on her ability to be a mother, on doctors, on society, and even on life as a whole. But she didn't. She kept her faith, sought an answer, and found one.

If in your gut you know there is a solution, just don't take no for an answer. Keep trying and you will succeed.

Some problems are beyond help. For example, the film *Lorenzo's Oil* portrayed a mother's search for a cure for her son's rare degenerative disease. Even her husband worried that she was becoming obsessive. She did find help because of her persistence and determination and faith. She did not find a total cure, but her faith empowered her to do everything she could. She knew she had made her love real for her child. She never gave up on her child, and his and her lives were better for it. When there is no cure, as with some birth defects, the family with faith finds ways to adjust with the greatest creativity and confidence.

Faith as a Weapon?

Many parents fear revealing the extent of their faith to their child because they are afraid to give up their ultimate weapon of control. They have been influenced by our culture to think that parental disapproval is a crucial tool, and they confuse disapproval of the child's behavior with loss of faith in the child's person.

The desire for approval is a powerful motivator for a child. When a parent is happy, the child's environment tends to be much more serene. The child likes it that way and is motivated to please. But a parent can be displeased without giving up faith. The threat that you will give up on your child is another matter. Do you need this threat? At what cost do you maintain it? What are the alternatives?

For a child, the threat of loss of faith is the threat of death. It's an excessive threat, the cost is too high, and the alternatives are far more effective, with no side effects. Let me explain.

Human emotions were developed in the context of life in the wild, formed as they were when we roamed as small tribes contending daily with the natural elements. If a parent lost faith in a child back then, he and the community lost interest, which meant the child would die of exposure.

The threat of lost faith, then, is the threat of death to a child, and a child who lives with that threat can never feel that the higher things of life are within his reach. Survival, not living, is the goal, and manipulation, not cooperation, becomes the child's survival strategy. That's too high a cost.

In contrast, when your child knows for sure that you will never give up on him, you have an ally in your parenting, where otherwise you would have a scared and desperate opponent. When you are clear, patient, honest, firm, and faithful, you will be successful not only at getting your child to change undesirable behavior but also at building your child's emotional health, mental skills, and confidence for the future.

A Natural Foundation of Faith

Jean Liedloff is a family counselor who has studied several Stone Age peoples of South America. As have researchers before her like Margaret Mead, Ashley Montagu, and others, Liedloff marveled at the ease and cooperation and contentment with which tribal peoples parent. She concluded that the core of their success was absolute faith that their children were good and whole and innately ready to be a valuable part of the family and tribe.

Liedloff asserts that the tribal parent's ability to make the children feel unconditionally "worthy and welcome" prevented the kinds of daily conflicts with parents, siblings, and friends that plague modern families.

Worthy and welcome. These Stone Age people would have no trouble at all saying, "I would never give up on my child." On a radio panel discussion on *Alternatives in Education,* Liedloff told this story of an enterprising father who invented a playpen.

Tribal parents usually carry small children everywhere with them until the age of four or so. But this enterprising young father built a little pen and put his child in it. The child immediately protested. So without a second thought—with absolute faith in the child's innate wisdom, said Liedloff—he smashed the playpen and discarded the debris.

Attacks on Parental Faith

In modern times, it might seem hard for a new parent to have that much faith in a child. If you buy a playpen and the child cries in it, you may think he should adjust because everyone else seems to have one, and it seems to be all right. Or you may get a sinking feeling that if he doesn't adjust as quickly as the kid next door, there is something wrong with him or perhaps with you as a parent. Or you may have never known a family that did without any playpens. You may feel you have no alternatives. Carrying the baby all the time may seem impossible.

Unfortunately, Madison Avenue knows just how to feed on our little slips of faith. There are plenty of products for sale to make the pen more interesting.

My mother told me I was never happy in a playpen. And I remember my sister and brother weren't either. Neither were my own children, unless I was right there playing with them. The pen was only helpful for the two minutes it took to pull something out of the oven, and I was talking the whole time, too. A playpen may substitute only briefly for the lap of a grandma or the hip of an uncle.

The Stone Age community nods knowingly and encourages faith in the child. Unfortunately, many of our own community's voices say things like this:

"Don't spoil him!"

"You can't be at his beck and call all his life!"

"He needs to learn to be without you!"

"He's just a momma's boy!"

"He sure has you wrapped around his little finger."

"Let him cry; it's good for his lungs!"

"Playpens are a great invention. Why stress your back and grow old before your time?"

Let the voices jabber. If you and your child decide the playpen works, that's fine. If you decide it doesn't, that's fine too.

Our egos feel safer when we follow convention, no matter how distorted it may be. If a conventional solution fails, people say, "Oh well, you tried." If it succeeds, they tell you how smart you are. But if something original fails, people shake their heads. And if something original succeeds, they declare you lucky.

Convention serves a purpose. It gives you a background against which to make your decisions. You don't have to start everything from scratch. But when convention conflicts with your deepest inclinations or those of your child, then faith gives you the natural foundation and courage to do what's right for you.

Applying the Secret of Faith Through the Years

At first, during the years of infancy, showing faith means mainly staying as relaxed as you can with your baby, knowing that you were chosen to be your baby's parent exactly because you are the most fit one for the job! When you believe in your child's inner capacity for survival, health, and success and in your own capacity for meeting his needs adequately if not perfectly and for learning all you need to know to do that, you will be more peaceful in your parenting. Automatically your baby will also feel more safe, secure, and relaxed.

As your child grows, the same faith allows you to go through all those exciting moments of first rolling over, first solid foods, first crawl, first walk, and first talk, as well as first cry, first fall, first parting, and so on, with the least stress possible. Faith in your baby and yourself helps you resist competition with other parents about exactly when and how these milestones happen. At the same time, it allows you to trust your own instincts about healthy development, so that you can get help with any problems in time.

In this stage, you can show your faith mainly by your smiles, your tone of voice, your affectionate touches, your encouraging words, and your being there as much as you can.

As your child becomes more verbal in the toddler stage, around 18 months to four years, your faith will take the form of affirming words that serve to empower your child to keep growing and learning and to show confidence in his ability to gain mastery in his life and your ability to guide him. When you set limits on your child's behavior, your faith in his desire to learn from you will go far toward inspiring his cooperation and to helping you avoid provocative tones that invite your toddler's antagonism.

Your child grows in freedom and begins to focus on interests of his own choosing from around age four to seven, what we can call the exploratory stage. Your expressions of faith in his own positive destiny, his many options, and his maturing inner guidance system will allow him to seek his potential with confidence. Even when your wills conflict, your faith will keep the conflict in perspective, so that you both will hang in there with love and respect until a resolution can be found. Patience and creative ideas come from faith. Words of appreciation, praise, and positive projections for your child's future are just some of the ways of showing your faith at this stage.

More challenges to your faith may come from the outside as your child interacts with other children, adults, childcare, or schools. In each case have faith that, whatever went on, your child is still the good little person you knew so well at home and if there's trouble, it can be resolved without your losing faith.

Disappointments can be dealt with in an atmosphere of faith, by readjusting your thinking to allow for new possibilities and to find the help you need to get over any hurdles and begin anew from your new position.

Your child begins to have a life outside of yours with school or other activities, from age 7 to 14, what we can call the growth years. Faith in your child and your own parenting so far will save you endless worry as well as ineffectual efforts to control situations now beyond your power to control.

We never get the chance to put finishing touches on our kids. By now they have some of their own ideas. Don't demand perfection of yourself or them. Meanwhile faith in yourself and your continuing importance and influence in your child's life will allow you to stay sensitive to any special situations that need your attention and to seek any help you or your child might want or need.

As your child moves through what we call here the stage of maturation, from age 14 to 21, faith is essential to your feeling comfortable and effective in your role as guide and mentor. As you let your child make more choices for herself and take on ever more responsibility in her own life, faith in your work together in the past will sustain you through some hairy moments, days, or nights. Faith in your parenting so far, as well as in your changing but continuing opportunities to exert positive influence, plays a large part in building your child's confidence in herself and in building the more adult relationship that will hopefully continue into your child's adult years and throughout your lives.

Words to Help Reinforce Your Faith in Your Child

To make the secret of faith your own, say it often to yourself: "I would never give up on my child." Imagine how wonderful it feels to know you never have to give up on your child. Rephrase the faith secret in different ways and use these new phrasings as positive affirmations to help reprogram your mind for faith-filled thinking about your child. Here are some ideas:

"I know my child will be all right."

"I know my parenting job will be good enough."

"I have faith in my child."

"I know God is on our side."

"I know my child will be successful in life."

"I can find many ways in which my child is lovable and endearing to me."

"I will focus on the bright side of parenting."

"I know my child will be able to forgive my errors."

"I know I will be able to connect with my child."

"My temporary upsets are normal and don't detract from my deep love for my child."

"Deep down I always love my child."

"My child is a part of me."

"My everyday experience with my child reinforces my faith."

"No one could ever make me give up on my child."

"My frustrations are mine, not my child's."

"I will always keep trying."

"My child will choose what's right for her as long as she feels valuable and secure, and these I can help ensure."

"My child is good, worthy, and exactly as he should be."

"Together we can solve any problem for our mutual benefit."

"I can be irritable or impatient or stupid on occasion without compromising my success as a parent."

"There is nothing so urgent it can't be dealt with in a way that leaves my faith intact."

"My love is openly unconditional."

"I'm a darned good parent."

If you like some of these affirmations especially, use them every day. If one or another seems hard to accept, use it as the focus for a few minutes' meditation and see what about it makes it difficult. Then let it go and think of it again in a few days. Chances are, your subconscious will have done some work on it, and it will be more natural for you to accept it then.

Take Care What Goes on in Your Head

Having faith in your child begins before you think about anything specific and long before you are in the room with your child. It's an attitude of mind that you will want to cultivate privately in preparation for each interaction. Consider these two fathers, Rob and Mick. They chose different ways of preparing themselves to deal with their children.

Rob and his 10-year-old son, Pete, are on their own for the evening. Rob's searching the refrigerator to discover dinner and thinking to himself, "I wonder what Pete's up to now. I bet his homework isn't done. I'm sure he overdosed on candy this afternoon before I got home. I just wish he would cooperate. I know it's going to be a trying evening."

In contrast, there's Mick, also with his head in the refrigerator while his son, Nick, is in another room. Mick is thinking: "It sure is quiet. I guess he's deep into something he enjoys. That's a good thing. If he spends some of his own time doing what he enjoys, he'll make the switch to homework easily, and he'll get it done with less hassle. I'm sure he makes OK snack choices while I'm gone. If it's clear he hasn't, I'll just have to remind him how it changes his mood. I'm looking forward to seeing him."

Which of these two dads has a better chance of having a positive moment or evening with his son when the boy finally appears? And which will more clearly show his parental love?

You know the answer without ever hearing or seeing what each father says or does. It doesn't matter the son's age or stage, the family's economics or marital status, or anything else. Rob is likely to say, without even looking up, "Is your homework done?" But Mick will say, "Hi, fella, how has your day been? Are you ready to tackle your homework yet?"

Which father would you respond to more cooperatively if you were a child? Rob got himself off track by worrying about his duty to supervise homework. Mick put his love and joy first.

Faith and the Optimistic Parent

Ralph Waldo Emerson said the birth of a child is a message of hope for the world. The very existence of your child can remind you that the universe has value and meaning, that history goes on for a purpose, and that life is a gift for which we can find reasons to feel grateful. Your child can give you ample grounds for optimism. To have faith in your child, cultivate this optimism in all your thoughts.

A father named Steve once told me about his son Fred's car collision a week after getting his driver's license. Luckily no one was injured. Steve said to me, "Fred just had his first accident." He said it as if at least one was to be expected and, what's more, the "first" implied a second. Steve went on, "I told him he was cruising for a bruising with his eagerness to drive. He should have waited until he was 17, like I told him." Steve's own prediction seemed more important to him than his son's actual experience or how he might support his son's struggle to become a better driver. With his pessimistic attitude, Steve was unable to help and support Fred in a way that would foster the boy's success.

With the optimism of faith, you will not be unrealistic. You will know that things can go wrong, but you will also know that one sad event doesn't mean anything about the future. Every trend turns around, as economists can attest. You may wonder if in medicine or psychology this may still be so. But for a healthy person, it is so, as most health professionals can affirm. The healthy body and mind are self-healing, self-correcting, and self-balancing—especially in children.

If you assume that a cough means strep throat, you have skipped the intermediate steps that can foster healthy self-care and healing processes in your child. A bout with the flu will pass whether you take medication or not.

Similarly, a fight between your child and his friend need not set off all the alarms. First try a little more guidance, more rest, or more love, and the system will self-correct 99 percent of the time.

Likewise with a negative emotion. The mind tends to self-correct too. If your child gets angry, that's fine. When you have faith, you don't give up on your child just because he is angry. His anger doesn't scare you because you know to keep it in perspective, even if it is directed at you. Something ticked him off. He only needs acknowledgment, encouragement, and guidance for how to handle his anger. Then the emotion can be expected to pass naturally, and he can make a calm decision about what, if anything, he needs to do.

Psychologist Martin Seligman, author of *The Optimistic Child,* has asserted that today's children need to be taught the skills of optimism. In a recent interview he explained that parents are often so eager to have their children feel good all the time—and particularly, good about themselves—that they give them no help in dealing with the inevitable downside and negative feelings in life. In his work with children, Seligman has developed a program for teaching optimism, one that can help us parents too.

Pessimism is not just about expecting bad things in the future. Pessimism is an attitude that also determines how you respond to present events. Likewise, optimism is not just about expecting everything to go well. More important, it is about how you respond to events in the present. As you read how Seligman contrasts pessimistic and optimistic responses, imagine how, if you had these different responses, it might either increase or decrease your faith in your child.

When something negative happens, a pessimist worries about three things: that the negative feelings or conditions will last forever, that they will affect everything, and that she can do nothing about it. In contrast, an optimist takes note of three things that are directly opposite to the pessimist: that the negative conditions will not last, that they will not affect everything, and that she can have an effect on the outcome.

If you know how to limit a problem in time and space and don't feel helpless to improve the situation, you will not give up or lose faith. You are immunized against hopelessness, depression, and despair. Seligman has in fact characterized his work as "emotional immunization."

Use this program to apply your faith to the events in your parenting. Remind yourself that any event you don't like is limited in time, scope, and power over you. It does not represent an irresistible trend or a permanent state of affairs. It will not poison everything in your child's life or other aspects of your parenting. Finally, you have—or can get—the information, knowledge, skills, and power to influence the situation for the better.

Even when you apply these strategies to your present situation, you may still be troubled by feelings from the past or projections into the future. So let's look at these.

To Have Faith in Your Child, Let Go of the Past

Haunting feelings from the past and frightening projections into the future are the most common threats to your having continuous faith in your child. Faith is an attitude of the present, independent of what has gone before or what might come after.

My client Joyce felt inadequate as a parent. It showed in her angry outbursts and heavy discipline, which she regretted later. She admitted she had been a very difficult child herself. She had been told so often in the past. She felt sorry for her mother for the bad things she used to do. But now she felt anxious whenever her own child showed signs of being the same. Deep down she feared that she was hopelessly handicapping her child.

When she examined her childhood again, Joyce realized her childhood behavior had been a reaction to extreme family stresses, with an alcoholic father and a frightened mother. Neither parent had ever expressed any faith in her, and her one goal had been to survive at all costs.

Now she could see that her parents were wrong to label her, and that she had been a normal child reacting to an abnormal situation. She had to put some blame on her parents to take it off her own shoulders, but then she also could forgive them, because she now understood, as an adult, how they felt trapped by their own history.

Once Joyce could see where her pessimism about her parenting came from, she could see that the hurts of her past did not have to last forever. They did not have to affect her parenting today. And she had the power to let go of them so that they wouldn't. She became more optimistic. She saw her faith grow.

Finally she was able to see that her own child's mischief was nothing to be afraid of or even ashamed of. And as her faith grew and she let it show in her words and actions, her child's mischief became less extreme and less frequent, until it was no longer threatening or worrisome.

If you feel troubled by thoughts of the past, then it's time to clean out the closets. Ask yourself where any feelings of ineffectiveness, guilt, resentment, and so on, may come from. Be as specific as you can with dates, people, places, events, and feelings. Then use your mature understanding of the situation to reinterpret it, so that now you will know how to limit its scope and become the parent you want to be.

To Keep Your Faith, Give Your Child a Future

Let's take a look at the impact of the future on your child and your faith. A recent national poll of young people found that a "high proportion of young kids fear dying young" because of violence and early death. "That fear is validated, rather than dispelled, by actual experiences" as teens, according to Lois Salisbury, executive director of Children Now, who completed the study with Kaiser Permanante healthcare providers. Of the children interviewed, who were ages 7 to 10, 71 percent worried they might be violently attacked. Of girls ages 14 to 17, 40 percent knew someone their age who had been hit by a boyfriend.

The authors of this study urged that parents make a special effort to combat this doleful outlook by talking about their child's future with optimism. Salisbury observed, "This generation is facing a unique set of fears," not the nuclear bomb of the previous generation that never went off, but little bombs of violence that are "going off all around them."

It's up to us as parents to be the first in line to believe in our children's futures and help them project positive expectations for themselves and their world.

Paul was a client who couldn't even think about trying to be optimistic about his child, because he really didn't think his daughter had a future at all.

"I can't do it!" he said. "What's the use? She's never going to make it." He added sarcastically, "At least one of us won't make it." I asked if he thought his daughter could detect this pessimism. "I'm sure she can. But I have to be realistic."

It is no wonder adolescence is so scary to parents, when they can't imagine a future for their children. Such dark visions trigger a parent's own fears of abandonment: if your child has no future, that means that after 20 years of your loving this child and doing the best you can by her she is going to abandon you! No wonder resentments can build and you can feel afraid to get close and invest in your child. But if you are ever in this fearful state, faith can pull you out.

I asked Paul to try this exercise. Imagine you are visiting your grandchildren at your child's house. Picture yourself arriving, being greeted by your child, seeing the grandchildren, and seeing and feeling warmth and hope and pleasure and pride.

Paul began to empathize with how bad his daughter must

feel knowing he had ruled out any possibility that she had a future. For two weeks, he found it too painful to imagine her married with children; the gap between his pessimistic projection and his heartfelt wishes was too great. But he worked to find lovable things in his daughter's life, as I'll describe in a moment, and soon he began to see in his mind's eye an image of his daughter grown into a capable young adult and the mother of his happy grandchildren. Before long Paul found it easier to relax around his daughter and to respond to her more constructively. She, in turn, became a gentler, more confident and cooperative person.

If you fear for the future or are tormented by the "what-ifs," lighten your load today by projecting positive images before you. At the very least, the decisions you make today will be consistent with a bright future. In contrast, if you assume things can only get worse, your decisions will be consistent with a dangerous and dark future, and you can set up self-fulfilling prophecies of doom.

Nature abhors a vacuum. If negative projections trouble you, you cannot simply wipe them away. You must displace them with positive projections. So in addition to the visit-to-grandchildren exercise, I want you to have some other ways to crowd out any negativity, pessimism, loss of faith, or hesitations in expressing your love for your child.

Every day, keep your eyes and ears open for things you can like about your child, as Paul did. If your daughter raises her voice, well, she has a good voice, and she's not afraid to speak her mind. If your son uses objectionable words to friends, well, he's not afraid of convention, and he lets out his feelings. And so on. This doesn't mean you don't object to things you don't like. It only means you don't let them poison your faith.

Set aside your fearful glasses and put on the ones that allow you to see in your child's everyday behavior the seeds of a delightful future. When you are not around your child, dwell in your imagination on the details of a future that is infinitely open. When you are around the child, speak freely of the options you are seeing unfold.

Feed Your Faith with Your Imagination

Here is an easy, fun way to stretch your imagination about a positive future. Picture a happy scenario for any quality you see in your child. For example, might your daughter be a great lawyer because she likes to argue every point?

> Will she be a wonderful mother because of the way she sings to her parakeet?

> Might she open a successful restaurant because of the original sandwiches she and her friends concoct?

> Perhaps your son will make a wonderful husband because he likes to talk things out endlessly with friends on the phone.

> Maybe he will captain a ship because he loves bath-time chaos.

> Perhaps he will run international rescue operations because of his insistence on collecting injured bugs in your sink.

There is no end to the imaginative possibilities we can create for our children. When you apply this kind of faith in your child, you begin bringing back the infinite faith your child wants and deserves, and the faith you want and deserve as a parent.

More Faith Builders

Here are a few more ideas for when you feel tempted to lose faith and give up on your child:

- Remind yourself that there are only a few reasons that a child will turn to the dark side, and pat yourself on the back that you will most likely have these bases covered. The reasons are basically these:

Bad or conflicted example set by the parent

Rebellion against parental neglect or oppression

Desire to be like friends

Escape from pain or helplessness

Ignorance or immaturity in thought or speech

With your growing faith in your child, together with the secrets to come, these reasons are least likely to exist in your family.

- State whatever is bothering you as clearly as you can in one sentence. Often this alone will shed the full light of day on your worry, and it will evaporate like morning mist.

- If a doubt lingers, imagine who in your past would be most likely to express that particular doubt, fear, or criticism. Have an imaginary conversation with them to find out why they would say it, and help them overcome their concern with courteous, careful listening and gentle, thoughtful responses.

- Imagine a conversation with your child. Let her tell you why your fear or doubt is misplaced. If the child is old enough to understand and to not feel threatened or confused by your thought, have a real conversation.

- Prepare a ceremony to free yourself from a particular doubt while you surrender to unconditional parental love. Here are a few ideas that I and other parents have found useful:

  Light a candle and watch it burn up emotional debris.

  Sing a favorite song from your childhood.

  Sing a contemporary song expressing love and hope.

Take a walk and see with child's eyes.

Peruse family photo albums, letting love greet each face.

Smile till your cheeks ache with joy.

Shed a tear for any regrets or disappointments.

Do a physical workout while repeating, "I would never give up on my child."

Call a parent and thank him or her for being your parent.

Call a friend who is a parent and give him or her praise.

With a stronger faith in your child, you will feel closer to your child. Now you have something very powerful and immensely important in common. You both believe in your success together. Your child is born with a natural faith, and now you share it. You are now on the same side of the fence. You now both believe everything is going to come out all right.

In a recent interview about his work to inspire corporate executives to find their poetic side, the author of *The Heart Aroused,* poet David White, told how real faith is the willingness to acknowledge that we don't have to do everything ourselves but that the world cooperates with us. He says this faith is what gets us out of self-pity and allows us to look around us with awe. Let awe and wonder and delight be part of your parenting life, and open up to the gracious cooperation that will be yours as a parent.

Now that you can see—and perhaps feel—some of the benefits of knowing you would never give up on your child, you may have noticed also how your thoughts, words, and actions naturally become more positive, and you feel more in tune with your child's natural program to grow and learn and thrive.

Words to Show Your Faith

Let me close this chapter on the secret of parental faith with some powerful words you can speak to your child. Sprinkle these into your conversations no matter what the situation.

"I'm glad you're in my life."

"I love having you around."

"You're a wonderful part of my life."

"I love you."

"I love the way you do things."

"It's great to see your enthusiasm for the things you do."

"Family is so important to me."

"You are becoming such a wonderful young woman (man)."

"I love you at this age. Actually every age has had its special gifts."

"I really enjoyed sitting with you yesterday (or reading with you, hanging out with you, going to the movies with you, eating with you, chatting with you, watching you work, seeing you play)."

"I love being your parent."

"I sure do work hard at this parenting, don't I?"

"I hope you will get as much fun out of parenting as I do."

"I don't know why some parents think this is so hard. You make it easy."

"You teach me what life is all about."

"You're so easy to love!"

"You do a great job being a kid."

"You are so lively, so awesome. I would never give up on you!"

No matter how many communes anybody invents, the family always creeps back.

MARGARET MEAD

For it is impossible for a man to put forward fair and honest views about our affairs if he has not, like everyone else, children whose lives may be at stake.

ASPASIA

Trouble . . . Why do we fear it? Why do we dread ordeal? Every good thing the human race has experienced was trouble for somebody. Our birth was trouble for our mothers. To support us was trouble for our fathers. Books, paintings, music, great buildings, good food, ideas, the nameless joys and excitements which added up to what we call "a good life" came out of the travail of countless hearts and minds.

LILLIAN SMITH

If you bungle raising your children, I don't think whatever else you do well matters very much.

JACQUELINE KENNEDY ONASSIS

"I pay attention first to my child's basic needs."

❖ **Attention** ❖

You may have guessed in reading the last chapter that the secret of faith is the most abstract of all the seven secrets of successful parents. Now you will be hearing about the most concrete of all the secrets, the secret of attention: "I pay attention first to my child's basic needs."

In this chapter you can find out how to make sure you are meeting all your child's basic needs effectively. I think you will come to appreciate how far this effort goes toward ensuring a happy, healthy child.

Without attempting to cover all the details about each basic need here, I want to touch on the elements that parents have the most concern about and those they have the most trouble with. I want also to give you the flavor of each need, so that you will be inspired to investigate thoroughly whenever you see a sign that a basic need may be unfulfilled.

Before looking at each individually, I want you to keep in mind these key ideas about meeting your child's basic needs:

• Basic needs are the foundation for everything else. I hope you will soon be gratified to see how the vast majority of parental problems and stresses disappear when you put your attention on the basic needs of your child. This is because nature has endowed your child—through hundreds of thousands of years of evolution—with a strong, internal program to grow and thrive under your responsive care and to mature into a successful member of the community, as long as basic survival needs are met. But these higher functions of the human child can only work when the basic needs are being fulfilled.

• Basic needs are the unique province of parents. No one else knows your child as well as you do, nor can anyone have as pure an interest as you do in the welfare of your child. So you are in the best position to recognize and fulfill your child's basic needs. As you focus more attention on these needs, you may be delighted to find that your child's basic needs are the one aspect of your child's life over which you have substantial control. So it is easy, natural, and effective to put your energy there.

• Basic needs are the place to begin in solving problems. As you consider particular aspects of each need, you are likely to discover that many everyday problems, even relatively severe ones, can be solved by focusing attention on basic needs. Those same problems may remain unresolved when parents or their advisers overlook basic needs and instead search for more complex, rare, or sophisticated causes that may not really apply.

• Basic needs can fool you. If you are facing problems in your parenting or just want to improve your parenting overall, you may want to check basic needs even though you are pretty sure they are all being met. With the material abundance of our society, it is easy to assume that basic needs are not hard to meet, that they are already covered, and that you must concentrate your efforts elsewhere. But for the individual child, one or another of his basic needs often goes unfulfilled because of particular circumstances.

In addition, many needs that historically were met automatically by a more natural lifestyle now need your deliberate attention.

• Basic needs are the best way to nurture independence. As you focus more of your attention on fulfilling your child's basic needs, you will probably notice also how you are increasing your child's sense of well-being, gradually transferring to her the responsibility for her needs, and empowering her to fulfill those needs in the future.

• Basic needs are finite. The needs of children are not infinite. If you are sometimes worried that, no matter what you do, your child cannot be satisfied, remember that with foresight and care the basic needs of your child can be met, and you have the power and privilege to do so.

• Basic needs can serve as a sound criterion for when to stand firm and when to be flexible. This is because if basic needs are met, even if your child is obstinate at times, he will eventually sort out his own feelings and wants so that you can help him deal with them. But when basic needs *aren't* met, he can't think clearly, assess his own needs well, or respond effectively to either you, others, or his environment. This creates a vicious cycle that can frustrate both you and him. Stand firm about basic needs whenever your child is caught in this cycle. You will see exactly how to do this at different ages and stages later in this chapter. Resistance will not last long, because your child knows intuitively that you're paying attention to your top priority and his: the basic needs that are elemental to his well-being.

In working with parents, I have learned that the more specific you can be about basic needs, the more effectively you will be able to fulfill all of your child's needs with success and confidence. So I have developed a very practical list of the 12 basic needs of children. You can use it often, whenever you want. The list encompasses all the essential requirements for creating, nurturing, protecting, and inspiring a healthy, happy child.

To make these 12 needs easy to remember, so you can focus your attention on them quickly at any time, think of the first six as physical needs and the last six as relationship (intellectual, emotional, social, and spiritual) needs:

PHYSICAL NEEDS	RELATIONSHIP NEEDS
Sleep	Safety
Food	Space
Light	Nature
Air	Companionship
Water	Activity
Comfort	Affection

Your confidence in your parenting efforts will grow as you begin to check this list often, to notice unmet needs, and to pay attention to their fulfillment. Check it daily if you like, and then also whenever things go wrong, and even when things feel just a little out of whack. Twelve needs may seem like a long list, but just remember that when these are done well, there is very little left for you to do but enjoy your child! I hope that as you hear soon about the details of each, you will see what I mean.

Applying the Secret of Attention Through the Years

As you consider how each basic need applies in your own situation, remember to bring to bear all you know about your child at his particular age, stage, and experience. In the infancy and toddler stages, through age four, the basic needs are up to you to meet directly or to insist upon their being met.

Then you will likely see a gradual transfer of responsibility for each need from you to both of you and then to your child, beginning in the exploratory stage around age four and ending, whether you are ready or not, near the end of the growth stage, at age 14. Examples throughout this book will help you see how to accomplish this transfer in different areas of basic needs with the least hassle and the most success.

You still have lots of influence even in the maturation stage that follows after age 14. Only now, your influence takes the form of highlighting likely consequences rather than trying to control, induce, or persuade. You can best focus on sharing information your child doesn't know, making your own boundaries clear, and giving lots of encouragement to your emerging young adult.

In this stage, your efforts to pay attention to basic needs can become a continuous thorn in the side of your relationship. Or, it can be a friendly sharing of useful information, packaged together with a healthy willingness to mind your own business and enjoy watching your child mind hers as best she can.

Twelve Basic Needs

Sleep

According to recent newspaper headlines, more than half of high school students are clinically sleep deprived. That is, they're too tired! Here are some symptoms of their exhaustion:

One falls asleep at school.

Another craves caffeine and other stimulants.

Another loses his appetite for foods of any kind.

Yet another is irritable and startles at any noise.

Still another feels paranoid ("My mother is trying to ruin my life!") or depressed ("No one cares. Why bother?").

One more starts frequent fights at imaginary offenses.

Imagine your satisfaction if a maddening problem like one of these were resolved with such a straightforward measure as insisting on more sleep!

Sleep is important for everything else your child does. While your child sleeps, her body and mind heal themselves from the day just past and build up the energy and stamina for the day to come. There are three important aspects of sleep for you to keep in mind: quantity, quality, and conditions.

My teenage son smiles only about half as often as when he hasn't had enough sleep. When I ask him about it, he is usually aware of it and already has plans to catch up. But if I didn't think of this basic unmet need, I could easily start a useless fight about why he isn't being more cheerful, helpful, forgiving, happy, or whatever. And he wouldn't have a clue about what I was talking about.

Even if your child is not dragging around looking tired, remember to still consider his sleep. Lots of nervous energy can come from adrenaline produced to overcome exhaustion. I have met children who have been tired so long that neither they nor their parents know how nice they could be if they were rested.

My client Dot complained that her 11-year-old son Rob's bedtime was a hassle, but she believed he got plenty of sleep. "He's asleep by 10 even when we have a bad night—you know, fighting over homework—and he gets up at seven o'clock to catch the bus. Isn't that enough?" For some children it might be. But Rob was an athlete and played hard almost two hours a day.

Rather than assume he was having an "early adolescence," Dot decided to try more sleep. It was easier said than done. Dot didn't want to start the bedtime routine earlier, because she would have almost no time to do other things after dinner and before Rob's bedtime. And on busy athletic nights, Rob would have no time to eat after practice, so he would have to eat before, and she knew he wouldn't like that unless it was junk food.

Rob, on his part, didn't want to give up his only free time on weekends to sleep, and he didn't want to go to bed earlier weekdays either. He didn't even want to talk about it. Finally, by chatting about it over the next few days, they decided to make lots of small adjustments. Rob went to bed just 15 minutes earlier and listened to his radio a shorter time in his room. He took a nap or rest Saturday morning instead of watching TV. They agreed that if he still seemed cranky after two weeks, they would review the situation again. But things improved in a few days.

Only you and your family can figure out how much sleep each one needs. I need 7 hours, my husband 8, my teenage son 9, and my teenage daughter 10. If we don't get it, we notice.

If your child is putting in the time in bed but not getting the benefits, check the quality of her sleep. Perhaps she never gets deep sleep because she's snacking too close to bedtime, or she wakes up a lot because she's drinking fluids too late in the evening. Or maybe nightmares keep her awake, and she hasn't linked that to the candy she has stashed by her bed.

If your child's habits aren't contributing to his poor sleep quality, then check sleeping conditions. Perhaps there's a distracting light or noise. Or consider the story of Holly, who described how her child had cried almost every night for eight years. She had tried doctors, psychologists, the works. Finally she discovered that the child was allergic to the flame retardants in children's sleepware! When she put him to bed in a T-shirt, on natural cotton sheets, his problems disappeared.

Check out the whole picture to discover how best to see that your child gets the sleep he needs.

Food

Diet gets so much attention today, I hesitate to begin. But I want to stress it emphatically, because time and time again attention to food has made the difference in children's lives.

It seems almost unbelievable that food could affect such a wide spectrum of elements in a child's life: from his weight and figure to his moods and emotions, as well as his strength, endurance, mental ability, concentration, skin, hair, immunity, nerves, hormones, and more. But I have personally known hundreds of parents over the years who solved difficult problems for their children by meeting the children's nutritional needs. They have freed a diabetic child from insulin, stopped earaches, ended colic, reduced allergic reactions, lifted depression, calmed hyperactivity without

drugs, moderated attention and learning differences, strength-
ened weak eyes and ears, cleared eczema, reduced tooth decay,
improved growth rates, avoided colds and flus, and more.

Research evidence helps explain all these effects of good
food. Everything your child does is dependent on the physical and
biochemical processes of her body. These in turn are dependent
on the raw materials you provide when you give her food to eat.
A child with no protein for her brain or no fuel for her muscles
can't benefit from school or play. Every function is compromised.

If your child has any problems that don't go away with more
obvious measures, check for unmet needs in nutrition. Putting
food first may require more of your time, effort, money, persistence, and even study. But I have never met a parent who regretted the effort he or she spent on feeding a child well.

You might think of food in terms of four crucial factors: food
quality, food mix, family attitudes, and eating environment. I
choose not to put the focus on quantity or on how often to eat
because experience has shown that, if the four factors above are
taken care of, these two issues are not a problem. They cause so
much stress and misunderstanding in the families I have known
that they are better left to take care of themselves.

First, let me make a pitch for breastfeeding. It's the best first
diet. Research has shown that breastfeeding can be successful for
at least 95 percent of new mothers if they get some instruction,
encouragement, and support. Feeding on demand and watching
your own diet for quality does the most to ensure a plentiful,
nourishing, and worry-free first diet for your child. Plus the
experience helps stimulate in you a pattern of responsive parenting that will help you for years after. I have heard quite a few
mothers who breastfed their second child and not their first, and
they always regret what they missed with the first.

Next, take your time with moving to table food. Learn about
the safest sequences for introducing foods. As soon as your child
starts to have some teeth, she requires very little special processing of foods, so don't feel bound to buy those overprocessed little jars. Just chop up your own healthy foods a little more finely

and make sure they are moist. Letting your child play with table foods and learn to feed herself is far superior to playing the comedy routine of stuffing heaping spoonfuls into an unwilling mouth only to watch them ooze out onto the floor!

As soon as possible, either all at once or bit by bit, establish a more healthy kitchen in your home. The foods you choose to keep in your home are your single greatest influential move when it comes to guiding your child's eating. Keep quality, moderation, and variety always in mind when shopping and then let a comfortable eating pattern evolve.

Think of your child's eating as a transformation process: your child transforms one form of life, food, into another, his own body. If you remember this, you will steer away from the lifeless concoctions of the modern food-processing industry and move toward living unprocessed foods or foods minimally processed at home. If you have only good foods on hand, your child will tend to select an adequate mix over a week's time, so don't obsess about it. Here are some other useful tips:

• Begin right now to stock your kitchen with the basic foods I'll describe in a moment. Throw out all processed white stuff: white flour, white sugar, white salt, and colorless oils.

• Teach everyone to cook a few simple meals. Even little ones can spread natural peanut butter on crackers. And involve even the littlest ones in food preparation.

• Have some not-too-awful snacks on hand. For older kids, buy some of the new sodas that are relatively free of preservatives and colors, have natural flavors, and are not too sweet. Dilute these and natural fruit juices, so they don't hype your child like candy does.

• Buy tasty organic fruits and vegetables instead of the sterile, bland, chemically farmed kind. You will have the advantages of avoiding toxic pesticides and other chemicals while getting superior nutritional richness, especially with all-important trace minerals. Plus kids can taste the difference. Organic foods cost more, but your children will eat more of them.

• Make sure you have plenty of chicken, eggs, fish, cheese, beans, and fresh seeds and nuts. These foods provide the all-important proteins that are so crucial to growing bodies and brains. Plan on buying these fresh and preparing them simply. Kids don't like a lot of gourmet processing, and as long as the raw ingredients are of high quality, the food will taste good.

• Find out how your kids like things cooked; don't overcook.

• Explore yogurts, preferably flavored yourself, and goat's milk and cheese, which is more easily tolerated by most children than cow's milk and cheese.

• Have peanut butter and more exotic nut butters on hand to spread on whole-grain bread, rye crackers, or finger veggies.

• If your child doesn't like cooked vegetables, serve them raw with a dip she loves. A popular one is half mayonnaise and half plain yogurt, with a little added herbs or salt.

• Try to create a rainbow of colors with your produce at each meal. Include something green, like iron-rich parsley; something yellow, like potassium-rich lemon wedges or bananas; something red, like digestion-helpful radishes; something orange, like calcium-rich carrots; and so on.

• Think of protein foods and produce as the core of your family's meals and snacks. Then keep a leftover soup on the stove and watch everyone help themselves, especially teenage boys. The heartier the soup, the better. Throw in lots of beans, onions, carrots, tomatoes (here's a great place to sneak in cancer-preventing cabbage), and a little brown rice or other whole grain; simmer it a long time; and add herbs and spices. If you find that your hodgepodge soup lacks character, add some natural soy sauce or tomato puree, and they'll love it.

• Use a naturally formulated vegetable salt instead of the white stuff, and let your kids salt to taste. Excessive salt comes primarily from preprepared foods.

• Try to fill your kids up at home with tasty good foods, so they won't be so tempted to snack at the take-out places.

• Only after protein and produce fill your menus should you add baked goods, bread, pasta, other grain and starch products, sweets, or products containing oil and shortening. All of these are easily overconsumed by kids because they distort the body's natural appetite mechanism. They do this because they are more concentrated than the foods to which our bodies are accustomed from our natural history. They are missing much of their original water, fiber, vitamins, and minerals, so the body doesn't know how to handle them and they lead to trouble. One expert on food addictions, Kay Sheppard, calls these sugary, starchy, and fatty foods the "sticky, pasty, and greasy" foods. That's a handy way to remember to minimize them in your home.

• See that grain products include the whole grain whenever possible, so that your child will get more of the basic nutrients from the original grain, especially the fiber.

• Encourage your child to chew thoroughly to get a head start on good digestion. A happy, relaxed atmosphere helps.

• Accept that your child, when outside your home, will inevitably get junk foods in the form of hoagies, rolls, pasta, french fries, condiments, pizza, donuts, cakes, puddings, ice cream, sodas, and candy. Don't try to compete with the outside. (Your children will still love you!) Just have a few not too objectionable standbys from the health food store, and pat yourself on the back that at home the diet is basically sound.

• Avoid making eating times stressful. If you have an important point of information about food or food policies to present, arrange to do it at another time. Use mealtimes instead as a social reinforcer—a purpose they have served for millennia, say leading anthropologists like Richard Leakey. Cheerful meals strengthen family bonds as well as health.

• When out on the road, decide ahead of time when and where you will eat, and be firm. Tell them your plan and stick to it. But make sure you stop often enough, because everyone gets hungrier, thirstier, and testier in a car.

• When eating out, don't make every poor menu choice a federal case. When kids forget, which they always will do, don't shame them or grill them or threaten to withdraw their favorite foods. Just remind them cheerfully and move on.

• Don't worry about what your children eat when they are out. For millions of years children have learned to eat properly by watching their parents. Today, overprocessed fats and sugars can kill a child prematurely, but in the old days the wrong berry could kill her instantly. Never underestimate your influence as a parent, by the power of example and good-natured reminders.

• Keep all food products fresh. Refrigerate produce and all meats, except dried or canned ones, and all fats except olive oil.

• Finally, insist on a complete vitamin and mineral supplement, one free of artificial additives. The extra insurance you get is worth the expense. And with the full complement of micronutrients, your child's appetite will tend more toward real foods and away from cravings. It's worth it to educate yourself to meet your child's particular nutritional needs. Do so early, while you still have some control and influence.

I do live in the real world. After your child reaches age eight or nine, it's all you can do to make him sit down to eat, much less get him to chew well, savor different dishes, and have some conversation. But accepting this reality doesn't mean food takes the back seat. Don't give up on family meals and wish things were otherwise, but instead make a regular effort to coordinate schedules and to set up the physical eating environment so that your child can sit to eat and you can be there when he does. You will be astounded at the payoff.

Before closing this discussion of the need for healthy food, I want to mention four food-related issues that come up with parents most often: fat phobia, sugar addiction, vegetarianism, and eating disorders.

If fear of fat runs your family feeding, get a hold of *The Health Revolution*, by Robert Atkins, M.D. Atkins gives a clear explanation of exactly how fat works in the diet and the body. It may seem controversial if you have been reading the newspaper headlines of the day, but it really isn't anything new.

Good, healthy fat has been with us forever. It's only the hydrogenated, overheated, overprocessed, and stale fats in processed foods that cause trouble. So read your labels and realize your child needs high-quality fat every day. Give her olive oil, butter, natural nut butters with no hydrogenation, and only expeller-pressed oils, and she won't overeat fat.

Don't scare your kids away from eggs because of their cholesterol. If eggs are fresh, not overcooked, and free of antibiotics, they are the best protein food around. Emulsifying lecithin balances the cholesterol, but if you're still worried, serve some cayenne pepper, powdered garlic, or fresh or dried onions with them.

As for sugar addiction, keep your home stocked with lots of fresh fruit and some not too obnoxious sweets free of chemical additives, preservatives, and colors. Educate yourself and your child about the physiological effects of concentrated sugars and starches. When your children want cookies at home, let them make them. They'll appreciate them more and also see how much sugar goes into them!

What if your child would rather die than kill? That is, she wants to be a vegetarian. If this is your child, learn more about her choice and talk to her about it. Don't try to talk her out of it, but explore the subject together. Remind her that being a "vegetarian" doesn't mean just eating vegetables. Historically the term refers to eating "vital foods"—foods that don't have to be killed but instead support life directly. Let her explore ethnic diets from around the world that don't rely on meat.

For adequate protein, just see that she gets lots of nuts, seeds, beans, and eggs and cheeses if she likes. And a vegetarian cannot get too much fat unless she is filling up on fried and baked foods.

Finally, a frequent concern of parents is how to prevent eating disorders. Research indicates that these are caused by many factors: addiction to refined foods, stress about food or figure, obsession with unusual and distorted eating patterns, and abuse of foods as stimulants are the main contributors. You can see how, if you follow the suggestions you have heard here, your child has the best chance to avoid these disorders and to treat eating as a natural, enjoyable, and moderated activity.

My client Tina complained about her daughter Drew's deteriorating looks and personality. Drew was a typical high school student and read all the labels for fat because she feared it would make her fat. Meanwhile, she was showing signs of fat deficiency: bad skin, frequent colds, food cravings, and fatigue.

Tina knew one of Drew's friends was binging and purging, so she was scared. Still, she was surprised to find out that her daughter needed fat and that many children with eating disorders abhor fat and are actually addicted to refined carbohydrates, especially sugar, pasta, and chocolate.

Tina and Drew let high-quality fat back into their lives, and Tina stopped hassling Drew about food. They soon noticed that irritability, fatigue, infections, cravings, and skin problems began to disappear. Even weight control got easier.

Girls are especially vulnerable to diet distortions because of the emphasis on the female figure. But boys are not immune. Jami complained to me that her 12-year-old, Tim, was starving himself to be under a certain weight limit for his wrestling competition. She went to his school and insisted he be put in a higher weight class, but this intimidated him because his opponents were now bigger. Eventually Tim gave up wrestling and switched to rowing. Basic needs must come first.

Light

Most parents take light for granted. Surely this need is still ful-filled by nature, you might think. But you need to ask yourself questions like these: Is my child's workspace well lighted so there isn't eyestrain? Is my child getting enough full-spectrum light to promote healthy development? Are halls and closets well lighted to avoid mishaps?

When checking your child's lighting, consider the quantity, quality, and timing of your child's exposure. Headaches, lack of concentration, and irritability can result from chronic eyestrain in light that looks adequate but isn't.

More and more studies are showing the importance of daily full-spectrum light exposure for hormone balance and optimal health. The recent attention given to the hormone melatonin reinforces this point. This hormone has a healthy, normalizing effect on daily mental and physiological rhythms. The body pro-duces it in response to exposure to sunlight.

We have also long known that the best source of usable vita-min D is not processed cow's milk but rather your own skin once it is exposed to sunlight. And consider also that full-spectrum lights are used in hospitals to cure jaundice in newborns. My Native American midwife told me the old way was to put the crib by an open window. It's the light of the sun when a child is born that stimulates the young liver to begin working. Can we assume that light's importance wanes thereafter?

See that your child gets outside for at least half an hour a day, no matter what the weather. Kids seldom complain about this, but they can forget about the outside with all the attractions and distractions of TV, homework, video games, telephone, chores, snacks, and exhaustion. The school we first sent our kids to made big points with us when they said the students all went outside at least three times during the school day.

Don't let recent attention to the risks of skin cancer scare your children inside because of the sun or missing ozone. Use natural sunscreens that don't irritate the skin or immune system, and encourage them to avoid the perpendicular light of midday. Send them out before and after school for a run or walk.

Consider replacing the bulbs in your house, as they burn out, with the new, environmentally friendly full-spectrum versions. Tests in schools and offices have demonstrated the beneficial effects. Health food stores and many home supply stores now have them. And make full use of your windows.

Remember that humans are diurnal mammals, which means that we are most lively in the daylight. It takes the artificial stimulation of caffeine, sugar, alcohol, or electronic visuals, or even the stress of illness to keep us up all night. If your child is a night owl, consider helping him reestablish a diurnal schedule.

As with other needs, focus your main efforts on those environments you do control. Only then consider trying to change other environments, like relatives' homes, school, nursery, or daycare. Institutions change slowly, and your child still spends more hours at home than anywhere else, no matter how busy he is.

Soon after my son turned 18, he set up a basement apartment so he would have more space and privacy; then he stopped getting up before noon. I nagged a bit but soon realized that he didn't know what time of day it was when he awoke. I cleaned out the window wells on each basement wall, and he started to get up in the morning again!

Air

Like light, air is too often taken for granted. Five key factors can affect your child's need for air: air quality, pollutants, breathing habits, airflow, and oxygen content.

Is the air fresh enough in your house? New insulation practices make our houses and buildings tighter now. The air can get very stale, especially in winter. Consider the air if your child has bad winters, gets frequent colds or sniffles, or seems to be allergic to more things every year. See that air circulates from the outside even in winter.

Avoid what appears to be the easy way to clean and freshen your house: using strong chemical cleansers, perfumed products, and chemical air fresheners. You end up polluting your own environment. Many kids develop sensitivities to these chemicals. If they don't get classic skin rashes, they can be affected in their moods, behavior, and mental abilities.

I know several mothers who found that their children would fall asleep in school or get into trouble with classmates only in particular classrooms. Recent pesticide treatments or fumes from new curtains or carpets were responsible.

Once we see that our air is fresh, what about breathing? I'm not kidding. Many kids don't breathe properly. Chiropractor Marsh Morrison has written that from the time a child first stands up, bad habits of breathing can begin. The diaphragm, the major muscle of breathing, is compressed both by uprightness and by sitting. It is soon neglected and weakens as children begin to breathe shallowly, instead of from the abdomen the way a concert singer breathes. Morrison has developed some easy exercises for reestablishing fully effective breathing habits. Yoga exercises can help. And martial arts classes also can help kids who need more discipline and incentive for healthy breathing habits.

Set an example of breathing long and deep yourself. If it helps your moods and stamina, mention how it has helped you.

Pay attention also to the flow of air. Some children like a breeze; some don't. Help your child set up his room the way he wants it for best airflow. Is your house downwind from an industrial installation? Or perhaps air can flow into the house from your garage? Arrange for airflow from the cleanest side of the room or house with fans or weather stripping. And check for contamination in air conditioners. What seems like a good thing—filtering, cooling, or moisturizing the air—may actually include spewing molds and bacteria into the room.

Invest in one of the excellent ionizers on the market today and watch your children's moods perk up. There are even pocket-size ionizers now available. An ionizer spreads negatively charged ions into the air. These make breathing easier, stimulate balanced nerve responses in the brain, and take allergens and dust out of the air. The room feels like a spring morning after a rain.

How about oxygen in the air? Health research is demonstrating how well-oxygenated tissues ward off disease. But the proportion of our air that is oxygen has actually gone down significantly in this century, due to the burning of fossil fuels and the destruction of the forests.

You might think here's something that is really beyond your control. But as with other needs, if you look not at the entire atmosphere but at the microenvironment in which you raise your child, there are things you can do. Having healthy plants in your house can filter the air and add significant oxygen. If you have any area under your control outside your home, you can plant some shrubs or trees. Meanwhile encourage your child to play in green areas. His moods will be better because his need for quality air is being met.

Water

Water is for your child to drink, play with, and bathe in. Today we are more aware than ever how it can dramatically affect our health. Also, thirst often goes unrecognized in modern America because drinks are always accessible. The problem is that only clean water satisfies thirst; other drinks just mask it. They offer water but also include dissolved substances like sugar, acids, and sodium, which can actually dehydrate our bodies' cells. So the water need goes unmet at the cellular level, where it is most important.

You can fulfill your child's basic need for water by paying attention to these four factors: water sources, any pollutants, when to drink, and how much to drink.

When I was growing up, Americans prided themselves on their safe water. We only had to be careful when we went to other countries. Today there are serious questions about the safety of adding chlorine and fluoride to our water and about the increasing contamination from industrial, chemical, agricultural, nuclear, and medical waste. We now know that these can affect us even in bathing and swimming, since scientists have found that a child's skin is much more absorptive than we used to think.

A quality water filter seems to be a wise precaution for any family. Filters can range from fancy to simple, but even a basic on-the-counter charcoal one is worthwhile.

Experts have long warned us to avoid pesticides to help prevent such problems as cancer and infertility for our children's future. The danger is scary, but real. Recently public awareness has grown tremendously about the toxic effects on children from pesticide pollution of water and food. Unnatural concentrations of metals are also a common problem, especially for children, affecting their growth, immunity, and behavior. Watch out for lead, cadmium, aluminum, nickel, and more.

Buy bottled water from named and known sources if you are not using a high-quality filter or don't have your own, properly tested well.

If people get cranky or the driver is nodding when traveling in the car, try this strategy. Stop for a round or two of water (even if they are all screaming for ice cream!). If you meet their water needs, you'll be back on the road in peace.

Other signs of thirst in children are sleepiness, loss of appetite, depression, bed-wetting, indigestion, chilliness, feeling overheated or light-headed, food cravings, irritability, under- or overweight, dry skin, rapid or slow heartbeat, congestion, and either reduced or excessive appetite for salt. In each of these cases, water deprivation has distorted the delicately balanced water content of the body and created changes in many organs that affect health, thought, and behavior.

If your child says she doesn't like water, then find a source with better taste. If she insists on other beverages, have her drink water first, even just a little. The chronic drinking of too much water can overburden the kidneys, but a generous glass of pure water first thing in the morning and a little while before each meal keeps your child fully hydrated. That's one more basic need fulfilled.

Comfort

Tending to the comfort of your child means accommodating temperature and humidity needs, seeing to your child's personal hygiene, and paying attention to the cleanliness and order of your child's body, clothes, possessions, room, and surroundings.

On the one hand, you certainly don't want to raise hothouse kids who have every condition perfectly controlled for their total comfort. On the other hand, these conditions can make a great deal of difference in a child's health, immunity, and level of contentment, so tend to your child's comfort at home.

Consider the situation where a child isn't sleeping well but wants to be macho and fails to mention that he needs another blanket on his bed for warmth at night. Perhaps a friend gave him the idea that only whiny little sisters need blankets. He lets it go until he actually forgets why he doesn't sleep well. He becomes more cranky in the morning. He starts roaming the house at night (to find a warmer room). Discovering donuts in the kitchen, he gets into the habit of chomping donuts out of boredom—a shot of sugar does get the blood flowing to warm you up temporarily—and he turns on the late-night adult videos.

What parent would think first about a second blanket when he finds out the donuts are gone, dirty movies are on, and the kid is obnoxious every morning? Yet that may be the solution.

It's a good idea to mention the elements of comfort at regular intervals, just as you would for a houseguest. Don't insist right away. Simply state that your child is welcome to consider a change. You wouldn't say to a houseguest, "You've got to have another blanket, or you'll be cranky in the morning!" Instead you would say something like, "It's been cool at night lately. Perhaps you'd like a second blanket. I'll leave one here where you can get it easily." That works well for guests and kids alike.

When considering your child's clothes, take your child's comfort into account. You may unintentionally steer your son toward styles that don't meet his comfort needs. You may like spiffy, tailored clothes, but perhaps he is uncomfortable in them. At his stage of life, he feels more at ease in big baggy stuff that offers no restrictions. Perhaps your daughter wants to wear skimpier clothes than you think appropriate. Something as simple as switching to natural fibers could solve the problem if your daughter does not know that the synthetic fabrics she is choosing make her feel hot. Help her experiment to find a style for each season that suits her comfort, taste, and modesty.

It is important that your child be comfortable with his body and personal adornment, even if it isn't to your taste. You might consider letting your child experiment with temporary and harmless changes in hair, makeup, nails, body hair, and jewelry, even if you are nervous about social consequences. Your child will learn what she should know about these soon enough.

For the sake of your child's comfort and health as well as your own, you do have the right to insist on body cleanliness. Take a firm stand but don't force; that won't work in the long run. Instead explain, coax, be patient, express your concern and frustration in words, or withhold privileges and favors if necessary, but focus always on your desire for her well-being and your comfort. If your desire is reasonable, she will come around.

Be careful to distinguish, though, between being clean and looking clean. A grungy style may look dirty, but if the clothes are washed, then hygiene and comfort needs have been met.

Avoid pouring too many chemicals on your child in the name of cleanliness. A well-rinsed body has its own natural oils and even benign bacteria that belong there. Aggressive soaps and deodorants are neither necessary nor good for kids. Let them hit their own stride as far as cleansing is concerned. But if you notice anything of concern (discoloration of nails, scalp, or neck; an unpleasant body odor; recurrent infections), that is the time to insist on more frequent bathing.

Your child's comfort may be more affected by temperature and humidity than you might imagine. We take these for granted now that our internal environments are highly controlled. But in ancient times, they were considered a major influence on health as well as comfort. Ancient healers manipulated the four qualities of wet, dry, hot, and cold in order to bring what they called the four "humors," or body vapors, into balance. We still talk about "humoring someone" and being "in a good humor." So get to know your child's "humor" (not just the funny side), and help her to get to know herself. Perhaps a child goes up to her room early in the evening only because the family room is too warm or cold. Or perhaps a child is grumpy in the morning because the kitchen is too hot or too drafty. Check it out; ask.

You can avoid much childhood discomfort by checking for allergens. Allergies are common and becoming more so, even without the classic symptoms. Strategies to reduce allergies include repairing a child's immune system through diet, uncovering hidden food intolerances, removing offending chemicals in the environment at least for a time, and limiting the total chemical challenge. Search for answers here.

Consider also the dangers to the nervous system from lead contamination, and avoid lead paint, car exhaust, lead-laced plates or toys, lead solder in pipes, and other sources of lead and other heavy metals. And when your child needs a dental filling, ask your dentist to use composite rather than a silver-mercury amalgam. That one measure can save your child from lifelong problems due to the slow leaching of mercury.

The child's sleeping area especially should be as allergen and chemical free as possible, because that takes care of a third of his life in one swoop and is totally within your control. In cleaning a child's room, use good old elbow grease—and not just your own! Make chores a social project and clean your child's room with him.

Finally, neatness and aesthetic appeal are important for comfort. Let your child arrange her space to her own taste, no matter how small that space is. Give your child the right to be comfortable, and watch other complaints begin to disappear.

Safety

Throughout history, no human parents have ever been so well-off that they could not think of fears for their child's safety that could keep them up at night. Nor has any parent been so badly off that there wasn't some grounds for hope. The starting point for meeting your child's basic need for safety is to be clear-eyed and honest about your child's situation and then to do everything within your power to protect your child.

Keep in mind these eight aspects of safety: the probability of risk, the seriousness of risk, your child's capabilities, people, places, things, supervision, and planning.

In the fast-paced world kids grow up in today, there are very few places, only a select group of people, and only some things—certain toys, tools, and activity props—that are totally safe. Accidents and violence can happen almost anywhere.

In a recent case from Pennsylvania, a federal court of appeals held that a school and its classroom teacher were not liable for damages to two students who were repeatedly sexually assaulted in a classroom during class, even though the perpetrators had been convicted. The court said that school did not create a "special custodial relationship" and that, even though students are required by law to be in school, the parents are still the primary caretakers.

Only under your direct supervision can you be absolutely sure. Everywhere else, you must know the risks and have a plan for you and your child. You will need to think ahead, let your child know your plans, and then follow through.

Sometimes parents can feel overwhelmed by the stresses of trying to meet this need. It is an unfortunate reality in society today that almost every parent must work for money. Few parents can then supervise their children as much as they would like. But don't give up. With some practice you can more easily find the sane middle ground between paranoia and complacency and can develop workable plans for day-to-day supervision.

Do put safety first. If you get a feeling and can't put a label on it, just obey it and explain later. Especially in matters of safety, trust yourself. Your child will test you if your resolve wavers, but if you trust yourself and speak and act calmly and firmly, your child will go along. Even if he complains, your child wants to believe you are keeping him safe.

Take each situation or risk and discuss it with your child regularly. As your child grows and needs less supervision, talk about threatening situations *before* they become a problem.

Take, for instance, the risk of fire. Does your child know the chief causes of fire? They are three: unextinguished cigarettes, careless use of appliances, and old wiring. Keep a safety dialogue going. For instance, talk out loud about your decision to put the iron away so your toddler can't reach it.

Does your child know what to do in case of fire? Does she know how to get out of her room if she smells smoke? Does she know to get out rather than to save possessions or pets? Fire-fighters say that pets are very good at escaping fires. Make sure your child knows this and other crucial information that matters to her. She needs to know safe neighbors, phone numbers for help, and how to use a public phone or to ask for help with a phone.

Make sure your child knows that you would rather see the house burn down than have one hair on his head singed, even if the fire were his fault. Also assure each child that there will always be adequate supervision so that it is not her responsibility to save other people. Then make sure this is true. If you want an older child to take responsibility, be clear and make sure she has a sensible plan for how to supervise and protect young or old.

Do this same kind of run-through with all issues that may threaten your child's safety, including violence in school, car accidents in the street, unruly friends, sexual advances, suspicious behavior from others, inappropriate questions, kitchen mishaps, thunderstorms, chemicals (in the garage, kitchen, or bathroom), medicines, dangerous tools, toys or activity props, the risks of sports, the effects of alcohol on otherwise trusted people, being stranded without a ride, and whatever other scenarios you might think of that could pose a risk.

The bottom line is, think through all scenarios your child might find himself in, have a plan for safety, share with him any safety measures he is old enough to comprehend, line up familiar, trusted people, and otherwise ensure adequate supervision to guard against any risks that are too invisible, scary, serious, remote, or complex for him to understand.

Take care also that your child *feels* safe. My clients Mary and Art complained that Chad and John, ages 8 and 10, were insisting on sleeping in their parents' room at night. Mary and Art had almost forgotten that it all started a month after their house had been burglarized. They had put the incident behind them fast. No one was hurt, insurance came through, and, well, it's a risk of modern life.

In their haste, they had left Chad and John feeling unsafe. They needed to acknowledge the breach in the family's defenses. They reassured the kids by bringing Chad and John along on the rounds to lock up the house, and they let the boys sleep with them until the boys felt safe again by themselves, which they did in less than a month.

If a child insists on a lock on her door, give it to her first and ask questions later. If we don't trust her feelings, she will stop trusting them herself, and she certainly won't trust us to keep her safe.

Let your child know he need never feel embarrassed if he seeks help to fend off a threat. Knowing his limits and seeking help is a sign of strength, not of weakness. Model this yourself. When safety is concerned, don't worry about what others may think. Seek out information, advice, and support until you know you have done all you can. Use social services, libraries, neighborhood clinics, employers, health professionals, clergy, friends, and self-help support groups.

Kids today are in over their heads much of the time. What they can handle for half an hour can get out of hand after two hours. No matter how savvy your child seems to be, go slowly. Remember how you were at whatever age your child is. Don't assume she is so different from you, no matter how different her life has been from yours. All the emotions are still there.

An old Hopi saying goes something like this: "We will know the end is coming when there is no one to watch the children." So if a child acts like you're supervising too much, become more a part of his life. He may really need more of you, not less, to feel safe.

Space

The need for safety is physical. The need for space is emotional.

Researchers are still a long way off from discovering what our needs are for personal space, if indeed it can be generalized beyond each individual culture. It is a known fact that each person has a sense of personal space. As parents we must respect that.

The need changes with your child's age. You begin with a baby who wants you there all the time, virtually attached to him. Before very long, you may have a child of 14 whom you love just as much as ever but who says to you, "Will you get out of my room and give me some space?"

Signs that the need for space has not been fulfilled might be irritability, chronic complaints, hypersensitivity to noise or touch, pushing, hitting, repeated rearranging of his room, estrangement, alienation, a compulsion to control or be the center of attention, impatience, and lack of concentration.

An important aspect of the need for space is privacy. Children need to know that their essential bodily functions are completely under their control, to the extent they are able to meet their own needs. Progress toward an adult private space can be a natural process that begins with the baby, whose natural dependency requires that the parent be very much involved in private functions. But even then, let the baby be free to explore her own body in any way that is physically safe. Very soon, a toddler wants to manage personal hygiene and body functions herself as her independence grows. This includes elimination functions, dressing, washing, and sleeping habits.

By the time your child reaches puberty, his bodily functions are largely up to him. His need for space includes the need to know that his privacy will not be invaded except in dire emergency.

The same approach applies to your child's sex life, whether early exploration of his personal sexuality or a teenager's developing relationship with peers. Though we may be tempted, if we invade a teenager's privacy hoping to offer tips along the way, we are liable to meet only resentment and excessive secretiveness. Instead, develop a healthy respect for the privacy of each member of the family, and offer your values, opinions, and pointers long before you think your child might actually need them.

As soon as a child is old enough to open and close her own door, for example, you need to establish a knock-before-you-enter policy, and set an example by doing the same with your door. Of course, make clear that there is virtually no reason you would not let a child enter after knocking. By establishing this policy you are demonstrating that everyone deserves a chance to make a choice, or to set their hair straight, before accepting someone else in their own private space.

Psychic privacy is essential as well. Dreams, goals, fears, crushes, and so forth can only be forced out of a child at the cost of breaching important personal boundaries. When you show respect for your child's inner life and create a safe emotional space for sharing within the family, that is the best way to encourage sharing of anything that needs to be shared.

Help your child identify her own psychic boundaries and don't take it personally when she draws a wider boundary than you would wish. Also, see that a child has enough space to do his many life functions. Is his bed too short now that he is a six-foot 15-year-old? Get a new one, even if it's a hand-me-down. Is your daughter feeling stressed because she has to share her bathroom with her older sister, who covers the area with makeup? Put a divider on the counter. For kids sharing rooms, check out new versions of the old screens, now becoming available to meet the needs created by closer living quarters.

Is your child troubled by either disordered space or excessively ordered space? Take these feelings into account. Let her have a space to herself that suits her personal sense of organization, even if it is different from your own. (And remember whose house it is, so that your sense of space is not preempted entirely.)

You can arrange even the smallest home so that basic space needs can be met. Don't deny the importance of these needs out of fear or guilt that they can't be met. Rather, ask for each family member's cooperation to help all meet their needs.

Is your son harried by hard rock CDs you insist on playing throughout the house? Another aspect of space is quiet. The constant noise in buildings, schools, stores, and now in electronically equipped homes filled with computers and appliances can be too much for a child. Find quieter fans, use earphones for personal listening, and leave each child with some quiet place and time when interruptions will be at a minimum. Also look for space and quiet outside.

Nature

Every child has a need for a direct, foundational relationship with the natural world. The depth of this basic need is just beginning to be fully recognized. Your child needs warm earth under his feet; the sensations of breezes, odors, grass, trees, and the vegetable world; and rich interactions with other creatures.

Researchers in the new science of ecopsychology are finding that emotional disturbances that won't respond to any other kind of therapy may still respond positively and dramatically to a return to nature. Nature nurtures the spirit.

Given that our entire emotional and physical character developed in the context of the natural world—not in the artificial one we are surrounded by now—it is little wonder that nature is a basic need. Just as a child who wanders a bit too far from his mother in a department store can panic until reunited with her, a child who reaches a breaking point from uninterrupted exposure to contrived environments, gadgets, tools, toys, voices, and sights can fall to pieces until reunited with Mother Nature.

Signs that a child needs nature include frantic activity; impatience; disorientation; lack of concentration; exhaustion; staring; lack of focus; disjointed sentences or thoughts; aversion to natural phenomena like bugs, birds, plants, or dirt; fear of or obsession with natural functions including his own; and compulsion always to be in control or the center of attention.

Give your child a regular experience of the natural outdoors. A direct relationship with nature helps ground the child's being in confidence, awe, and wonder. It's a source of spiritual strength and renewal. You will love to watch your child embrace the simplicity of life on the one hand and its complexity on the other.

Think of nature when nothing else seems to solve a problem. Perhaps, as Popeye said, "Too much is enough. I can't stand no more!" Take time out and have your child walk with you in the park or, together, open a window and listen to a bird, lie down on the ground and stroke a cat, wade in a stream and chase fish or frogs, sniff a flower in a supermarket, watch the breeze play with leaves, or chase butterflies down the sidewalk.

Give your child a plant for her room or start some sprouts growing in the kitchen, and watch them together. Buy goldfish or whatever more ambitious pets you want, and enjoy them together.

Even a teenager needs nature. Social concerns, books, and papers may take over her life. But when you think about it, even your child's physical activity at school takes place more and more in neatly antiseptic gyms rather than outside. Find activities that get your child outside and among the vegetation (but not on chemically treated lawns). Locate local parks, arboretums, and neighborhood gardens. Expose your child to kiteflying, skateboarding, biking, gardening, and so on.

When you are outside, don't think of learning names and categories, but rather about experiencing. Think of nature as aromatherapy, color therapy, and soothing subliminal audiotapes wrapped up into one. Relating to the natural environment is not a privilege or luxury; it is a basic need and right of children.

Companionship

The need for companionship comes from that fact that we are by nature social beings. Children thrive in the company of other people. Your child needs regular human interaction of a kind that is encouraging and reinforcing to his well-being and growth. They need a familiar group of reliable, loving, accepting, and forgiving people to help them learn skills, language, and a sense of their own value. You and your family, relatives, friends, and mentors can serve this purpose.

It's a mistake to assume that because we live in a crowded world children get plenty of companionship. It is easy to forget, for instance, that though a child is surrounded by other children at school, school can be a tense place with difficult pressures created by various artificial circumstances. These include virtually absolute authority of one adult over 30 children, segregation by age and skill level, constant interruptions by bells and commands, and competition for social, physical, and academic attention and achievement. These pressures make the free, voluntary, patient, and nurturing interactions of companionship hard to count on. This is why kids so often declare that lunch and recess are their favorite school times.

At home, too, children have little time to just be with friends, siblings, or parents. Adult functions in this society leave no room for kids to hang around, watch, and learn. Shopping is about the only thing some children actually do with their parents. Time with siblings is cut short by chores and homework, and visiting with friends after school requires special planning and often extra effort from already exhausted parents.

Easygoing companionship is the rule rather than the exception among traditional societies, which give us a peek into the circumstances under which our psyches developed. A tribal child has few pressures. Ages and skill levels mix freely, and a number of adults supervise the children cooperatively. If competition arises, the kids make their own rules and can break them at will.

In contrast, my client Paul reported that he could go for weeks on end with his only interactions with his son Hal being interrogations about homework, orders and follow-ups about chores, chiding words about bedtime or missed buses or overused telephones, and calls to turn down the music or the video. Paul wondered where the rewards of being a father were hiding.

By recognizing his child's need for companionship, Paul tried to downplay other kinds of interactions in favor of words and deeds that showed appreciation for Hal just as he was. He lightened up and tried to leave time in his expectations for his son to hang out with local friends. Soon Paul noticed he was getting a lot more cooperation, and he was feeling a lot better about being a parent.

Signs of unmet needs for companionship include loneliness; lack of interest or enthusiasm; obsession with winning or keeping friends; possessiveness over friends, family, or things; chronic discourtesy; and depression. Stay attuned to your child's need for regular human interaction based on acceptance, courtesy, tolerance, admiration, and shared interests. Much as you would like your children to find good companions, you can't make it happen. But you can facilitate valuable relationships your child may find and create opportunities for more.

Don't try to fulfill all your child's companionship needs yourself. Your relationship with her is her first model for human interaction. But then she needs to widen her circle steadily over the years. Trust this process as the best way to meet this basic need.

Activity

Your child's activities and the activities going on around her provide the energy that motivates her to be interested in life, to be alert, to learn, and to grow.

When your child is at rest, she wants things steady, predictable, comfortable, and safe. But when she's awake, she wants to see what's happening, try something new, do stuff, go places, find new things, get into the action, do old things new ways.

A child who has unmet activity needs might be bored, hyperactive, fatigued, sleepless, drowsy, restless, unmotivated, always or seldom hungry, resentful, paranoid, withdrawn, or controlling. Without appropriate activities, she feels more like a victim of life than like an active participant.

The successful parent tries to provide healthy stimulation, interesting activities, and timely rest for his child. The most important elements to consider in fulfilling the need for activity are these:

- Encouraging any relatively safe activities that your child discovers on his own

- Adding activities that appeal to your child and stimulate growth and learning naturally

- Seeing that activities aimed at a particular purpose, like education, continue that natural process (the only way they will really be effective)

- Affording opportunities for frequent physical activity and for frequent unstructured play

- Finding a balance between different kinds of activity and rest

The last element comes up most often in the mad rush of activities that so many families today fall into after school and on Saturdays.

From the beginning, the activities going on around an infant in a healthy family environment stimulate his brain to build the nerve connections, or synapses, that can increase his mental and emotional skills. Colors, music, loving human voices, melodic sentences and rich vocabulary, lots of touching and carrying, and changes of scenery and physical objects create this stimulating environment. A parent must keep life interesting.

Music likewise has a profound effect on brain development. Research has shown that music stimulates valuable new links between different parts of the brain. Children respond to rhythm, dance, and song right away. So make music of any or all kinds a regular part of the activity around your child.

Once your child reaches school age, try as much as possible to take the attitude that formal education should be a continuation of childhood's fulfillment of the basic need for rich, stimulating activity. Children learn naturally this way. Unfortunately, few modern school experiences fill this bill. But a child is interested in schooling exactly to the extent that it offers interesting activity that moves away from the status quo while still offering security and support. A child responds to new friends, new events, new ideas, new authorities, new skills to master, new ways to feel, new places to explore, new things to investigate, new forms of expression, and new sources of inspiration and love only to the extent that these are presented in a way that trusts the child to know what he needs and wants. Meanwhile, he will embrace the familiar also, as ground and home base for new explorations.

These experiences must keep coming, and appear in a context of trust and support, or your child can lose interest in formal education fast. A good teacher keeps them coming. A poor teacher doesn't know how.

If you see school in this perspective, you can be successful in hanging on to your best role as a parent. You will see that your role is to support, help interpret, guide, encourage, and then also always to offer opportunity for rest from the stimulation. You will be able to avoid becoming obsessed with achievement of any particular goal in school. Rather you will be able to watch with pleasure as your child's learning unfolds naturally in response to school-based activities.

If you choose to school your children at home, as we have for the past 10 years, you may see clearly how schooling is indeed a natural extension of the guidance you have given them as younger children. Since, of course, most of my clients are sending their children out of the home for institutional schooling, I know from them how hard it can be in this more usual situation to keep this perspective. But those parents who work at it find that it enables them to be far more helpful and supportive and that their children's success in formal education increases.

One of the reasons my husband and I decided to teach our children ourselves was that in my parenting classes I found that almost 90 percent of family problems stemmed from three things: getting the kids to get up to go to school, getting them to do homework, and getting them to go to bed so that they could get up again to go back to school. Most kids want to play and explore at their own discretion first thing in the morning. They are more eager to tackle purposeful tasks later, but only if they've had sufficient sleep. Likewise, homework is of dubious value, accomplishing little after a full day at school except to transform perfectly normal parents into frustrated substitute teachers. And similarly, at the end of the day when the child finally expects a little discretionary time, it's off to bed!

One more school-related source of problems for families is dealing with the stresses and strains of the artificial environment of school, in which bells tell you when you can talk or not, schedules tell you when you can play or not, teachers tell you when you can interact with others or not, and the very structure of the institution forces you to be with the same group of children all day whether the group dynamics work or not—all under the authority of a nonparent who may be effective or not.

These four problems boil down to the existence of an authoritarian institution outside the home that affects every decision made within the home. It seems a natural solution to get rid of the outside voice. And indeed it was so for us and for dozens of other families I have known and worked with. As I gained more experience with the natural development of children outside school, it seemed more and more that "school" was wholly beside the point in our children's education and growth process. Because parents express so much curiosity about the home education option today, I have included an appendix about home education at the end of this volume.

The physical activity of your child is every bit as important as the emotional and intellectual activity we have been discussing. Muscle and bone development both depend upon regular physical activity, as do heart and lung capacity, digestive functions, and the workings of the lymphatic system that cleanses the body. In turn, adequate energy and nutrients to the brain are dependent on these. So keep your child active.

Many experts feel that our society's requirements that children sit for hours at a time in school from as young as four years old prevents them from fulfilling this need and compromises both their physical fitness and their learning.

Experimental schools like Montessori and Waldorf schools have moved away from the desk-and-pencil model for children under age 7. Some say kids needn't really settle down to book study until 14. They note that Abraham Lincoln didn't do schoolwork until that age.

It is up to you to determine what level of activity your child needs each day and to be alert to signs and cues. I have seen many children who have been labeled poor learners simply because their physical activity needs were not met in the early years and they weren't able to move on to sedentary pursuits.

You might consider, then, letting a preschool child do all the running around, playing catch, handstands, bed jumping, and so on that he wants. And later, if you find that homework cuts into your child's afternoon activity, even though you would like him to get it done right away, let your child meet his need for activity.

When my children were smaller and reached a limit on long drives, we discovered a special use for rest areas. After the third time they said, "When will we be there?" we would stop the car and ask them to run from one end of the area to the other. They never needed to be asked twice. And then they were good for another couple of hours in the car. It paid to stay alert to our children's need for activity.

Set a strong example for vigorous physical activity in your own life, whether it is formal exercise or just hard work around home or neighborhood. Don't be too particular about what form your child's exercise takes as long as it does not endanger your child or others. Consider some with you, some alone, some with other companions, some with teams. Just keep that little, or not so little, body moving.

Give your child rackets, balls, ropes to jump and climb, bikes, sticks, beanbags, paddles, skateboards, ice skates, in-line skates, minitrampolines, pogo sticks, kites, rockets, bubble makers, any kind of musical instrument that gets children drumming or dancing, or whatever catches your fancy or theirs.

A longtime physical education teacher told me that he had seen many children whose early team sports resulted in burnout and exaggerated competitiveness instead of long-term fitness and love of athletics. So let your child take her time getting involved in these.

If a child tires of an activity, don't worry about her switching to another. Even if you have spent a thousand dollars on dance lessons, it doesn't mean your money was wasted if she decides to move to soccer. The love of activity is what counts.

Regular opportunities for unstructured play are every bit as important as the various structured activities in your child's life. Play allows your child to process experiences and emotions in her own way as they arise. Play must be voluntary, open ended, experimental, and often imitative. Your child plays for the sole purpose of pleasure and learning, with no goal in mind. Play is most productive when safety is ensured by the parent and when safe props and people are readily available but not at the center of the activity. If a child seems bored, burned out, depressed, or irritable, encourage play.

Too many activities without frequent breaks and time to rest and play will only confuse and exhaust your child. Try to establish a balance, day by day, among your child's activities.

A gentle stream of activity that you monitor carefully is the surest way to nurture health, vitality, and learning. Find a comfortable balance between physical and mental, passive and active, visual and aural, solo and group, outdoors and in, away and at home.

Affection

Affection is the outward expression of your parental love. It's not only the finest support for your child's well-being but also your greatest reward as a parent.

Infants in orphanages have had the unwanted distinction of proving the necessity of human affection for child survival. Though all their physical needs may be met, they lose their will to live and many die if they are not touched and warmly spoken to at least to some minimal extent. Your affection energizes your child to seek life, to grow, to learn, to mature, to explore, to connect, and to enjoy. Your affection is the switch that turns on your child's internal "software" that sets all these functions in motion. It lights up your child's heart.

Signs that a child is in need of affection include sarcasm, rejection of well-meant gestures, irritability, short attention span, poor physical self-image, frequent infections, competitiveness, listlessness, and depression. Almost any behavior will improve when the child experiences your affection.

Don't worry about giving too much affection. It can't happen. Affection is a simple expression of your love for your child as a person, with all his weaknesses and strengths. It is not a reward nor does it ask anything back, but expresses itself simply and gratuitously in your words, touch, tone, and body language. It is not a fawning adoration that idealizes the child nor is it spoiling the child. Spoiling substitutes things like gifts, praise, favors, and permissiveness for true signs of affection.

Undoubtedly you already have your favorite ways of showing affection. Here is a little catalog to encourage their frequent use.

Eye Contact. Whether you are in your car, walking together, watching TV, or doing chores or homework, you may find it hard to make eye contact. Yet it's the quickest way to build faith and understanding, as long as your gaze is warm and accepting. Avoid glaring, staring, or narrowing your eyes. That's not the kind of affectionate eye contact you need. Your look should be a gift of full attention and love.

Don't insist on eye contact from your child. A number of emotions can prevent eye contact, and forcing it misses the point and breeds resentment. If your child is comfortable enough with you or the situation, then eye contact will naturally follow.

When you want to speak with your child, you will know you have her attention if you address her and then wait patiently until she looks up. And when your child addresses you, look up. If you can't, say, "Just a minute" and then stop as soon as you can and look up.

Focused Attention. You need to focus your attention completely on your child, with no distractions, several times a day. Try to have a balance between your initiative and hers. Focused attention is the quickest way to convince your child that she is important in this world, especially in your world. Research has found that, on average, children get only eight minutes of focused attention from a parent per day. Be sure you do more.

Words. Talk a lot to your child. Cultivate a balanced, cheerful tone that reassures even when problems arise. If you converse for about five minutes, you will have shared about 1,000 words. That's a lot of opportunity to do some great parenting, if you think first a little before you speak.

Even when you're angry at your child, your words can remain friendly as long as you don't threaten, frighten, or put down your child. If you find yourself screaming, for example, let out your distress to the ceiling (as Haim Ginott once recommended), and let the child observe your example of how you handle strong emotions without malice!

Proper Names. Use your child's name often, at least five times a day, and in a respectful, affectionate tone. Don't use it to shame or degrade, no matter how angry or frustrated you may be. Use the form of the name she likes best. If you don't know, ask. You might be surprised how many adult clients have complained to me they still feel angry that a parent refused to use the form of their name that they wanted.

Greetings. Say "hi" and "bye" no matter how many times you part in a day or for how long. Make each one affirming of your love. With a hello, inquire about how your child is and what he has been doing, before laying on him your own story or ideas of what he needs to do next. This is a strong acknowledgment of your child's personhood. Similarly, with a parting always let a child know who is accountable for his safety in your absence and exactly when you will see him again. Avoid last-minute messages about your expectations or special requests. And for younger ones, make sure to put your return time in terms of familiar events, like dinner or bedtime.

Laughter. Life gets so serious. I find parents don't laugh enough with their children. Discover what tickles your funny bone and share it with your child. Also, notice what she enjoys most and try to participate. Make a joke, laugh at her jokes, laugh at something silly or careless you have done or thought of, read the funnies together, watch a sitcom with her, share a political cartoon and explain its irony, or make up a voice for your cat, bird, dog, goldfish, or puppet. Look for funny things when you're on the road together.

Don't laugh *at* your child, only *with* her. And if she brings home inappropriate humor from school or elsewhere, resist being outraged. Simply explain why it doesn't work for you and find something else funny to share.

Sharing Space. At least once a day, make an effort to be where your child is. Not to do anything, but just to be there. This is an easy and powerful way to let your child know you want to be in his life and are glad he is in yours. Sit on the same sofa, make up something to do in the same room, hang out while your child makes a snack, stand at the doorway and make small talk as he puts finishing touches on his looks, sit on the floor near where he is.

Smiles. Smile with every greeting and as you begin and end each conversation. Avoid sarcastic or self-pitying smiles. Keep it simple and easy. Even if the situation is tense, as long as you are keeping things in perspective you will be able to smile at a lighter moment. Smiling never gives away your power; it only enhances it, because it makes clear you are in control and your optimism and affection are steadfast.

Hugs. Try for three or four a day, especially mornings, partings, and bedtime, but also in between, at any opportune moment. Explore all the different kinds of hugs, from a quick cheek-to-cheek hug to a big bear hug. You can even find one that a macho 12-year-old boy will tolerate, if you are sensitive to his wishes.

If you notice a wince or a wiggle when you offer a hug, choose another kind of touch next time or ask what your child would prefer. In front of others, kids may prefer a pat on the shoulder, a wave, a salute, or a message like "Have a good time" or "See you soon."

Likewise kids may be uncomfortable with sitting on laps, chest-to-chest hugs, or lip-to-lip kisses. Do whatever both of you are comfortable with and nothing else. No teasing, tickling, or ambiguous or aggressive moves should be tolerated. Be clear or stick with words until you can be clear.

Favors. These are little gifts. You do something just because you care and think your child might like it. Be careful not to overdo material gifts, like candy or a toy. Instead give of your labor or time, like feeding the cat because you know your child will be home late from school that day. Once or twice a week is enough. Don't overdo it.

"I Love You." You need at least some version of this daily.

Keep it light and real. If you want to get deep and serious, make sure your child is in the mood.

Touches. Hugs are just one kind of affectionate touching. Try a light and friendly touch on the arm as you make an interesting (but nonaggressive) point; a casual massage of back, neck, or feet while watching TV; a friendly tumble or wrestle if the child is in the mood; a pat on the shoulder in admiration for a chore completed; or a handshake or high five in celebration of just about anything—a good idea, a helping hand, a creative effort, or a good plan.

Keep touches away from private parts and delicate tissues. The only exception is when you are actually helping a child who is sick, disabled, or in pain. Even then, ask, explain first, and wait for permission. Touch must be consensual and appropriate to ensure your child will know and respect her own physical integrity and interpersonal boundaries with others. Don't surprise a child with bodily contact, even intended as affectionate. The mixed messages are just too hard to sort out. Children need regular touch by loving people, but if in doubt, don't. Try to use all the opportunities you see for unambiguous affection. And go ahead and be corny and mushy if you want, but always respect the child's express instructions.

Once you appreciate how much of your parenting effort can be profitably devoted to simple affection, you may well agree that expressing your affection is not the icing on the cake but the cake itself.

A Success Story

I want to end this chapter by telling you about Tina, whose two teenage daughters were always fighting. Tina had done everything she could think of. She had tried keeping them apart, punishing them when they were rude to each other, and sending the aggressor to another room or outside or even to a friend's.

Finally Tina decided to focus her attention on meeting the girls' basic needs instead of being police officer, judge, and enforcer.

She hovered around in the morning to make sure they ate at least something for breakfast. She hung around at night to encourage each to brush teeth, change to a nightgown, calm down, turn down the lights, and read with a night-light or listen to music so that sleep would be the next step. Then she made an extra push to show her affection. She found opportunities to touch them more often on the shoulder, pat a hand on a counter, or administer a hug on the way out the door. And she tried to show them a few more smiles.

When Tina paid attention to these three things—food, sleep, and affection—they did the trick. At first Tina worried that she might be manipulating the girls to be nice rather than just "making them" be nice. After all, she thought, they should be nice even when they are hungry, tired, or not getting enough affection from Mom. But this is a mistaken interpretation of manipulation. If Tina fed them candy or some mind-altering drug to make them nice, we would have to say she was manipulating and, worse, hiding the problems from her children so they couldn't learn to deal with them.

In contrast, showing children what their basic needs are by meeting them and having them see the beneficial consequences is quite the opposite of manipulation. It is empowerment. If a pattern of conflict emerges again, instead of keeping up the confrontation or appealing to Mom as judge, they may think of postponing further unpleasantness until each has paid attention to her own basic needs.

Knowing when your basic needs need attention is at least as important as having conflict resolution skills. Experience shows that you'll need the latter less often if you have taken care of the former.

So don't fall victim to the idea that it's a cop-out to put off ending hostilities until basic needs are met. Even on the international scene, stalemates in negotiations resolve after a good night's sleep.

In three days, Tina noticed less tension in the air. The girls were sharing stories from school and talking about the next CDs they wanted to buy. And even when one did say something careless and hurtful, the other shrugged it off and went about her business. It seemed like a miracle, but it was just one more case of a parent doing what a parent is best at doing—paying attention to a child's basic life needs.

I hope you, like Tina, will set aside that urgency to fix the problem right now, no matter how well you think you understand the situation and know what needs to be done. If a troublesome event in your child's life keeps recurring, postpone your plans to "teach the child a lesson," to "make sure it doesn't happen again," to give instructions about prevention, or any similar urge. These solutions may make you feel good for the moment, but they won't really help the child.

Instead resolve to pay even more diligent attention to your child's basic needs. Then watch the miracles happen!

Summary of Basic Needs

Pay careful attention to these physical needs:

1. Sleep. Consider regular hours, adequate space and quiet, seven to nine hours.

2. Food. Consider unadulterated, simple foods, homemade whenever possible. I invented the acronym WOLFSPRING to remind me to check that my family's foods are as Whole, Organic, Local, Fresh, Simple, Pure, Raw, In season, Not irradiated, and Genetically traditional as I can get them.

3. Light. Consider variety, intensity, color, natural sources when possible; sensible hours in sun.

4. Air. Consider filters, ionizers, and outdoor exposure.

5. Water. Consider filters, springwater, pools, waterfalls, water as first choice for thirst.

6. Comfort. Consider temperature and humidity. A few degrees can make a big difference in moods, comfort, stress, and immunity. Also, consider personal hygiene. Give regular access to shower, sink, soap, comb, toothbrush, and toothpaste.

Pay close attention to these relational needs:

7. Safety. Consider effects of storms, precipices, tools, fire and heat sources, cramped enclosures, persistent wetness. Also, protect against environmental poisons like excessive medications, illicit drugs, alcohol, household and industrial chemicals, radiation, and agricultural, biological, or environmental waste.

8. Space. Consider adequate privacy, frequent breaks from work or study, and room for meditation and renewal.

9. Nature. Consider getting back to basics, with green below and blue above, yellow blossoms, and things that grow without the aims and efforts of humanity.

10. Companionship. Consider family meals, daily greetings, weekly time with friends, and mixing different ages and sexes. Share family lore, religious traditions, classic stories, and even good-natured teen gossip to bring the larger community into your home.

11. Activity. Consider room to move and good reasons to engage in life. Cultivate group and individual activities, any exercise that suits. Spend time setting limits on safe activities and promoting possibilities. Give frequent updates on family plans, goals, and schedules and create opportunities to develop ethics in action.

12. Affection. Consider all the options mentioned in this chapter and create a warm, emotionally safe, and loving environment for your child.

It is not a bad thing that children should occasionally, and politely, put parents in their place.

COLETTE
(SIDONIE-GABRIELLE CLAUDINE)

God sent children for another purpose than merely to keep up the race—to enlarge our hearts; and to make us unselfish and full of kindly sympathies and affections; to give our souls higher aims; to call out all our faculties to extended enterprise and exertion; and to bring round our firesides bright faces, happy smiles, and loving, tender hearts.

MARY BOTHAM HOWITT

Children require guidance and sympathy far more than instruction.

ANNE SULLIVAN

"I always hear my child out."

❖ Listening ❖

Once you've made positive steps toward building your faith in your child, and once you've begun to focus more attention on your child's basic needs, you may discover that the next thing you can work on most profitably is your parental listening skill. The third secret of successful parents is this: "I always hear my child out."

You may have heard about good listening skills so much today in talk about relationships that it sounds almost trite to recommend them to parents. But I find that in my parenting seminars, although parents know listening is important and often try very hard to do it, they may never have had any real instruction in the delicate and powerful art of listening.

I hope you will benefit from the explanations, stories, examples, exercises, and suggestions you will be hearing in this chapter. First, here are some crucial ideas to keep in mind about listening to your child:

- Your child always wants you to hear and understand, no matter how much it may seem to the contrary.

91

- Nothing is so urgent that it prevents you from hearing your child out—unless one of you is literally falling off a cliff.

- By always listening in nonemergency situations, you actually build your child's ability to respond immediately in an emergency. If your child is used to your good listening, she will recognize instantly any situation where listening is impossible.

- Listening is as much for you as for your child. You will learn far more than you ever dreamed when you become a truly skilled listener. You will save yourself endless words and worry.

- Begin always with an open mind. Situations that seem totally clear and wrongs that seem to need immediate righting are often the events that require the most careful listening. A child's most mischievous or outrageous behavior is usually a desperate move to get the listening attention she deserves.

- Always pat yourself on the back for your loving example of listening. Never feel guilty for saying less and listening more.

- Listening is the single most validating, empowering thing you can do for your child when you do it with loving responsiveness.

A Sunlit Web of Love

Good listening is like a spider's web in the morning sun—delicate and strong at the same time. To catch the meat of what is being said, you must create a delicate, almost imperceptible net of kindly attention that can catch every nuance of meaning and hold it firmly in your understanding once captured.

Unlike with a spider web though, your own little prey—your child's message—really wants to be caught. That is, your child yearns for your understanding and validation of his feelings, thoughts, motives, reasoning, actions, and decisions.

Barriers That Can Keep You from Listening

If you worry that there is tension and distance between you and your child, you may, as do many parents who hear that listening helps, feel you are way beyond any help of such a subtle kind. They say, "My child won't even listen to me! Why should I listen to her!" Or, "You wouldn't believe what comes out of his mouth. I can't listen to that!"

Listening *can* do wonders, even in the most severe standoff between parent and child. Even when there seems to be an impenetrable block, as long as your child is saying something—anything—you can use specific listening skills to begin to remove the barriers.

"Ears Up!"

Musician Kit Stewart, lead singer and composer for the Kit Kats rock group, now dedicates his musical skills to inspiring children and families to live healthy lifestyles. When he has a special point to make, he likes to say, "Ears up!" Once you have absorbed the soothing truths in this chapter, you will know exactly when, like an attentive fox, to let your ears pop up.

What's more, as you apply the techniques you'll read here, you'll be amazed at the new and more satisfying responses you can get from your child. Here are some strategies I hope you can make your own.

- Whenever your child initiates conversation, you will need to listen.

- If you ask your child a question, listen to the answer.

- If you want to be understood, take time to listen to your child's response to what you say.

- Don't interrupt unless absolutely necessary—and that means only in a real emergency.

- Rid yourself of urgency. You will always have enough time to set a child straight *after* you listen.

- You can learn the patience you need for responsive listening with practice. To borrow from Ben Franklin, listening is "a stitch in time that saves nine."

- Listening is the best way to discover unmet needs.

- Listening is an excellent way to show your faith in your child.

Now let me tell you a story from my own parenting notebook.

Listening Can Save Worry

A few months ago, my son was taking a class in the city and was commuting to and from our suburban home. He hadn't decided yet which was better, train or car, and was trying both out on different days. One day he came home and said, "I can't do this! It's not worth it. I'm not really interested in this class!"

I felt temporarily dismayed. He had really wanted to take the class, and it seemed just the thing. I began to question myself in guiding him to the class and to worry that he had lost his motivation. I began to respond with cogent points about why he chose to take the class in the first place and how he should stick with it and give it a chance. Then I remembered. I hadn't really listened yet!

By this time my son was wandering around the room, waiting for me to stop talking or to say something useful. So I quickly backed off and said, "But wait a minute. What you were saying was that you're discouraged about your class today. You're not sure it's worth it." Then I listened.

He said, "Yeah, I decided to drive in today, and there was a horrible tie-up on the expressway, a jackknifed tractor-trailer or something. I was two hours late and missed half the class!"

My son hadn't given up on his class, after all, or changed his interests suddenly, or even gotten lazy about getting to the class. He had simply had a bad day that could make anybody react as he did.

By listening, I avoided a whole stream of motherly fears, worries, projections, and quandaries. The next day he got up cheerfully and took the train to town.

Listening May Run Against the Parental Grain

When you are trying particularly hard to be a good, careful parent, it may be especially hard to listen. You may tend instead to be thinking miles ahead of the conversation. You're assessing the risk or the damage of what's being proposed. You're anticipating contingencies, formulating an intelligent response, and most of all working up a great solution. And of course, you hope it's the very best solution!

With all that on our parental minds, no wonder we have trouble really hearing what is being said.

Even when you think you know exactly what your child is saying—actually, especially then—you need to back off and listen. If the same thing comes up again and again—"I've heard all this before," you're thinking as you watch your child's lips move—then chances are that the matter hasn't been handled effectively before and listening may be just the approach to get you where you want to be.

Language Is Inherently Imperfect

No human communication is perfect. No matter how much in sync you feel you are with your child, if she feels the need to say something, you will need to listen. Human language is an amazing device for getting another person to think similar thoughts to your own and to have them understand who you are and what you want. It is a brilliant supplement to the body language, facial expressions, noises, and invisible vibes we began with as babies.

Still, language is imperfect. Unless we really listen, we can run around with a half-baked idea and wreak havoc with our parenting for no good cause. If we have heard something a thousand times, we probably need to listen more, not less.

Just think of the times that you have repeated things yourself. It's probably not because you have had a silly idea or haven't been listening to good advice. Nine times out of 10, it is because you are not being heard. Someone you want to have understand you, or just to validate your right to think what you're thinking or feel what you're feeling, isn't listening to you.

Your child is just the same. No matter how strange, ridiculous, confused, misinformed, offensive, or repetitive your child's words may be, you need to listen.

Listening Through the Years

Listening is one of the skills that is dramatically easier to pick up if you have lots of time with your baby from the very beginning. Listening doesn't start when your baby begins using words, or even hand gestures. It starts with the first whimper. If we as parents experience from the beginning our ability to grasp and respond effectively to our child's basic needs, ongoing parenting will be a lot easier. Some parents who have had smooth birth experiences and on-demand breastfeeding, for instance, report that their baby never cried full throttle until the first parting, immunization shot, or other stress imposed from outside. Babies don't need crying for lung exercise.

Listening can be challenging in the toddler stage, as kids pursue all kinds of playful repetitions, delusions, fantasies, falsehoods (known or unknown), and experiments with the incredible power of words. Just knowing that this is normal, and that ideally we were allowed to do it ourselves when we were kids, can reassure us that we can just listen and enjoy the process while relating as genuinely and encouragingly as we can.

At the toddler stage, gentle guidance is usually all that's required to steer the child through this important verbal learning. So resist overreacting to behaviors that would be atrocious at an older age. Here is the best time to focus extra effort on giving your child a vocabulary that he can use to share his feelings, make requests, register discomfort, or express anger as well as delight and satisfaction, so he doesn't have to act these out on other kids, adults, or things.

In the exploratory stage, expect your child to branch out and try her new skills on others as well as trying some new ideas out on you. Take special care to be familiar with the kinds of things your child is being exposed to on television, video, and computer or when in the care of other adults. You will need as much context as possible to interpret what you are listening to, because your child is likely to have limited ability to explain to you the ground and meaning of new ideas she wants to run by you.

Needs can seem vastly increased now too, and you may need to think often, hard, and fast to know what you are comfortable with in each area, so that you can set reasonable limits for your child's explorations. Can the kids still take baths together? Can bedtime be a bit later? How many people can be invited to one party? Your tone of confidence and flexibility and your willingness to listen in these situations can often be more important than the particular stance you take.

As children enter the growth stage, roughly the years from age 7 to 14, your child wants even more to be heard. He is starting to want to make real decisions that have an actual effect on his life. You may want to hone your listening responses by practicing the suggestions in this chapter, so that even if you must say no, your child will know you are listening.

When your child is in the maturation stage, from 14 to 21, you may be asked to listen less often than you would like. Here your listening attitude must include a clear acknowledgment of the limits of your actual power and your simultaneous desire to stay a part of your child's life. Create casual opportunities for listening as often as possible, since your child's emerging sense of independence may discourage him from bringing questions to you in any kind of planned or formal way.

When you hear or overhear bits and pieces of things, as you most likely will, try not to waste too much time speculating and scaring yourself. But rather, make further inquiries with your child, not accusingly but with affectionate curiosity. Or if you know it's not your business, let go of your worries and dwell in your faith.

Combine Faith, Attention, and Listening

As you listen, nurture your faith in your child. Think to yourself, "If my child wants to say something to me, it is important because he is important and he has a capable mind and important thoughts." Also be attentive to basic needs. Ask yourself, "Is he crying out for help in meeting a basic need? Is he in need of affection, companionship, food, safety, air, activity, and so on? What need may be behind his present frustration, anger, distress, or confusion?"

With a little practice, you can quickly develop the ability to deeply understand your child's words without getting hung up on her particular choice of expression. Sometimes the generation gap in modes of communication becomes so great that parents don't listen at all to the message but only react critically to the choice of words or expression.

Focus on the Message, Not the Medium

As you hear me urging you to focus on the message, let me emphasize that good listening doesn't mean you ever have to tolerate intolerable forms of expression. Good listening simply means you don't let the message get lost while you are making appropriate responses to the form of expression. That sounds very theoretical and difficult. Let me make it more concrete and simple.

Marsha's son has been at football practice every afternoon for a week. When he comes home, he goes straight to his room after a quick complaint that there's nothing good to eat in the house. He turns on his CD player loud, does a little homework, and then comes down to watch MTV. He's 13. Marsha fears the vacant look in his eyes after a half-hour of that MTV stuff. Today she asks if he has done all his homework. "I don't give a sh**!" he says.

It's easy at that moment to feel like a failure as a parent. Here Marsha has given her son a home, all the essential middle school electronics, a caring family, a good education, and support at his football games. She deserves this? How many times do you think she has reacted to this situation with: "What kind of attitude is that? Don't talk to your mother like that! I care about your homework, and you should too. Turn off that stupid TV right now! Show me some respect, after all I do for you. . . ."

This time Marsha remembers to listen. "I always hear my child out" was the parenting secret she rehearsed in her head. Instead of launching into her usual diatribe, she says, "So you don't care about your homework right now. I can hear you loud and clear. But I wish you would say it in friendlier language. I find it impossible to listen to you when you choose to use offensive words."

Then Marsha has a shock. Her son looks up at her. She can't remember when he has voluntarily made eye contact when she has interrupted his MTV viewing. "Yeah," he says. "The math teacher is really dumb. She gave me a D."

Again Marsha is tempted to begin, "A D! But you're good at math. What happened? That's why homework is so important!" But she listens again.

"She gave you a D?" she asks.

"Yeah, she said my work wasn't neat enough for her to read. And I had the right answers!" He continues, looking back at the TV, "She's just too lazy!"

Once again Marsha wants to attack, but she just listens. She waits, with an attentive "Hmmm."

Then she gets the shock of her life. Her son says, "I guess I'll just have to write neater for her. What a pain!"

After You've Weathered the Storm

Now listening gets fun! Marsha says, "Yes, I guess you're right. It'll be a pain, but if you write neater she probably will get off your back." How wonderful it feels to say to your child, "Yes, you're right"!

Her son smiles. And so does she.

After that day, Marsha knew that she had a vast new power at her fingertips to help her relate to her son. She could find out what was on his mind and help him to help himself, and still she could look out for her own sensibilities about how he talked to her—all without worrying, giving up, or screaming!

If Marsha's story sounds too good to be true, try to believe. I have heard this story over and over through the years from hundreds of parents I've worked with, parents who thought they would never have a comfortable or even respectable conversation with their child again.

There is incredible power in listening. It works because you are demonstrating both faith and attention. It is irresistible to your child. So let's look at exactly what it involves.

The Techniques You Need to Be Successful

First, watch your body language. Stay relaxed. If you have already tensed up at the first angry, frustrated, or disrespectful tones in your child's voice, loosen your shoulders, unfurl your brow, and relax your fingers. Then make eye contact and relax your lips. Ears up!

Next, face your child. No matter what you're doing, try to take a break and turn your chest parallel to your child's. Unfold your arms in a gesture of openness and receptivity. Face the child.

If you are right in the middle of something, give a true estimate of how long it will be before you can stop, ask for your child's patience, and finish your work. Then stop when you said you would, thank him for his patience, and turn on your full listening art.

Have More Patience than Your Child Has!

A child under age 5 can wait only a minute. A child 5 to 12 can go up to 10 minutes. Only teenagers can wait 20 minutes or more without feeling neglected or unimportant in your eyes. So keep your postponements short. Remember, few things are more urgent than listening to your child.

This means you can let the phone ring, let the page you were reading go unfinished, let the sentence you were typing wait for your return. Go ahead and turn over the pancake, or turn down the soup that's boiling over, or close the front door that's letting in rain. But put off cleaning the drain or finishing the shopping-list inventory. Make time to listen when it is most effective—that is, when your child seeks you out.

Monitor your tone of voice. If you feel a whine coming on because you've been interrupted umpteen times before, ask for a minute and use it to collect yourself. Remind yourself of your true priorities and refresh your mind with your listening skills.

Interruptions: Snares on the Path to Mutual Understanding

Talk quietly but energetically. And resist interrupting, even if the first few sentences your child speaks may not make any sense to you. Resist asking detailed questions at the outset, even if these seem to show your interest. They may easily sidetrack your child, especially if her message is a hard one to express.

Imagine what happens to you when someone interrupts or asks too many questions and all you want to do is set the context for your story. Imagine Nancy, who says to her husband, Bob, "Oh, guess who I saw at the store?"

Bob says, "You went to the store? What store were you at? Did you buy anything?" Nancy's likely to say, "Oh, never mind." Wouldn't you be tempted to do so?

That's the kind of frustration you can easily impose without knowing it, if you are too inquisitive from the start. Whatever you need to know about your child's experience will come out in good time if you listen closely and follow along with the child. Just as an impatient listener can destroy a storyteller's narrative, so an impatient parent can block the very message a child wants most to share. It's a case of never seeing the forest because of a narrow focus on the trees.

Pay Attention to Your Environment

You may have heard how businesses are beginning to pay more attention to what is called *ergonomics,* to increase worker productivity, health, and job satisfaction. Adopting the Asian concept of *feng shui*, designers are paying attention to the atmosphere in which people try to accomplish things. Why is it, after all, that people congregate in the kitchen?

You probably already know from your own responses and experience—if you simply pay attention to them—where in your house you are most likely to have a constructive, comfortable conversation with your child. If your child's opening words sound like a serious bit of conversation, take the time to move into an environment that is conducive to conversation.

If you are standing at the ironing board working on a collar for work tomorrow and your child brings up a problem at school, he'll feel the pressure if you give your thoughts while holding the iron poised to continue. Put down the iron and lead the child to a place where you can both be comfortable and focused on the dialogue. A place with some natural light and space to sit is best.

You may feel that your child deliberately chose an inconvenient time to talk, but that doesn't mean you shouldn't oblige. The seriousness of the issue may have actually scared your child, and he wants to treat it lightly, at least to start, by bringing it up casually. Sometimes, too, your child may be subconsciously testing how high a priority his problems are for you. Will you take a break for him? Or are you simply a hard person to find standing around doing nothing?

Try not to resent this kind of interruption. But rather, take a moment to switch gears and then give your full attention to listening.

If, on the other hand, all your child wants is to give you a quick reminder that he needs a ride to the mall, eye contact and a cheerful response are all you need.

Have a Little Patience with Yourself!

Take your time responding. Many parents think they look bad if they don't have an answer ready for every situation. They think they should know everything all the time to be good parents or at least to appear authoritative to their kids.

This isn't the case. It's better to show your child how life really is. We don't always have all the answers. Lots of things take thought and some time to mull over. Don't we want our children to feel comfortable and secure thinking through answers when they are asked important questions in life?

Just think. One day your darling may hear, "Won't you please stay over?" or "Why do you think you have to call your parents?" or "Can you think of any reason I should hire you?"

If you have let your children know by your own example that good answers require first good listening and then good thinking, they will never be embarrassed to take the time they need to answer important questions.

Take your time listening. Let your child ramble on if you are not ready to respond. Practice nods and grunts that symbolize listening and interest.

The Sounds of Good Listening

Notice your own style of listening in other contexts, where your parental self-talk isn't a distraction. Think, for example, about how you listen when you're talking to friends. Use the same words or noises for your child.

How do you encourage a friend to tell the rest of a story? Perhaps you say, "Oh, really?" or one of these:

"You don't say!"

"Hmmm."

"Uh-huh."

"Yeah . . . interesting."

"Go on. . . . And then?"

"Wow! I don't believe it!"

"Gee!"

"Oh, yeah? Man!"

"So then what?"

"I can hardly believe it!"

"Mm-mmm."

"Right. . . . Way to go!"

"Go figure."

Read this list to yourself a few times, or make your own and review it. Can you imagine not being encouraged to continue talking if you heard a few of these when you spoke? Make frequent sounds of listening.

Be sure, however, that you *are* listening. It won't take long for your child to discover when your mind is elsewhere and you're faking at listening. Even if he doesn't call you on it, he will know. He may just be too disappointed to say so.

How to Catch All the Information

Indulge in multidimensional listening. Notice your child's words, tone, body language, intensity of expression, pace, rhythm, eyes, and facial expression.

You probably do this naturally. But when your parenting cap is on, you can get so emotionally involved that you may filter out some of the most useful information. Only with all the signals as well as the words will you get the whole message.

Often I find parents are afraid to absorb the whole message. They may be easily distracted by what they think is most important: their own impending wise words of advice. Or they may be uncomfortable with, for instance, their child's body language or attire. As a parent is often all too aware, the child's clothes or stance may be specifically designed to appear disrespectful to authority figures, and that means you.

A parent can't afford to take these things personally. In such cases, I recommend that you take the general message of distracting clothes or postures in stride. Accept that the main message a child intends with these is self-assertion; she wants to be her own person. Simply assume she isn't directing the most obnoxious implications of dress and posture at you personally. If you doubt yourself, your child will doubt with you. If, in contrast, teenage symbols can't startle or distract you, they lose all their power with respect to you.

If some body language or dress or adornment is truly distracting, simply say so: "I'm sorry, I just can't listen effectively about such a serious matter with your hair covering your eyes." You'll get a better response this way than if you let it interfere with your concentration or if you let your anger build up and then say something like, "Get the stupid hair out of your face!"

Use the multidimensional cues you are accumulating to focus in on the real, particularized message that is meant for you only. Obviously an outrageous outfit that you see on your child every day doesn't tell you much about what's on his mind right now.

So if you are offended by the outfit, don't let that response color your perception of exactly what it is you must listen to now.

"Mork Calling Orson"

Think of yourself as a detective, or better yet an astrophysicist, trying to find out what planet your little astronaut has visited most recently. If men are from Mars and women are from Venus, you must assume your child has just come from Pluto. Every little thing can be new and interesting.

You're the seasoned scientist on the ground. You have done your own exploring in your day but are now trying to debrief and interpret what this new explorer has found and also to inform her, so that her next exploration will be even more productive and meaningful, to her as well as to you.

Notice every bit of evidence, and even when you think you have a theory of what's up, don't get cocky. Just as with the story I told earlier about my son's class and the traffic, what seems like one problem that is scary and unmanageable almost always turns out to be another, with a solution that is well within your—or better yet, your child's—reach.

It can work the other way too. If you don't listen carefully, you may miss an important problem while solving only its symptoms. For example, Ernest told his father that he didn't want to go swimming anymore. Trying to be an understanding father, he agreed to let Ernest skip swimming for a couple of weeks. When that period ended, Ernest was even more adamant. His father then got worried.

By listening more carefully, he noticed Ernest's squirming and new shyness around friends. He realized the boy was going through puberty a little earlier than his friends and was scared and embarrassed by the changes in his body. His father finally addressed that problem with some open-ended questions, some sharings, and a few encouraging words. The boy was being teased by a coach. The father brought the problem to the attention of the coach, and soon swimming came back easily into Ernest's life.

Keep your mind open to the idea that what seems an insurmountable problem may have a simple solution if you keep listening. Meanwhile you must also avoid missing what may be an important problem to address.

Use Frequent Reality Checks

You will need to use frequent reality checks and midcourse corrections. Test out your working theory of what the problem is. Ask, "So you're concerned about such and such?" Whatever the child's response, it's another clue to what's important and where he's going with it, so listen.

Don't worry about making a wrong guess. Your child will care less about your mistakes than about the wonderful feeling of being important enough to be listened to. Your child won't fault you for mistakes, only for not trying at all—much as you probably do with her.

You'll know your child has gotten to the main message when you perceive a sense of relief in the child's voice or demeanor or breathing pattern. She may sigh, finally look into your face, project a questioning look, or ask a question.

At this point, resist jumping in with all your well-thought-out solutions! Take your time. Sigh with her. Say something along these lines:

"OK. I see."

"Hmmm, so that's what's on your mind."

"So, you would like my help with that?"

"All right, let's see."

"I get it. I think I understand."

"Is this something I can help you think through a little more?"

"Oh. Let me see if I've got it right."

So often parents will freak at this point, even if they have gotten this far with patience, because they are imagining all the things they could or should do to help solve the child's problem. Remember then that you are only about halfway through the listening! Now that you know the problem, it's time to listen to your child's thinking about the problem, so that she herself can hone it down to a doable thing.

No child's request is truly unreasonable if we take our time and listen hard through this process. If your child's plan sounds impossible, you can bet that your child knows it. She can't yet see the practical solution.

Socrates said that our biggest challenge is not finding the right answer so much as asking the right question. Your child needs the validation of your listening to help her focus more effectively. This is powerful stuff!

The Impossible Request

Frank's daughter had an elaborate plan to buy a gift for a birthday party. The plan involved his driving all around looking for a gift that she hadn't given much thought to yet. He imagined spending hours waiting—in the gift shop, the record store, the jewelry store, the novelty store, and the department store—for her to make up her mind what was exactly the right gift.

Frank was ready to scrap the whole idea and lecture her about planning ahead and not leaving gifts to the last minute. But instead he listened. He listened more. And then he listened again.

Apparently his daughter was distraught, because last year she had overheard the birthday friend complaining about someone else's gift, a gift that had seemed perfectly fine to his daughter. So Frank found out by listening that she had put off buying or even thinking about the gift because she was afraid of getting the wrong gift and being gossiped about and criticized for it.

Frank had used his new listening skills to hear his daughter out as she articulated the pros and cons about different gifts and finally got to the central issue of her friend's silliness. While he listened, she let go of her fear and suddenly remembered over-hearing the same friend listing favorite music groups. She proposed a quick trip to the CD store, and the problem was solved.

Frank felt like a wonderful father, full of patience and good advice, and yet all he had done was listen! He hadn't felt so good about his parenting in a long time. He made a quiet remark about how friends may talk but real friends are never malicious about their criticisms, and his daughter actually thanked him for his advice.

Once a solution presents itself, good listening requires a pat on the back for your child. Stock up on useful phrases like these:

"Well, you got that one solved."

"That's done. Good for you!"

"Good plan. Nice thinking."

"I like it when I get to see you think things through like that. You're a very smart kid!"

"What a good problem solver you've become!"

"All right then! Nice going."

Discover your own favorites. I like the Australian one "Good on yuh!"

Meanwhile pat yourself on the back too. You've used your intelligence, perception, patience, experience, and love to their full advantage and to an excellent outcome. Good for you!

Distinguish Reaction from Response

As you are practicing these listening techniques, you probably experience the vast difference between reacting and responding. Reacting comes from an emotional place, where the first emotive message takes over.

If you don't like your daughter's tone, you may react by turning critical.

If you don't like your son's hair, you may react by becoming angry.

If you're tired of requests, you may react by acting impatient.

If your child's words are the latest in a long line of interruptions, you may react by brushing her off.

In contrast, when you respond instead of react, you take into account all your immediate and possible reactions and choose a response that best suits the situation as a whole.

What is really best for you and your child in the situation?

What really meets your highest priorities?

What avoids sacrificing one important goal for another?

What's most constructive and least destructive to the relationships involved?

You may recognize these kinds of questions as related to what has been called transactional analysis (TA), which according to some popular opinion is divorced from values or priorities. On the contrary, as TA is used here, your thoughtful response to each immediate situation as it presents itself serves to help keep you in line with your most important values and priorities.

You won't get far if you limit your thinking to the transaction itself and see how you can get out of it with the least emotion or trouble. On the contrary, you become successful by expanding your thinking beyond spontaneous emotional reactions and looking at the whole of the transaction in the context of the whole of your relationship and even your life. You try to see how that transaction fits into the larger picture. Only then can you face the emotions and do the work that must be done to have the best outcome possible.

How to See Both the Forest and the Trees

Let's take another example. Twelve-year-old Max is calling 10-year-old brother, Ed, ugly names because Ed won't leave him alone at the video screen and is bugging him to come outside to play stickball.

Their mother, Judy, has seen this hundreds of times. She could react as she usually does, yelling at the boys to get along, trying to figure out whose turn it is to give in to whom, lecturing them about bad language and bullying, or just yelling to vent her frustration over their chronic bickering. But this time she decides to listen hard and to respond instead of reacting. She resists her automatic reactions to the noise, the tones, the nasty words, and her own anger and frustration. Instead she listens, so that she will know how to respond instead of react.

This squabble may be like every other, but maybe it is also a unique transaction that needs a fresh look. Judy moves herself quietly into the boys' presence and just listens. "I could hear the noise downstairs. What's all this about?" she asks good-naturedly. "Anything I can do?"

"Make him play with me." "Yeah, get him off my back." "He called me a nerd." "He's always bugging me." "Make him leave me alone." "He yelled a bad word!"

They have lots of ideas for her, but she resists reacting or agreeing to any of them. "I meant, what can I do to help you work this out for yourselves?" she continues, feeling her blood pressure rising, but sticking to her plan.

"Well I'm in the middle of this game, and he won't let me be," says angry Max. "But he never plays with me! I'm not good at that video game, and I want to play outside!" snaps back self-pitying Ed.

Wonderful plans rush through Judy's head: they could take turns inside and outside, each could spend 15 minutes on the other's game, and so on. But instead of the quick fix and a nice authoritative imposition of her nice plan, she listens, watching for cues toward a helpful response. "OK. Max, you want to play at the computer, but Ed isn't good at it. Ed wants you to play outside."

Max looks up at Ed. "You're not so bad at the game. I just always win." He smiles.

"So you always win, Max?" says Judy. "Yeah, and he's nasty about it," says Ed.

"Max is nasty when he wins?" Judy continues to listen. She wants to tell Max off for the hundredth time but resists. "Yeah. Make him stop," interjects Ed.

"Max, when you win, you rub it in and make Ed feel bad?" Max says, "I guess so. Oh well, let's just go outside and play stickball for a while, Ed. How about I teach you more about this game later?"

Judy can't believe it. But it works like this again and again. Just when you think you are running out of ideas for listening and don't know where the conversation is heading, the children solve their own problems.

Judy stayed aware of the whole transaction. She reminded herself she was not a helpless stranger in the middle of hopelessly squabbling bullies and victims. She remembered instead that she was the loving, caring, almost patient parent of two nice boys who get on each other's nerves when they are tired from school and probably hungry and wanting to relax with their favorite activity—and hopefully a willing brother.

If Max hadn't come through just then, Judy had some other options. She might have suggested a bit more of a chat over some fresh water and crackers. Attention to basic needs could break the ice. Or she could simply keep repeating what had been said in her own nonthreatening restatements until one of the boys found a solution.

How to Keep Listening for a Solution

If a silence were to take over before the family reached a solution, Judy would still have these options:

"OK, what shall we do about this?"

Or, "All right, what do you guys want to do now?"

Or, "Hey, guys, I need to get back to work. What more can I do for you?"

Here are some more possibilities:

"Tell me, can I leave you to work this out on your own now?"

"You're both quiet now. So have we talked about this enough?"

"Can you two finish this for yourselves?"

"Great, we've got all the thoughts out. Do we need to do anything more?"

You can probably think of other things Judy could say, now that you have a sense of the good-listening attitude she wants to use here. So think of Max and Ed when you must choose between a reaction and a response.

Level One: Reflective Listening

You do your best listening when you reflect what you hear like a mirror. Reflective listening is effective because you repeat more or less what you hear as the listener, rather than projecting what you want to hear or think or feel. Its great power comes from its validation of the speaker: someone is actually listening. That one event means, all at once, that

- the speaker is important enough to listen to,

- his thoughts are valuable to you,

- he has the right to think and express his thoughts, and

- he is acceptable to you, at least enough to be heard.

Being listened to empowers a child to think more for himself and eventually to solve his own problems.

The first level of listening, then, is to repeat exactly what you hear with only the pronouns and expletives changed—and perhaps the loudness and tone. For example, if your child is supposed to be studying but runs by you yelling, "Mom, I'm going over to Jimmy's. Bye!" you might be tempted to say, "No way, get back to your homework," and so on. But the child may just keep going and will want to go by even faster next time, perhaps saying nothing at all. So instead of an attack, you might say, "You're going over to Jimmy's?" You just listen, and reflect back exactly what you've heard.

Your child might say something like, "Yeah, he just called. He has a new whatever." If you stick with reflective listening, you can say, "Oh, Jimmy called to tell you about his new whatever?" The conversation will almost certainly eventually get around to whether your child has allowed time for his studies. The difference is that the child will bring it up, and you will not be the heavy. In fact, you have exhibited your faith that he can manage his own affairs.

Of course, if it becomes obvious in the conversation that he isn't planning so well, you will have ample opportunity to guide him to a better plan. You will have established some faith, some rapport, and a commitment to a conversation, so your child will be able to hear you.

Reflective listening, then, begins with repeating just what you hear. No matter how expert you get at listening, this is always the best fallback strategy. If you don't know what to say, repeat what your child has just said. Even if it's, "You hate my guts right now!"

"I'm Outta Here!"

Many parents I have worked with have had wonderful success with just this kind of first-level strategy. Consider, if you will, a mother named Henna, whose 10-year-old son, Bob, came downstairs with his backpack full of toys and a change of clothes. "I hate this family. I'm leaving."

Bob had done this before, and Henna had cried, yelled, and spent an hour convincing him she loved him and wanted him to stay. She also had tried to shame him about his ingratitude to his family. In the past, her own guilt and fear had made her react. But this time she responded thoughtfully, "So you really hate this family and want to leave us all."

The boy dropped his backpack. He said, "Yeah, Dad yells at me too much, and you never play with me." They decided to make some changes and ask Dad not to yell so much, and the crisis was over.

Level Two: Receptive Listening

The next important strategy for listening is to be receptive to your child's actual message. Be aware of the elements of time and context in her communication. Then you will be able to grasp her multiple levels of meaning, both emotional and practical, general and specific.

First, get time on your side. If you don't do this consciously, your child always has the time advantage, because you are almost always in more of a hurry than she is.

You get time on your side simply by taking all urgency out of your demeanor and voice and by adding a time element to your restatement of what you have heard. A time element helps your child accept his feelings as feelings and not necessarily as a permanent state of being that requires he take action.

For example, your child might say, "My teacher hates me." You might respond, with first-level reflecting, "Oh, your teacher hates you." If you add the time element, you might say, "Oh, your teacher hates you today."

In your wisdom and experience, you set parameters and limits to the bad news your child is sharing. If you are wrong, it's OK; your child will give you more information. "She's always hated me!" Then you can say, "You think she has always hated you!" It will keep your child talking.

In addition to the time element, in this second level of listening you can add other clarifications of your child's relationship to her story. It's affirming to the child for you to be noticing her and her feelings, and it can help her recognize what is going on for her.

You can add things like "Oh, OK, you think . . ." or "You feel . . ." or "You're angry that . . ." or "You're upset that . . ." or "You're excited that . . ." or "You want me to know that . . ." or "You are trying to get across to me that . . ."

Naming your child's emotion keeps your attention where it needs to be in listening: on your child. You can remind yourself that you care more about how events affect your child than about the details of the events themselves. You also help your child right away to get a little perspective. For her, too, it is how the event affects her, not the event itself, that is important.

Consider 14-year-old Sandy, who shared this with her dad, Mel. "Dad, Tisha stole my notebook!" Mel could get furious at Tisha. Stealing is wrong and obnoxious, and this is not the first time Tisha has been a bother. But he resists reacting with an explosion. Instead he says, "What, Tisha stole your notebook? You must be angry."

Then Sandy says, "Yeah, I am. I wrote some stuff in it about her and Bill, and she threatened to tear it up." Mel was glad he hadn't exploded. He could see there were two sides to this story. It was a friend's squabble, not a thief and victim.

Reflective listening gives you the power to avoid overreacting and the additional power to give your child the accepting atmosphere in which she is more likely to tell you the whole story. In Sandy's story, once she knows that her father is interested in her and not in justice for Tisha, she feels good enough about herself to own up to her own responsibility in the matter.

If you find that your child is objecting to your embellishments as you are exploring this more sophisticated level of listening, fall right back to the first level. It will work just fine. You can then start again, using more subtle interpretations to build more sensitive listening.

When I am helping parents learn to listen, I begin with exactly what words to say, because experience is the best teacher. The positive feedback is so obvious and direct that parents quickly get past some doubts and hesitations that might otherwise discourage them from trying these techniques. But let's now look at some of these doubts and hesitations.

How to Remove Blocks to Your Listening

You may be hesitant about repeating what your child says, because you don't like what she has said and you don't want to reinforce it. Or you may worry that reflective listening requires endless patience, self-control, and empathy that you fear you don't have. Or you fear that this technique doesn't make use of your excellent store of knowledge and experience.

If you fear the positive reinforcement of your child's negative thought, consider the fact that your child shares the facts or events primarily to get affirmation from you that there is a solution and that he is capable of finding it. Your child wants to feel more alive and capable by having your input. So when you repeat what your child has said, you may be reinforcing the thought to some slight extent. But your child has already thought the thought—and thought it strongly enough to articulate it to you. When she hears it back, she is more likely to look at it critically than to embrace it even more.

Especially when you say it as we have reviewed here, as a caring parent who respects a thought solely because your child has thought it, the child can step back a bit from the thought. Here you can use your faith in your child that a bad idea will also look bad to your child, once she has gotten it off her chest and heard it again from your mouth as simply a thought or feeling she has a right to have.

As for finding the necessary patience, self-control, and empathy, parents are often quite sure they don't have these and will never get them. But let's look at your motivations as a parent. That can be the key here. If you try to be patient and controlled and empathetic because you "should," you'll feel from the outset like you're fighting your own human nature. You may drop your good intentions as soon as you perceive your child as not meeting you halfway. It just doesn't seem fair for you to work so hard when your child isn't trying at all.

In contrast, with a little experimentation, you may discover that patience and self-control and empathy aren't for the child's benefit so much as for your own! They work! The more difficult and uncooperative your child is being, the more productive these skills are.

Look at your other options. Sure you know you "shouldn't" be impatient, out of control, or unempathetic. But the only reason you will give up these attitudes is that you realize that they just don't work. When you use them, you will likely feel like a failure.

Ask yourself why you are acting as you are. Are you struggling to do what you think you ought for your child's sake, or are you logically thinking through what is going to make life better for you, altogether and in the long run? If you take the time to consider what is really going to work for you and your child, you will find patience you never thought you had and a lot more self-control than you may have felt before.

Your Empathy Is Essential

As for empathy, there's a public perception that this is a skill you are either born with or not. It is seen as a characteristic of do-gooders and people pleasers, and few have time for it.

Not so. Empathy is the most powerful of a parent's good listening skills. And it can be learned. A friend of mine focused her doctoral thesis in psychology on whether empathy could be learned. Her study convinced her that it could be, but that teaching it to someone else was tricky.

In fact, you can teach empathy to yourself simply by repeating back each time exactly what you are hearing from your child. This is because when you say the same thing someone else has said, you will tend to feel the way she does and even to begin to stand and look the way she does! Give it a try. It's the same thing actors call on in their acting.

Remind yourself that every one of us has a wonderful imagination and a full palette of feelings. If you stand and talk like someone else, you will begin to understand what he is going through. An old Native American saying holds that to understand another you must walk a mile in his shoes.

Again, don't torture yourself that you aren't good at knowing how others feel. Perhaps you haven't even been that good at knowing what *you* are feeling most of the time. But good, careful, reflective listening will overcome all these hurdles, and you may become a more patient, self-controlled, empathetic parent— and person—before you know it.

When do you get to share all the knowledge and experience that you have saved up to pass on to your child? You will get your chance, but only *after* you have listened and listened well. When you seek someone else's advice, do you want to hear their answer before you have told your whole story? Never! You want them to get the whole picture, to understand why you feel the way you do, and to affirm that your position is reasonable and appealing. Then only are you ready to hear their take on it. So it is with your child.

Again, think of patience and self-control and empathy as self-serving. They enable you to get to the heart of each matter so that you will also get the opportunity to share your experience and knowledge and wisdom. More about this in the chapters on secrets 5 and 6.

The Buddha Posture

One of my favorite listening strategies is the Buddha posture. If you have not often used the listening techniques revealed here, then your child won't take them seriously at first. She may test your resolve to listen. She may provoke you in old accustomed ways. When this happens, remind yourself first that you are the parent.

This is not so you can assert and impose your authority and insist on obedience. But rather, it is so you can relax in the certainty that your child is thoroughly programmed as a human child to believe and know that you have the knowledge and experience and love she craves. You don't have to assert, impose, or insist on anything. Instead you can simply show what I like to call your moral authority. This is the quiet authority that comes to you by virtue of being your child's parent. Your child expects it and counts on it.

This moral authority harbors no aggression but rather is patient, unmovable, and beatific, like a Buddha statue.

You need not be perfect or always right. You must simply show more patience than your child. You must be willing, like the sincere, confident statues of Buddha, to sit there as long as necessary with a serene expression on your face, to listen to anything that must be heard.

I've seen many parents laugh at themselves as they retell how they "tried the Buddha thing." But every time, their bottom line is that it worked. When you exercise your moral authority by showing you have infinite time and faith in your child, you are irresistible to your child. You are exactly what she needs for a parent. We could even say that you fulfill your destiny as a parent. It can certainly feel that way when you do it.

Of course, if sometimes you just can't muster the patience of a Buddha, it's not the end of the world. You can salvage the situation with humor, particularly at your own expense. Throw your own little tantrum and laugh at it with your child. She will understand that it's OK to be human, that you're still on her side, and hopefully that she really would like to cooperate. Remember even Buddha statues seem to smile at themselves from time to time.

With multilevel listening and an attitude of moral authority, you are now ready to truly understand the meaning of what your child is saying. So let's look at that.

Why Your Child Speaks

When you are trying to listen receptively and carefully to your child, it will be helpful to you to realize that people speak to each other really for only two basic purposes: either to share themselves or to make a request. That is, either to express who they are or to express what they want.

First, they want to feel more alive and real by sharing themselves with another and by having that other validate their existence. Second, they want to bring about a change in the other, to get the other to do something that promises to make their life better. Both purposes reflect the basic will to survive and thrive and feel alive.

Test out this idea over the next few hours and the next couple of days. Each time someone speaks to you, decide whether, on the one hand, they are sharing and want to be heard or, on the other hand, they want you to do something—and consider whether there is some third motivation. Even if at first you suspect other motivations, you will find that these will eventually resolve into one of these two if you just keep listening. Either they are totally satisfied by being heard out and really listened to, or they want some action from you. That's pretty simple, isn't it?

Think of these two options when you are listening to your child. With each pause your child gives you for your response, ask yourself, is this a time to validate my child or to commit myself to action? If your daughter wants the window opened and can't reach it, then you can commit to action. If she wants the window opened and *can* reach it, maybe she wants you not to open it but to notice and validate how hard she's working on her homework or at washing the dishes or whatever. She might actually want to open the window herself, by way of taking a break, once you have taken notice of her hard work at her task.

Sometimes the distinction is subtle. That's the bad news. But the good news is that when your child speaks, she asks nothing more than one of these two things of you. Keep it simple. Listen with your whole heart.

Level Three: Naming Feelings

Whether your child wants to share or to make a request, the third level of sophistication in your listening will be naming the feelings you are hearing. This allows you to get a better grasp of what your child really means to say. American culture, particularly European-American culture, has a lot of trouble with feelings. We are educated to care only about facts and events and rational thoughts and actions. But our humanness comes to the fore first with our feelings. We find no direction to guide our actions if we are not in touch with our feelings.

We may have the best of intentions, but feelings will trip us up every time if we don't acknowledge and deal with them, incorporating them into our deliberations if necessary. Just like us adults, your child will be empowered to deal with feelings and get on with sound thinking and appropriate action only if you validate those feelings as they are shared.

You may fear that if you validate a feeling, you are saying that it is good and should motivate your child's actions. Consider revenge, for example. If your child expresses a vengeful feeling, you may (like most parents) want to say, "Oh, you shouldn't feel that way. Revenge is destructive." But feelings are never destructive. Only what we do with them can be destructive. Experience will show you how an acknowledged feeling is much more likely to go away than a feeling you think you shouldn't have. Feelings are neutral until you act upon them. Accepting a feeling actually frees you up to not act upon it but to move on.

Just try this with your child if you have not already done so. When you hear a negative feeling, or one that you fear is bad or destructive, try acknowledging the feeling and your child's right to feel that way. So many parents I've known have been astonished how quickly the child moves on to a more benign feeling when they do this simple thing.

The third level of reflective listening, then, is to take a guess at your child's feelings. As you have heard here before, your child may well correct you, but so much the better. He is now talking about and refining his understanding of his feelings. When your child knows his feelings, he can see better where his thoughts are coming from and can begin to correct those thoughts as need be.

As your child gets more familiar with his feelings, he will even begin to examine where they come from. If he is making false assumptions about the world that make him feel bad often, he will begin to change these too. All because you knew how to reflect his feelings!

When you are identifying a feeling, err on the side of more intensity. It is more important that you don't underestimate your child's intensity than that you get the particular feeling right. If your child is furious, resist saying, "Gee, you seem a little upset." Rather say, "Oh my, you are totally enraged about this!"

You are giving your child permission to feel anything he wants, so that he can take a hard look at it. If he must spend all his energy getting you to appreciate how strongly he feels, he will keep the focus on your supposed thickheadedness and not think to look to himself.

The Basic Feelings

Whenever you feel stumped about feelings, just stick to this simple list.

Bad,

mad,

sad, and

glad.

It covers just about everything. Your child can relate to all of these.

I used to worry that it seemed only one of the three was a positive feeling. But from working with people over the last 20 years, I am convinced that true sadness holds a lot of acceptance and peace and renewal. For example, when a good friend moves away, a child may feel angry, resistant, threatened, lonely, and so on. When she finally reaches sad, she will find peace. She will have accepted the necessity and reality of the change, gotten in touch with the hurt it gives, and accepted that she can get past this change and look forward to her future.

It has been said that depression is suppressed anger and loss. Once you get to real sadness, depression is impossible. If you are allowed to be sad, you don't need to depress all your feelings and your affective self to avoid the sadness. Instead you can dwell there comfortably until you are ready to move on.

We hear so much now about the dramatic increase in childhood depression. Certainly our kids face stresses galore. But what do you think about the idea that a major cause of this new epidemic of depression may be the lack of adults in the children's lives who can listen and validate the children's rights to their feelings?

Once a child gets to sad, you can let her have as much time as she needs for it, but glad will then be not too far off.

If you feel unoriginal in choosing feeling words, just pick the one of these four—bad, mad, sad, glad—that comes closest to what you perceive to be your child's present state of mind. Validate her right to be there, even if you don't like that place.

Suppose your 10-year-old son says gleefully, "Jimmy really got Matt today, and Matt went crying to the principal." I'd be the first to want to say, "Why are you happy? That's terrible! Beating people up isn't any way to solve problems. What did the principal do?" But you get a lot further saying, "So you're glad Jimmy beat up Matt today. Why is that? That's a funny way to feel about someone getting hurt."

"Matt's a big bully and has been calling me names all week. Jimmy just got sick of it. He didn't really hurt Matt, but he threw him on the ground."

"So you feel satisfied that Matt may have learned something from this?"

"No, it just feels good to get him back."

"It feels good to you that he knows now what it feels like to be bullied?"

"Yeah, but Jimmy's not a bully. He just couldn't take it anymore."

"You like the way Jimmy handled it?"

"Well, not really. I wouldn't have done that. But it still felt good to see it. Maybe Matt will leave us alone now."

"Are you still a little afraid of Matt's bothering you?"

"Yeah, I hope he stops."

"You hope he'll be nicer to you."

"Yeah, if he doesn't, we're just going to ignore him and tell the teacher on him from now on."

This is a typical conversation when you are listening really hard. You will be reassured that your child's head is screwed on straight if you just hang in there and let the process play itself out.

Once you are familiar with the basic four feelings and use "very" and "a little" and so on to vary the intensity, you can increase your feeling vocabulary. Here are some suggestions for naming your child's emotional intensity:

How to Help Your Child Express Mild and Intense Feelings
INTENSITY INDEX

MILD	AVERAGE	INTENSE
Hurt	Bad	Awful
Bothered	Mad	Furious
Down	Sad	Miserable
Good	Glad	Excited

If in doubt, pick a more intense phraseology. You can be delighted with the relief you feel when your child corrects you with a less intense feeling. "No, Mom, I'm not totally bummed out. I'm just a little miffed!"

How to Use the Feelings Grid

Having explored all these aspects of hearing your child's feelings, you may be ready for what can be one of your most valuable tools in your seven-secrets toolbox. The feelings grid is a diagram of clusters of feelings. It explores the relationship between fear and love and can help you get in touch with the full array of feelings your child is capable of. By understanding how fear affects the emotions, you may be able to understand better some of the more offensive emotions, so that you will not lose faith or panic if you hear them from your child. Likewise, you can develop a deeper consciousness of all the subtleties of the positive feelings, so that you can give your child the great gift of self-knowledge about his own happiness.

Just think how little time we give in this culture to reveling in good feelings. We feel satisfied for a moment and then run off to take on the next stressful challenge. Out of an exaggerated fear of complacency, and not trusting ourselves to reach out for new adventures, we suppress our good feelings almost as eagerly as we tend to suppress the bad ones.

If instead we take time to explore the richness of our brighter feelings, they tend to crowd out the dark ones.

Feelings Grid

HIGH FEAR

Escape	Protection
Hate	Control
Anger	Judgment
Rage	Attention
Alienation	Reverence

LOW LOVE ——————————————— HIGH LOVE

Disdain	Joy
Superiority	Celebration
Put-down	Peace
Abuse	Acceptance
Dissociation	Trust
Indifference	Empathy

LOW FEAR

You may not agree with each placement of these feelings in the different quadrants. Take time to explore what each of these feelings means to you when you feel it or when you see it in others. Get to know your own full feelings grid and then use the feeling words with your child as you think is appropriate to his age. Help him build his feeling vocabulary.

Once you have explored this diagram a bit and have begun to use some of these words in your listening, you will have on the tip of your tongue perhaps the most valuable communications tool you will ever encounter.

Before going on to the exciting power of the next secret, let's take one last example here and see how Rick listens carefully as he deals with his son's request.

Greg, 14 years old, wanted to go with friends to a pop concert that required advance ticket purchasing. He told his father, Rick, that he had to go with his friends to sleep overnight by the ticket booth if he was to have any chance at a seat. When Rick heard the idea, he began picturing the stadium, which he knew to be in a dangerous part of town, swarming with drug dealers and his sweet boy in over his head with street toughs and brawls and exhaustion.

Rick wanted to say, "Absolutely no way! Wait until you're 18 or, better, 21 or never!" But he knew this would estrange his son and encourage Greg to do things without permission or even without notice. Rick felt he needed to handle this sensitively or the next few years would be awful. So he took a deep breath to clear his head, sank to the bottom of his breath like Buddha, and began this way:

"That sounds really neat. You love that group. You would have so much fun with your friends. And staying out all night—what an adventure!"

"Yeah, wouldn't it be great, Dad?"

"You've never been out all night. But you have been to concerts, and you know how fun they are. It's a Saturday so you wouldn't miss any schoolwork."

"Right."

"I know concerts are fun. I've been to a few myself, and I loved them. But there's a lot of stuff that goes on at concerts, and I'm concerned you're pretty young to be on your own, especially overnight at the ticket booth."

"Yeah, well, Ryan did it before, and he said it wasn't bad. He said it was crazy! I mean he saw some other people getting crazy, but he just watched. We would just watch, Dad."

"I know, Greg. But you can understand why I'm concerned. Let's see. You want to go to the concert, and part of the fun is staying out all night getting the tickets. And you want to know if I will let you do that, right?"

"Yeah. I'll be really careful, Dad."

"I know, but there are risks on the street that you may not fully appreciate and that I feel it's my job to take into account in my decision. Let's see. What are the options here?"

"Well, one of the other guys could buy my ticket. Each person is allowed to buy four tickets. But I want to go!"

"OK, that's one option, but it's not your favorite, of course. I could say no altogether, but I'm trying not to do that. I could go with you and stay there all night with you, but it's not my idea of a fun time! Still, it would be nice to hang out with you and your friends one night."

"Yeah, you want to? It's kinda weird though. None of the other guys . . . well . . ."

"Or we could go really early in the morning and hope the tickets aren't totally sold out."

"Yeah, I guess so."

"Can you think of anything else?"

"No, what am I going to do? I want to go."

"OK, let's see. You absolutely want to go. I think I'm pretty clear that I don't want you out all night unsupervised at your age. For now, what I propose is that I go with you and camp out in the car. If anything gets too weird, you'll come home with me and let someone else buy your tickets. But meanwhile, how about you check today with your friends to see what the other guys' parents think of the idea, and then let's talk about it tomorrow."

"OK, Dad. Thanks."

The next day, Greg said that two of the guys, one younger but a lot bigger than Greg and one 16, had permission or didn't need it. But his best friend, Walt, wasn't allowed to go without a parent and thought Greg's dad was the greatest to offer to come. And another friend's dad wanted to go.

Rick thought about letting the other dad handle the whole thing but decided it would be a blast to go with the kids and have another adult to hang out with, so he agreed to go. The fathers filled the car with sodas and pretzels and stayed out of the boys' way. All had a great time, and Rick and the other dad even bought tickets to the concert—but nowhere near the boys' seats, they were cautioned.

As you practice listening, you will discover that it calls all your wisdom and experience into play in ways you never would have imagined. As you live ever more in harmony with secret 3, knowing "I always hear my child out," you will see the tremendous response you will get and you will feel your trust building in yourself, your child, and your parenting.

And you will know more clearly than ever before what exactly your child's needs are and how best you can meet them. You will know this because you will know how to let him tell you and how to match your powers to his needs.

A mother is not a person to lean on but a person to make leaning unnecessary.

DOROTHY CANFIELD FISHER

The beginning of love is to let those we love be perfectly themselves, and not to twist them to fit our own image. Otherwise we love only the reflection of ourselves we find in them.

THOMAS MERTON

Parents who expect gratitude from their children (there are even some who insist on it) are like usurers who gladly risk their capital if only they receive interest.

FRANZ KAFKA

It's always been my feeling that God lends you your children until they're about eighteen years old. If you haven't made your points with them by then, it's too late.

BETTY FORD

"It's my child's life, not mine, after all."

❖ Letting Go ❖

By beginning to play with some of the ideas revealed to you through the first three secrets of successful parenting—faith, attention to basic needs, and listening—you've probably begun to discover how these bring more peace, satisfaction, and joy into your family's life. Now, as you become more full of faith in your child and more attentive to basic needs and more skilled at listening, you may want to know, like so many other parents I meet, how far to go in parenting.

Your guide to that is the fourth secret: "It's my child's life, not mine, after all." It's the secret successful parents use for letting go.

At first this secret may seem a bit of a cop-out: if the going gets too tough for us parents, well, we just back off and let the kid make his own life. But that's not it at all.

Ascertain Your Real Power

Letting go is about knowing both your full power and the limits of your power. Only when you have done that can you give the very best guidance possible, especially if your child seems to be fighting you and trying to take over the reins of his life.

Letting go is an art that requires finely tuned skills. You'll be well on your way to mastering this by the time you have explored the ideas, stories, and practice exercises in this chapter.

Here are some important ideas to keep in mind and develop as you grasp the full impact of knowing that your child's life is, after all, her own.

• Your child is a fully formed person from birth. Her life is as full spiritually, physically, emotionally, and intellectually as your own. She has a life path beyond your direction or control. We no longer subscribe to the idea of a clean slate that we must write on.

• Your child's best guide in life will be his own deep satisfaction and happiness. You will help him most by reinforcing with joy his attempts to seek out those qualities in his life and by facilitating his attaining them.

• Imitation and experience are your child's real teachers. Though less bound to instinct than other animals—in fact, exactly because of this—human children have fantastic learning capabilities. At first they rely on delicate programming to imitate in minute detail your behavior and that of the other people around them. Then after they achieve a sense of mastery in each area of their lives, they will switch to learning from their own experience.

• Your job is to stay on your toes so that you can see when this shift is taking place in each area. If you acknowledge a level of mastery and offer guidance during experimentation, you can maintain lifelong influence without stifling or trying to control.

• This means letting go is best done gradually. Only a parent can be attentive enough in all the different areas of a child's life to facilitate these transitions most naturally and successfully.

- It is not only OK but very helpful to be open and clear with your child about your efforts to let go. Your child will appreciate your efforts to do it thoughtfully and gradually, with a minimum of risk to his safety or to the trust between you.

Letting go is not something you do suddenly when the time is right. There is no magic moment when you know your child is all grown up. You never really know for sure in your mind when to let go. You really only know it in your heart, trusting your intuition. And it's an intuitive sense you can hone with experience, one day at a time. It's not a conviction that hits and sticks.

Letting go starts at the beginning of life and goes on for at least two decades—sometimes by fits and starts, sometimes with a push from you, and sometimes with a pull from your child. The process takes place in years, not days or months. And as you will find out in this chapter, it's worth it to try to work on letting go each day, trying to keep it as gradual as possible.

Letting-Go Checklist

You might ask yourself these questions each morning:

- What little tasks in my child's life am I holding on to that both of us are really ready for me to turn over to her?

- For what activities might my child need or want a bit more instruction or further demonstration, before I turn over the reins for that activity?

- In areas my child is experiencing now, is there any follow-up I need to do, or any pointers I could share with him?

- Is there any area of stress between us where I'm holding on to too tightly?

- Is there any area of stress where I'm assuming too early that it's time to let go?

Getting in Touch with the Sad Side of Parenting

I often tell parents that from the moment of your child's birth, parenting has a sad side. You are letting go of something you love. You'll never be as close as you were in the birthing period.

By the way, though popular wisdom has it that men may bond only later, when the child walks and talks, this is only a consequence of the unfortunate state of affairs where others often take over the role of the father at birth. Today, fathers who are close to the infant and mother at birth, even if not at the actual event, can also feel the closeness of the parental bond. Fathers also experience the gradual letting go as their children have more and more of their own say in the matter of living and growing.

Your baby obviously makes a big physical break from his mother at the moment of birth. But even after that occurs there is a continuous physical letting go, from breastfeeding and being held and sleeping close to sitting up and crawling, then to walking, then to walking out of the house, then to staying over elsewhere, then to driving, then to moving out—and today, in our supermobile society, even to moving to another community or country.

The physical progression is only the most obvious part of the letting go. Studies have shown that a mother and her nursing baby actually share patterns of brain waves. They are literally synchronized. I have had more than a few parents tell me, by way of example, that their newborns have the uncanny tendency to awake when the parents achieve sexual orgasm. Obviously, the bond is far beyond our current comprehension, despite our scientific confidence.

Psychic and emotional bonds will loosen too, just like the physical, until finally you realize you no longer can read your child's mind nor guess how she will react to a suggestion you have. This is sad, but not bad. It is parenting.

Once you have accepted the sad part of parenting, the glad parts become much more obvious, immediate, and real. Once you have accepted that parenting is letting go, you will be less tempted to hang on too long or too tight, causing unnecessary rebellion and frustration. And you may also feel less fear and guilt when your child pulls away. Likewise, you will not blame yourself if you find yourself moved to give your child a little nudge forward.

In fact, you can feel real joy as you watch your child move toward more independence, because you will know this is what is supposed to happen. It's a sign you're doing your job!

Applying the Secret of Letting Go Through the Years

The skills described in this chapter for the daily process of letting go can be both subtle and challenging. The communication skills can apply across the board to all stages, once your child understands your words. But it is essential that you speak with a vocabulary and tone that is appropriate to your child's age, speaking neither condescendingly nor over his head.

Just as your vocabulary in letting go is age sensitive, so is the extent to which you are letting go in each area. Don't be reluctant to let your child lead the process, within reason. Your child is the best indicator of all about how quickly or slowly you can or should be letting go.

Be careful, especially regarding basic needs, that you don't just drop the ball and expect the child to take over the responsibility. At each juncture, if at all possible, let the child first give hints of wanting to be allowed to make decisions or to take independent action. Then talk about the transfer of power and plan for a long, flexible transitional period. Trust that even if the neighbor's child is way ahead in one area or another, your child's time will come if you keep on parenting with the seven secrets in your pocket.

Let each stage evolve at its own pace, and stay alert to changes. For example, if 10 seems old enough to let a child feed his own gerbil, avoid a sudden pronouncement. Instead plan to do it together for a month and then let him do it every Monday for a month and so on.

Don't expect to be able to let go in all areas at the same time to the same extent. As a child is exploring one area courageously, she might in fact be surprisingly dependent in another area, if only to keep a kind of balance as it were. A child who is winning squash tournaments at the state level, for example, may still be afraid to be left alone at night.

Only you can feel out the rate of letting go in each dimension of your child's life. But some obvious cases may give you a feel for the process. For example, you would not want to yell at a three-year-old toddler to get her shoes on this minute or you'll leave home without her. Yet this might be fine with a child of 10, in the growth stage. She might even feel flattered that you thought she would be OK alone.

You might admonish a child of six, in the exploratory stage, to be careful not to eat too much birthday cake Friday night if he wants to do well in his soccer game. Yet you would be frowned upon and even humiliated for saying the same thing to your 14-year-old, who has just entered the maturation stage.

Rapping an infant on the knuckles for spilling milk implies you think he is up to taking on responsibility for what happens when a glass of liquid receives a slightly too forceful nudge. Yet how does that fit, he might well wonder if he could, with the fact that you want him to try to pick up that glass in the first place? Not until later can you expect to be able to let go of the responsibility for overseeing your child's interactions with things that can go awry and cause you a lot of cleanup or other bother.

In this chapter, you will see a number of families working through the process of letting go. I find parents often are astonished by how early some things come up in their children's lives today. You must be ready for some surprises. For example, in this next case history the boy is 12, but in a different family he might have been 15 or only 9. Yet all of these would be perfectly healthy, success-bound young people.

Coming to Grips with the Push and Pull of Parenting

Perhaps, like other parents, you get very uncomfortable with the mixed feelings of parenthood. You may fear you are doing something wrong whenever you feel those moments of push and pull with your child. When you don't understand where the mixed feelings are coming from, you can either try to suppress those feelings or vent them by injecting them into the situation at hand. Let's look at these two dark alternatives.

If you want to suppress unwanted feelings, your mind has no other choice but to suppress all your feelings, the good with the bad, to some extent. Then you no longer can feel the joys and fun of parenting as you are meant to. Eventually you can sink into the all too common chronic depression many parents suffer. You may start to feel you can do nothing right and that the good times don't feel good enough to counterbalance the hard times.

If, instead of suppressing your mixed feelings, you inject the unwanted feelings into the situation at hand, your judgment can be clouded. You may not handle the situation as well as you would have otherwise. You can overreact to small provocations and not even know why.

But you are not stuck with just these two alternatives. When you accept that parenting will touch all your emotions, then the glad emotions will far outweigh the sad and will even make them disappear like light dissolves a shadow. When you allow yourself the full range of feelings, and expect them and even welcome them, then you can pick and choose which ones to act upon. You can be fully responsive instead of merely reactive, as I hope you remember from secret 3 (listening). And you will also be well on your way to developing an excellent intuition about when to hold on and when to let go.

Let's look at an example. Nell's son Ken was 12 years old. He was a responsible kid, cheerful, social, and doing fine at school. Then a new kid, Jon, joined his class. As usual, Ken made friends quickly, but the new kid was rough, used offensive language, and had little respect for adults, let alone parents.

Nell reported that Ken seemed intrigued with Jon's attitude and it was beginning to rub off on him. She forbade Ken to hang out with Jon, but the bad behavior continued. She called Jon's mother to explain that the kids were getting out of hand, but Jon's mother took it all personally and said Jon could do anything he liked.

Nell didn't know what more she could do. She was frightened she was losing Ken. She had never been heavy-handed with punishment and now regretted this, because Ken didn't seem at all intimidated by her desperate threats. Guilt, worry, and fear tormented her daily, in addition to the extra hurt when Ken spoke rudely to her.

Nell decided she had little alternative but to let go. "It's his life, not mine, after all," she began repeating to herself. At first she wanted to let go angrily. She tried saying to him, "I've done all I can with you. I got you headed the right way, but you insist on undoing all we've done together to make you a fine young man. Why are you throwing all that away? I'm not going to try to help you any more when you're so obnoxious to me. Your life is your own! I can't live it for you!"

This seemed like letting go, but Nell was still holding on to many strings. Her emotional attachment to Ken's failure and her own would not permit a real letting go. Neither could be empowered and content with the new state of affairs, if it was really new at all. The anger, frustration, and misunderstanding were still all there.

Nell felt worse than ever when Ken reacted by yelling, "Fine, good. That's the way I want it!" At other times he began to weep, saying, "You don't even want me to grow up. I have to do it myself. You don't like my friends, and I don't care. Why can't you just leave me alone? I'm not doing anything bad."

Letting Go with Acceptance and Love

Nell thought this letting-go stuff was as bad as her old ways, but she was not really letting go. This was angry, vengeful, guilty abandonment. Letting go is an accepting, loving act, not an aggressive one. It requires you to accept the child just where he is today and to maintain hope and faith that the child's inner nature will lead him to a better place tomorrow. Nell's anger was a clear sign that acceptance was a long way off.

If a child makes choices that are beyond your tolerance, your most difficult job is to decide whether this is a situation you can and must control or one in which you can and must let go.

Ken was old enough that Nell couldn't control whom he chose as friends. After all, he could see Jon at school every day, completely out of her control. She could, if she chose, exert a certain amount of control through teachers, but the parents I have seen who try to do this are usually disappointed. Teachers often do not see the situation in the same light as the parents, and the children may even act very differently at school. Plus teachers rarely have the time or attention span to consistently monitor and guide a particular schoolyard relationship; they just have too many other responsibilities.

Bobby, a boy of nine, told me story after story of what went on at the playground. Even taking into account that he was good at exaggerating for dramatic effect, the basic stories still described situations well beyond the healthy range of playground behavior. Each time I would ask, "But where were the teachers? Were there no adults around?"

He always said, "Oh, Miss So-and-So was there, but she was at the other end of the yard, talking with Ms. Such-and-Such. If I ask her to help, she just says, 'Be nice, boys,' and goes on talking."

Teachers who get special requests from home often change their opinion of the child and may even perceive the parent as a problem. It's better to let the teachers do their job and to focus on doing yours. If you find evidence that teachers are not doing their job, then of course complain, but don't heap new duties on already overworked and undersupported teachers.

Nell rightly chose not to try to control Ken through his teachers. Could she control him through punishment? In the busy lives of parents today, enforcement of punishments they have previously imposed is almost impossible and a chronic source of new strain. If you ground a child, who is there to see that she stays grounded? If you take away something she enjoys and hide it somewhere, who is there to see that she doesn't spend all afternoon turning the house upside down to find it? If you destroy something or give it away, can you prevent her from replacing it or going to a friend's house to enjoy the friend's version of the same thing?

Unfortunately all some parents think they are left with is physical punishment. It's one way to impose the full force of the punishment all at once, so no supervision or enforcement follow-up is required. But when a child is pulling away and trying to grow up, punishment can backfire dramatically.

Punishment Is a Poor Substitute for Healthy Letting Go

Punishment just won't work here. For every imposition of punishment (whether physical or emotional), the parent hopes the child connects the pain directly to the transgression and feels a deterrent to a repeat performance. But the main message that really gets through is that this parent, who is supposed to want her happiness, is deliberately inflicting pain. All other points pale to insignificance. If a parent is deliberately inflicting pain, it's pretty easy for a child to justify any rebellious or disrespectful urges she gets.

In the vast majority of cases when your child does something wrong, you know your child knows already that it is wrong. Punishment, then, is not designed to teach but to frighten. In the few cases when she doesn't know it is wrong, are you not on weak moral ground to punish?

Physical punishment doesn't make your point. Plus, as you will be hearing throughout this chapter, there are far more satisfactory and comfortable ways of making any point. In addition, once a child is in the preteen years and certainly by the age of 14 or so, physical punishment is about impossible unless the child is already completely submissive to it. Your child's size and speed become comparable to yours. And even though you can push a child around as long as he weighs a good deal less than you, such physical invasion of the child's security and personal integrity is totally unnecessary even in the younger years, if you have mastered the seven secrets. I hope, as you are experimenting with the first four secrets now, you are already coming to agree.

Once a child is bigger, any kind of force is useless, whether it is punishment, pushing him into the car, or making him sit down at the table. Someone is liable to get hurt and to have a hard time forgiving themselves or each other. Physical force is even less useful than angry emotional abandonment.

Punishment Shows Weakness, Not Strength

Nell was small, and Ken was gaining in height. To decide now to push him around when Nell had done little of it before would have been only another sign of Nell's desperation. She had done well to develop a good relationship of respect and trust with Ken over the years. When she wished that he lived in fear of threats of physical pain from her, it was simply a natural feeling arising out of her total frustration.

So punishment was out, angry abandonment was out, and control through teachers was out. She let go of the idea that she could force Ken to avoid his rebel friend, Jon. She let go of the idea that she could use pain to deter him. She let go of the idea that she could control things at school. So what was left?

Limits of Control

Nell began to see that she had to let go now out of strength, not weakness. She began to take a hard look at what was truly in her control and what was not and what to do about each.

At home, of course, she could control where she drove Ken. In this case, Jon lived too far away for Ken to walk there, so she could refuse to let them get together after school. This she decided to do for a few days. (Of course, if a pal is in walking distance, the parent doesn't even have this option for exerting control.)

In Nell's case, she realized that, realistically, the extent of her control was limited to a decision not to drive Ken to Jon's house or permit him to be driven there by Jon's mother. She found out that the latter was easy; in addition to letting Jon do anything he wanted, Jon's mother did very little for him, not an unusual state of affairs for friends who cause trouble.

Nell also had to accept that she couldn't control Ken's feelings toward Jon or even the behaviors he wanted to take on. But she discovered that she could control her own thoughts and the feelings they engendered, once she knew how to include the natural process of letting go in her thinking.

Ask Yourself What You Can Control and What You Can't

Nell soon felt secure in knowing exactly what she could control and what she couldn't. Now she had to get comfortable with that by thinking through what she *ought* to control and what she ought *not* to control.

When she thought hard about it, she realized that she didn't really want to orchestrate Ken's feelings or his friendships. And she accepted that he needed to learn for himself what was nice behavior and what wasn't. She could see that she had set a good example and walked him through the motions of courtesy and kindness, and he had taken to these well. But now his training was being challenged, and she knew it was time for Ken to convince himself, by his own experience, of the value of what he had learned. Nell concluded that, hard as it was, she wanted to let go of trying to control Ken's feelings, thoughts, and behaviors.

Through this process, Nell got realistic and comfortable about what she could and couldn't control, what she ought and ought not to control, and what she wanted and didn't want to control. Now she had to figure out how this scenario would fit with her relationship with Ken.

Nell asked herself whether she was holding on too hard in thinking that she should be able to orchestrate his friends. She realized that she needed to let go of trying to control his friendships. And what's more, she realized this was not a failure on her part but a natural development, a milestone, a triumph even.

If she didn't have to feel guilty or angry about these developments, then Nell could consider soberly what her real options were. When she let go of things that were now really Ken's responsibility, then she could focus her energy on things that were truly still her responsibility and in her control.

Here's what Nell did.

A Letting-Go Chat

One day after school and over a snack of hot soup and crackers with cheese (paying attention to basic needs for them both), Nell and Ken sat down for a little chat. She had told him in the morning, "Look, Ken, I've been very angry at you lately, the way you've been acting since you became friends with Jon. I don't want to do this anymore, and I want to talk it over with you this afternoon, just for a few minutes. OK?"

Ken was skeptical, but said, "Yeah, whatever." Nell took that as an assent.

As they sat down that afternoon, she said, "I care about you and want you to be happy, but I've been wrong the way I reacted. You are old enough to make your own friends. I've taught you well, and you can see the good in people even when they seem offensive, like Jon does to me. Your friends are your business, and if some of them turn out to be not so nice you will know what to do. Right?"

Ken said, "That's what I've been trying to tell you!"

Nell continued, "But some behavior is just unacceptable to me. You can understand that, right?"

"Sure," said Ken.

"OK. So I like that you can see the good in Jon. But if hanging out with him makes you behave in ways that aren't like you or that are ugly to other people or offensive to me, I can't just do nothing, right?"

"Well," said Ken, "I don't see why you can't leave me alone."

"OK, I think you're saying you're trying to grow up and make your own decisions and decide for yourself how you want to act, and I'm not letting go fast enough for you. Right?"

"Yeah."

"Well, see what you think of this. I do want to let go of you. I want you to grow up and make your own decisions. It's natural—and to be expected—for us to disagree at times about when it's time for me to let go and when it's time for me to still try to have control. That's OK. But what I need to do each time is to get myself feeling comfortable enough with your level of maturity in each area to be able to let you take more responsibility for yourself. Does that make sense?"

"I guess so."

"OK. You've always been a courteous child and told me your plans and things, and now suddenly everything seems different. Can you see why as a parent I might freak?"

"I guess so," whispered Ken. "Are we almost done?"

"I think so. Thanks for listening," said Nell, nodding. "So I need to stay on the sidelines and build my confidence that you know the limits of bad behavior and that you're just experimenting with different behaviors so you can make your own choice. While you're doing this, I'm going to be absolutely clear about what I don't like, and if I can't stand the way you're behaving, I'm not going to want to be around you much or feel good about doing things for you, like driving you to the mall to meet friends and stuff like that. Does that make sense?"

"I guess so." Ken was starting to squirm a lot. Nell worried whether he didn't really go along with what she was saying or he was just tired of talking. She gave him the benefit of the doubt and tried to wind up quickly. A week before, she would have assumed the worst and started to argue.

"OK, so let's see. I'm going to work harder to let go and to let you carry the responsibilities that are yours in your life as a 12-year-old. And you're going to try to make careful choices about whom you hang out with and which of their behaviors you take on for yourself and which ones you bring home. I believe you're going to make wise choices. Does that sound like a good plan for us for a while?"

"Sure, OK. You'll get off my back, and I'll try to be nicer, right?"

Nell smiled and gave him a little hug. "Right! Thanks, Ken. Parenting isn't easy, but neither is being a kid!"

Ken smiled.

Shifting Boundaries

I hope you have seen from the details of Nell's chat with Ken how much skill is involved in letting go. You most likely will have dozens of chats like this as your child moves out into the world, from the day he reaches his hand out to another child to the day he pays his own rent. And each family is different in what particular issues need letting go at what age. It will depend on your and your child's relative sizes and personalities, your level of mutual trust, the extent of your child's experience and maturity, and other things as well.

You will be most successful in empowering your child to grow at a healthy pace if you remain aware of the power of the bond between you and of the boundaries that differentiate you and your areas of responsibility in his upbringing. Check regularly for the inevitable shifts in boundaries. Things once subject to your control can be suddenly subject only to your persuasion. Treat letting go as a regular privilege, not as a rare tragedy.

Nell found new satisfaction in her ability to use her good intentions to good effect. She had always wanted Ken to grow up, but every prior attempt to make it happen backfired miserably. With her new skills in letting go, her desire to have him grow up became a strength, not a weakness, in every conversation. By appreciating his efforts to grow up and accepting them for what they were, she empowered him to make real choices for himself and freed him to appreciate that her efforts were to help not hinder his growth.

Meanwhile, Ken could appreciate her efforts and actually help her feel better about letting go. He felt more secure about his freedom to see Jon and spent less energy pressing for frequent contact. Ken became more open with his mother about things he didn't like about Jon, since he no longer feared her condemnation and restrictions. In turn, Nell felt better about turning over more responsibility to Ken because she could see him exercising his maturing judgment.

As you apply these letting-go skills in your own life with your child, you too can feel new power in your knowledge that you're no longer at odds with your child's efforts to grow up. In fact, when you get rid of the adversarial postures and get on the same side of the fence, you will see how your child's efforts can make your guidance more effective, not less.

In my own parenting life, I have often felt that the natural urge to grow provided just the energy my child and I needed to go forward to the next stage in developing a more mature relationship.

By keeping in mind that your child must find his own life and that you can't find it for him, you can set up the most effective natural relationship of trust, understanding, and guidance between you and your child.

"But, I'd Be Happy to Let Go If Only He Were Ready!"

Often parents aren't ready to acknowledge new boundaries to their power and control over their child, because they don't think the last ones were respected adequately.

The new boundaries apply anyway. Let me show you what I mean. Another family was having the same kind of problem (as Nell's) with their 16-year-old daughter. The daughter was out of control. They hadn't sought help as early as Nell did, so they hadn't done any letting go.

As these parents began to learn about letting go, they wanted to start back again as if their daughter were 10, when they first felt things were going awry. That was not possible. The boundaries of control had shifted, even though earlier ones hadn't been dealt with well.

Their 16-year-old wasn't going to tolerate their forbidding her to go to the mall. They no longer controlled that, because she could drive. They could forbid her from using their car, but that just tempted her to take it when they were out and to not come home to give them a chance to take it back. Besides, she had a zillion friends who drove and were eager to come pick her up, even if she was grounded. New boundaries required new letting-go decisions.

The same basic chat applied. The 16-year-old girl was more skeptical than Ken, and more rebellious, because she had had six more years of experience with the idea that her parents didn't understand her, didn't want her to grow up, and would never let go.

Her parents' obviously earnest intentions to learn how to let go eventually won her over, and she became more communicative and cooperative. They never got their little obedient 10-year-old back, but they found they had a reasonable, responsible 16-year-old they could enjoy with new serenity.

The earlier you learn the art of letting go the easier parenting is going to be. I urge parents to give their children room from the very beginning. Giving children room means, to us parents, giving them room to make mistakes. Letting kids make mistakes can seem not only scary but wrong. Let's look at this in more detail.

Room to Make Mistakes

When your baby is first born, you want to protect her from any pain or trouble and teach her how to be safe in every possible situation. It's a natural urge, one that has stood us in good stead for eons, making us good protectors of our children.

As our child grows, however, we will have much disappointment if we think we can protect her from everything. Life happens. Learning to cope with life, its ups and downs, is part of growing up.

We need not impose any early lessons about life's difficulties—I would never advocate that. But at the same time, we should not try to hide them altogether. Even if we try to protect our children from every pain, they will naturally seek out their full range of options in life and will only resent and rebel against misplaced efforts to protect. Eventually, no matter how carefully and gently you protect, those honestly motivated efforts will look and feel to them like control and distrust.

Parenting is a perpetual task of deciding how much protection your child needs and how much freedom. You'll see the process at work every time you watch a parent spotting for a crawler trying to walk. Do you hold on to prevent a spill? Do you cushion every fall? Do you watch from afar? Do you "child-proof" the furniture?

Think about your own inclinations. Do you, or did you, trust your child to get his bearings and pull himself up gradually and not let go unless he was steady enough on his feet, or did you assume you would have to coach him and spot him every step of the way? See how your own early attitudes hold true through the years. Now, as you become more aware of the options you have, with faith and attention and letting go, begin today to make any changes you want in your attitudes about protection from risks, mistakes, stumbles, and falls.

If you let your child make little mistakes from the beginning, your child can learn her own powers and limits in the most natural and safe way, under your watchful eye. Think of a child gifted in gymnastics, for example. If the parent were to prevent every move that might lead to a fall, the child would never discover that talent. She might actually become afraid of the natural urge to jump and tumble. She could spend the rest of her life wondering what it was she was meant to do.

This lesson holds true for the much less dramatic case of the typical child, who is a bundle of small or large undiscovered talents. If you let your child make what might be called manageable mistakes from the beginning, she will learn two important things that will help your parenting immensely: first, that your example and your advice are valuable and, second, that you want her to grow up and will not hold on too long or too tight.

It all starts with things as simple as what to wear, or which food to eat first, or even which end of the spoon to hold. If you let your child make harmless mistakes, she will do her own experimenting, notice what you do and what you advise, and then make her own choice. And she will also realize that you have tolerated all of this and will welcome her growth.

If the mistake is harmless, then an unwanted consequence will teach your child the better way to do things at minimal cost. At each stage, your job as parent is to decide what mistakes are harmless enough for you to leave your child with full or partial discretion and what mistakes are too serious to allow for full freedom of choice.

Fear of Flying

I'm reminded of the notorious case of Jessica Dubroff, a seven-year-old who was permitted to fly a plane under the guidance of her father and flight instructor in an effort to cross the country. Jessica's parents let go too soon. They did not assess the dangerousness of a mistake that any seven-year-old could make. Though the child had had successful flight instruction, she was still only seven. The plane crashed, killing all three. Whether it was the weather or another cause that actually brought the plane down, the risks of any number of normal seven-year-old reactions were just too great.

My 18-year-old son said of Jessica's case, "A seven-year-old just can't have the concentration you need for that kind of thing!" Her parents needed a healthy fear of flying to protect her from her own premature ambitions or their ambitions for her.

Which End of the Spoon?

Flying a plane is at one end of the spectrum of risk; holding a spoon is at the other. Holding a spoon has few risks. Holding the wrong end is obviously a harmless mistake. Yet parents can get wrapped up in the idea of getting table manners straight from the beginning or showing off to Grandma how quickly the child learns, and so forth.

Yet the child will be frustrated if you don't let her experiment and will remain unhurt if you do. You may feel some frustration yourself for a time, when you know from your own experience how efficient a spoon can be. But there's no harm in letting the child experience it herself. One experience is worth a thousand words.

Dessert Before Veggies?

When you move on to what to eat first, most parents wouldn't want to take the risk, with a two-year-old for example, of putting dessert out first. The flavors are so concentrated and irresistible in today's desserts, and the applicable nutritional concepts so difficult for a child, that you would of course avoid letting a child choose for himself whether to eat the tuna or cookies first. But even there, if you are out at a rest stop with a boxed lunch and all is there in plain sight, what's the risk? Let go.

I use this example in particular since many parents find travel especially stressful. They try to impose all the same rules that they have at home, without realizing that the child knows just as well as you do that the circumstances are dramatically different and that some flexibility wouldn't do any harm. You can make travel fun by letting go.

As far as choosing clothes, many parents are surprisingly torn (pun intended). You may want grandmother to dote and fellow shoppers to ooh and aah, but if the child wears an old, stained T-shirt and ripped short shorts on a rainy day, that's not what you are going to get. Here's a good exercise in letting go!

From the child's point of view, is it a harmless mistake to choose this outfit? It would seem so. But as a parent, you may worry that you want him to know he should dress more warmly in the rain, or that clean shirts look nicer to people on the street, or that grandmothers like you to dress up for them.

Will your child miss any of these lessons if you let him choose his clothes today? Must all these lessons be learned or foreshadowed at three years old? Or can they wait until age six? Or can they be learned harmlessly by trial and error between now and then?

Mixed Motives Can Trip You Up

You may want to ask yourself if seemingly logical rationales are perhaps covers for other concerns, like a concern that people will think you an irresponsible parent to let a child wear shorts in a cool rain, or that you have failed to supply your child with clean clothes. Or will grandmother think you socially inept? Which of these are consequences you can live with, and which can you not tolerate?

Let go of whatever you can for the child's sake, and hold on to whatever you must for your own. But be clear which is which, and let go of as much as you can. Perhaps you don't really care about what other shoppers think, but the risk of a sarcastic comment from grandmother is too much for you. Go ahead then and insist on a clean outfit for grandmother and let the other go.

Be honest with your child that you want him to dress a certain way for your sake, not for his, and that it's a favor to you. That will make clear to him that you are not trying to restrain his freedom to grow up in general or judging his taste deficient in particular; you are asking a certain behavior in a certain situation for your own reasons.

Still, a time may come when you discover that your child doesn't want to go to grandmother's anymore because he can't choose his own outfit. He may even be uncomfortable with the fact that you are so eager to please grandmother at his expense. Perhaps he doesn't want to be that beholden to you when he is finally all grown up and you are grandparent to his kids. Consider if you really want him to feel that way toward you in 30 years.

If you notice your child's urge to freedom coming into conflict with your own ideal scenario, it's time for another review of whose life it is anyway. It's time to think again about letting go, for your sake and your child's.

The only bad mistakes are the ones that cause permanent damage and the ones you don't learn from. As for permanent damage, it's a parent's job to let go only so far as she is comfortable in light of the severity of the possible consequences of your child's mistakes. As you read earlier about attention to basic needs (secret 2), your first duty is to protect your child from the threat of permanent harm of any kind. So don't talk yourself into letting your child take unreasonable risks in the name of letting go, like the parents of Jessica, the seven-year-old pilot, did. It's your job to think through the whole situation and anticipate the risk. Permanent damage and your own regrets and guilt are too great a cost. Neither pride (in the case of Jessica) nor petulant anger ("Oh, OK, go ahead if you insist. You're just too pigheaded!") nor any other motive can justify letting down your parental guard.

Facilitating Learning from Mistakes

One famous entrepreneur put it this way: "If you aren't making any mistakes, you're not trying hard enough." When you realize that a potential mistake threatens only some consequence that's not permanent, you may have a wonderful opportunity for letting go. Trust your child to learn. If the child in the shorts gets wet, cold knees, he will learn. If grandmother says, "Honey, don't you have any cleaner shirts?" he might learn. Being embarrassed in school because of a silly choice is a temporary setback and gives room to learn. This is a healthy letting go.

Letting go comes with its own set of caring responsibilities. But even then, when you let go in certain situations and let your child make a mistake that has consequences you can live with, you still need to anticipate these, explain them if you can, and be prepared to help your child interpret them if and when they happen.

What if the World Doesn't Cooperate?

A frequent error parents can make in their efforts to let go a bit and allow children to face the natural consequences of undesirable behavior is to let the outside world carry the whole burden. For example, 10-year-old Bill had begun calling his brother nasty names. His mother, Nan, decided to handle it by warning him that people wouldn't like his using such names and he would lose his friends. But soon it became obvious that his friends thought his language was macho and cool. The outside consequences Nan had hoped for, and was counting on to teach Bill how to behave, didn't happen, at least in the short run.

Even if you expect some natural consequences to result from bad behavior out in the world, those consequences are outside your control. You still need to let your own natural consequences flow. In Nan's case, in addition to warning Bill he might lose friends, she needed to assert her own boundaries in the home by saying, "What you say to your friends is ultimately up to you, but in my house and my presence that kind of language to your brother is unacceptable."

If a behavior is intolerable to you, stick up for yourself. Lots of parents forget that their own natural responses can serve as the most important consequences of a child's behavior. Your responses count. The natural consequences of behavior within the home are actually far more important to the child, even if he wouldn't admit it, than are any artificial consequence the parents might dream up, or even any on the outside. And your own response is much easier to orchestrate, because it is in your control and natural to you.

For example, instead of grounding a rude child, so you have to be around her even more, avoid the child for a time. First tell her exactly why and ask her to let you know when she is willing to stop the rudeness. Instead of washing the child's mouth out with soap, like some parents did in the old days, you might say simply, "I'd love to talk to you more, but when you talk like that to me I don't want to be around you. I'll ask you in a half-hour whether you have finished speaking so rudely."

You may think this is too simplistic to apply to much more serious transgressions. This firm but gentle approach will work for these too. But start with the smaller transgressions first and you will see one of two things happen. Either the child's behavior will get better over all and larger transgressions will stop, or you will become so skilled that you will handle larger transgressions in a way that eventually leads to their ending. Thankfully, the first is the most common result, though you can take comfort that you will be able to handle the second if necessary.

With your new skills in letting go, you'll make it vastly easier and safer for your child to learn from his experience. But what may be even more important than learning from a particular mistake is learning how to handle mistakes.

Life and Love Compared

My father used to share a joke that has some bearing here. He would ask, "What's the difference between life and love?" As a physician specializing in infertility—or, as he saw it, the business of making couples happy—he loved the punchline: "Life's just one fool thing after another, while love is two fool things after each other!"

Life is about experience, and experience is about mistakes, and mistakes are about taking risks. If you avoid mistakes at all cost, your child will fear life. If you tend to stomp on your child's growing sense of self-determination in order to make sure the child does things "right" or if you invade the child's space by offering too much unsolicited advice, by punishing, or by taking over, then the child will be ever more afraid of being less than perfect. Life becomes a minefield in which your child won't want to move.

A child who fears mistakes may approach life timidly, with fear and hesitation. Or, in contrast, she may dive headlong into life, denying her mistakes or minimizing them or their consequences, or trying not to remember them, not to think about them, not to learn from them, or not to make amends for them afterward. A child in denial is sure to make the same mistake again. Love itself is a risk, but it must be taken.

Understanding Shyness

Researchers have found that many people who are excessively shy in adulthood have come from parents who were highly critical, so that they learned to be afraid to make mistakes. In his book *Shyness,* Phil Zimbardo explains that shy adults are afraid to take the initiative in any situation, especially with other people. He says the cause is their fear of being judged or criticized.

As explained in *Overcoming Shyness,* by Blaine Smith, this kind of shyness can be overcome only by learning that negative feedback is not necessarily a reflection or judgment on you, but is instead usually merely a reflection of the mood of the other person. To overcome shyness, you must learn that positive feedback will come if you just get some practice taking some risk. Usually a shy person must rebuild her self-image as a competent, attractive person before she has the courage to take that risk.

These researchers have found also that shame is often deep-seated among shy people. In fact, even though a child tries to be perfect, she always knows she is not; even if she can hide her mistakes from you, or especially if she can, she can accumulate a significant burden of shame that makes her feel less and less competent in life. Self-doubt becomes a constant companion that gives rise not only to shyness but also to a general fear of stepping out into life.

Let your child know that mistakes are natural and that you do not expect or demand perfection, nor will you criticize unduly when imperfections show themselves.

If you let your child have enough freedom to make some mistakes, she will know that mistakes are a part of life and that each mistake is to learn from. Also, if she can make small mistakes, experimenting gradually as she goes a long, she is much less likely to risk all on one big mistake.

Little Mistakes Prevent Big Ones

I think of learning and growing as a process somewhat like the movement of the earth's continental plates. They have to move. It's only a question of whether it's with a series of tremors or an earthquake. Likewise with the development of different species. As Stephen Jay Gould has shown in the biological field, change is sometimes cataclysmic and sometimes almost imperceptible.

In parenting, luckily, we have a lot of control over which way growth occurs. But we must always be aware that it will occur regardless of which way we handle it. Here's a common example of letting the little tremors come in order to avoid the earthquake. Consider the parent who forbids a child to dye her hair blue or forbids the second hole in the ear. Later, when this child can get around on her own, she is the one most likely to come home with a permanent tattoo or something even more disturbing. Hair grows back, but tattoos are permanent. Protest the little tremors if you wish, but don't be overbearing unless you want to invite the earthquake.

Mistakes with mild, temporary consequences that a child can learn from are preferable to mistakes whose permanent effects can outweigh any lesson learned. When your child has been allowed to have discretion within age-appropriate limits, he is more likely to have confidence in himself and in his judgment and to shy away from unreasonable risk.

Whenever your child is pressing the envelope, remind yourself: "It's my child's life, not mine, after all!" A bit of hard thinking at the right time can save you endless hours and perhaps weeks, months, or years of worrying, of wrangling with your child, of apologizing for unnecessary interference, and of nursing regrets for too much or too little advice or control.

Letting go is a tough job but yields great benefits. Letting go may be the hardest thing a parent must do, especially in the stressful moments when it must be done. But when done well, it is among the most rewarding of parenting tasks. It leaves your child feeling proud of your faith in him and empowered to consider his choices wisely. And it leaves you knowing you are on his side in his efforts to grow up strong and true.

The Chicken and Egg Problem

Many parents find themselves in a catch-22. Of course you want to let go and give your child more freedom, but you don't want to do it until the child shows she can handle it. Yet you suspect your child can't do it well until she feels that you believe in her and trust her with responsibility.

What to do? The trick is to back off from the immediate crisis that both you and your child feel so strongly about and begin to turn over responsibility for smaller tasks. This way your child sees your good intentions and enjoys new responsibilities—gets to test her wings—and you get to watch her evolve into a good decision maker while you keep the situations within tolerably scary limits.

Let Go of Urgency

The hardest part of a crisis is remembering right up front, in the moment, to back off a bit. Helen and her 15-year-old daughter, Jen, went through this.

Jen and several friends had met some military trainees at the mall and had been hanging out with them for a few weeks while they were on leave. Several weeks later, Jen announced to her mother that she and her friends were going to drive down to the military base, about three hours away, to see their friends for a weekend. She explained that the guys said they had rented a room for the girls at a motel where they could stay together and all would be safe.

Helen freaked. No way, she thought. Not in a million years. But the most scary part was that she realized she couldn't prevent it! Half of Jen's friends had cars, and she couldn't see how to lock her daughter up all weekend.

Luckily Helen's mind went into gear. She went through the thoughts I laid out for you earlier. "It's her life, after all, not mine" reminded Helen that she would have to handle this delicately, not with a bludgeon.

Jen thought her particular friend among the trainees was totally above suspicion, so Helen saw there was no way to intimidate her daughter with dire fears and predictions of sexual assault. She couldn't give Jen this freedom, but she couldn't really control the girl either. She listened hard, worked on her faith, and tried to think as clearly as possible. Was there anything less than this weekend trip she could let her daughter have a choice about? Was there a way to back off of this crisis and let Jen have more freedom in less dangerous venues?

Helen expressed her fears and tried to show faith in Jen's thought processes. She made this suggestion: "How about you and your friends meeting the boys midway for the afternoon? There's a great tourist center and fun area right between you. I'd be OK with that. What do you think?"

"Oh, Mom, that wouldn't be any fun," whined Jen.

"But it would be better than not seeing him at all, right?" asked Helen. "Could you just do this first? I would be a whole lot more comfortable with this, and then I can work on the weekend idea later."

"Look, Mom, I'm going whether you like it or not."

"Yeah, I know you really want to go, and there's no real way I can stop you short of calling the police or your friend's military commanders, but do this for me. Arrange this shorter visit first, OK?"

"Yeah, whatever," Jen said. "But I'm not giving up on the weekend."

An hour later Jen returned in tears. "Mom, he didn't even sound interested. He said he wanted someone who was all grown up. He said he didn't want to see me for lunch, only overnight with his buddies and mine!"

Helen cried with her daughter, knowing more than Jen could imagine about what had really motivated the boy. Meanwhile she congratulated herself for resisting the urgent all-or-nothing tone of the situation and finding an intermediate solution that quietly flushed out the truth.

Avoiding the Black and White

Whenever you think you are in an all-or-nothing situation, think again. No choice is so urgent that you cannot wait until the best answer is clear. If a matter is truly life and death, you will know what to do. If you do not know what to do, then the matter is not really life and death, though it may seem so. There must be other alternatives that you haven't yet thought of. So take the time to think, and use the skills you have been adopting from this chapter. Calm yourself, slow down, look at the reality of the whole situation, and resist the pressure of artificial urgency.

Remember, kids are great at creating urgency: "Dad, quick, she's on the phone now and she has to go and she's going to her aunt's for the weekend and she won't have a phone!" Or "Dad, I can't make the team unless you decide today!" Or "Mom, this is it, I don't want to ever speak to you again if you won't let me do this!" Or "I'll kill myself if you don't come through for me now!"

Remember always, just because you are letting go doesn't mean your child doesn't still need a parent. It's your job as the more mature and experienced of the pair to see through artificial urgency and to know what's real and what's not. We're back to Buddha again. Practice your reflective listening until a real solution comes. Knowing it's really your child's life, not yours, can give you the impetus you need to take your time and involve your child as you think problems through together.

Attention to Needs Versus Letting Go

A particularly difficult area of letting go is basic needs. In the chapter on secret 2, I gave some examples of how you can empower your child to gradually assume responsibility for his own basic needs. Often this requires a lot of experimentation, since kids naturally wonder if all the trouble they see you go to is really necessary. It's a trying time for parents.

To get through these trials, you may have to muster all your faith, your wisdom about basic needs, and your listening skills. You will need to be on your toes as far as letting go is concerned. When basic needs are at risk, ask yourself these questions:

- What basic needs are threatened here?

- How serious is the threat—relatively tolerable, like a day without food, or relatively intolerable, like a week in the streets?

- How lasting would be the consequences?

- Will my child's judgment be directly impaired by the unmet need so that nothing much can be learned and choice cannot really be exercised—such as under conditions of overmedication, drug use, exhaustion, terror (as with a horror movie at too young an age)?

- What lesser freedom can I allow that would show my faith without threatening this basic need?

If you decide you can let your child take the risk, see that all other basic needs are met to the best of your ability, especially food, security, and love. Then her mind is more likely to be operating effectively to meet any new contingencies.

Don't be afraid of being too simplistic or repetitive when you are reviewing basic needs. It doesn't hurt for a child to know what her basic needs are in your opinion, even if she wants to put each one to the test. As your child takes over responsibility, don't assume you're off the hook either. She may come back to you for advice or return sheepishly after she has gone too far in ignoring basic needs.

Allow your child to save face. Welcome her home with no shame for having tried. Resist the temptation to say, "I told you so," or "See, I knew you weren't ready," or "I guess now you know I was right." Instead say something more like: "I admire your desire to test things out for yourself and find out what's really good for you. But I was worried about you and I'm glad you're discovering what your natural, healthy limits are."

You may be surprised at how willing your child is to take advice when it is given in the context of letting go. As Mark Twain pointed out, it's funny how much wiser a parent can grow just in the space of a few short years.

My very first family counseling client had a child who had been overseas with his father since age 10. The boy came to live with his mother, Ava, at 16 in hopes he'd have an easier time of it.

For six months Ava did everything she could think of to make her son feel at home, to help him adjust to American schools and kids, and to show her love. But he didn't give her the time of day. She was heartbroken.

She washed his clothes, made him a great breakfast, made his bed and cleaned up his room, drove him to school and to all his activities, helped him with his homework, and helped him plan for college. But nothing was coming back to her. Ava felt more and more bitter that she spent so much of her energy trying to help him and he seemed to appreciate none of it.

She decided to let go. She said to herself, "It's his life, not mine, after all. If he doesn't appreciate all I'm doing, I should stop, and instead learn how to simply show my love."

Ava stopped cleaning up his bed and room, she showed him how to do his laundry, she waited to be asked for a ride to activities, she stopped offering to help with homework, and she stopped talking about planning for the future. Meanwhile she invited him to have lunch with her on Saturdays and to go to the movies one night a week. She made a point of being around in the morning, and she smiled and chatted and touched him on the shoulder.

At first her son made no response at all to these gestures, but she kept at it. It was as if she was domesticating a wild bird. Then, two weeks later, she ran into my office, gleaming. "He hugged me good-bye this morning as he left for school and asked if he could have my advice about a term paper! I never would have believed this could ever happen!"

Letting go brought them closer, in a healthier, happier way.

The "Hurried" Child

The great value of appropriate letting go is not diminished by the fact that children today are left on their own far too early. It is when we don't understand the delicate process of parental letting go that we fool ourselves into thinking that our children are more ready for independence than they are. As a society we need to take notice that our children are being deprived to a large extent of all the parental modeling and guidance and all the more general cultural cues that have helped children develop in the past.

When I appeared as guest therapist for troubled families on TV talk shows such as *Gordon Elliott, Geraldo, Ricki Lake, Montel Williams,* and *Sally Jessy Raphael,* at least half of these families had children who were given too much responsibility for themselves too soon.

David Elkind has been the leading whistle-blower on this problem: pressures on the modern family to make ends meet and stay healthy fall disproportionately on the children. In his groundbreaking book *The Hurried Child* and subsequent books, Elkind points out that intelligent transfer of responsibility is completely different from pressuring children too fast, too soon, to be out on their own in society. Yet the media, schools, politicians, and even many child experts get it wrong.

Madison Avenue knows how vulnerable kids are to the "keeping up with the Joneses" urges. Just when they are trying to discover for themselves what their basic needs are, advertisers are happy to tell them these include $90 sneakers and a bottle of No-Doz or Tylenol. Meanwhile the news clips every night show us that unsupervised kids are running amok in our inner cities and in communities around the country. Instead of asking where the parents are, we often blame the kids, the schools, or the police force.

Meanwhile, to prove they are preparing children for great futures, schools are responding to pressure by pushing for achievement in academic subjects too early and then discovering that the children aren't ready. It has gotten so weird today that one child in seven nationwide is on Ritalin, a drug that has no other purpose than to make these children adapt better to sitting quietly in a class that doesn't interest them. In some schools, half the children are on Ritalin, often in order to keep them from being distracted from activities that are obviously inappropriate. Just because some kids *can* do something doesn't mean all *should.*

Political candidates urge us to lock up all these "troublesome" children, force them to be more responsible with tougher discipline in and out of the home, and treat them the same way criminal adults are treated. Some experts even advise making kids more responsible earlier and earlier. They see that some kids are superresponsible early on, and they assume it's a good and harmless thing. They marvel at young prodigies and see it as a tragic but unconnected thing when youngsters burn out early, show themselves to be socially or kinesthetically underdeveloped, or become chronically stressed, depressed, or suicidal.

Millions of adults are struggling today with the effects of not having had a secure, cared-for, gradual, nurturing childhood. Some experts call for more consistency, more consequences, more rules, more structure, more activities, more discipline, more daycare, more schooling, more responsibility. But few of them realize that the child just may not be ready for any of these.

Trusting and waiting patiently as the child gradually asks to take over his life may be the best approach. It is scary to think that many specialists base their conclusions on a sampling of children that may not include even one child who has grown up with an optimal rate of transfer of responsibility—with a truly healthy letting go. It's as if a doctor were to study babies in a modern suburban subdivision and conclude that all babies needed glass bottles instead of plastic bottles, not knowing that the healthiest thing of all is a mother's breast.

Luckily, each parent can discover for himself the best rate of letting go for his family. And don't feel bad if you discover your rate is a lot slower than your neighbor's. The friction this causes is not overwhelming so long as you practice the letting-go skills in this chapter, along with the other secrets you are learning in this book. Trust yourself and your child to make a smooth transfer of power in the rich years you have together.

Remember, once you have let go, you are still a parent. After a child ventures out, takes risks, triumphs, and learns lessons, he will often want to come back to the family cave, as it were. Don't grasp on tight again or try to keep him home, but instead make letting go a lifelong spiritual exercise in responsive parenting.

Striking Bargains

Sometimes parents try to strike a bargain with their child: "I will give you certain privileges so long as you fulfill certain responsibilities." This can be useful, but only in a loving, respectful, and flexible context that always holds the child's basic needs more sacred than any bargain. Negotiations can degenerate suddenly and quickly, especially when your child moves into a different stage of development.

A child who has been dependable about chores for months may suddenly take on different interests that leave less time for chores. Or he may expect more freedom simply because of his age. At that point, insisting on the old arrangement will probably fail. It's time for a new negotiation.

As soon as possible, rather than bargaining, try getting across the idea that your child's chores are a voluntary contribution to the community of the family and that the freedom he deserves as a maturing child is not contingent on performance of these contributions. In the long run it will feel better to you as a parent if you know that your child didn't buy his freedom with chores and obedience but rather did chores and obeyed out of gratitude for your faith and guidance and letting go. And your child will feel better knowing he made a contribution for its own sake, as a token of his love and goodwill toward the family.

As your child becomes ever less dependent on you, he will have more and more freedom to choose. First your child is part of your family because she has to be; but later on, it's because she wants to be. What a pleasure!

The Scariest Times for a Parent

The hardest times are when it seems all too obvious to you that your child is not maturing as he should, isn't shouldering the responsibilities kids usually do at that age, or isn't contributing anything to the family workload. But even then you must resist making decisions that your child should make for himself. Living his life for him or treating him like a child of a much younger age can be only shaming and debilitating.

If irresponsibility persists and your child is old enough to be physically beyond your control, then the strategies of "tough love" are a natural continuation of the letting-go strategies. If you get no cooperation, then figure out exactly what boundaries of acceptable behavior are comfortable to you, make them perfectly clear, negotiate as much as you are willing so your child can buy into the final arrangement, stick to the plan, and get all the support and advice you need to carry through.

Going into the details of these tough-love strategies is beyond my purpose here. For one thing, the details have been described admirably in other books, such as Katharine Levine's *When Good Kids Do Bad Things*. For another, if you raise your child using these seven secrets, the chances are excellent you will never need to resort to those difficult strategies!

You can best liberate your child to achieve her greatest potential by freeing her a little bit, one day at a time.

You Can't Live His Life . . . and Vice Versa

Just one more important point before I introduce you to the wonderful power of the next secret. Be careful not to live vicariously through your child: "It's my child's life, not mine, after all." All the things you wanted to do and didn't, or would like to do but think you can't, are part of your life, not his.

You will inevitably influence your child in many ways toward or away from certain activities and paths. If you admire musicians, for example, your child will be more likely to be interested in music. Or if you abhor politicians, she may never show any interest in a popular election, even for class president. This is just the real you coming through, and it's inevitable. Your child is meant to feel your influence.

But it's a step too far if you consciously or unconsciously act out your own desires through your child. If you always wanted to be an athlete, you must guard against pushing your child in that direction or shaming him for not being interested. Or if you hated your own shyness, you must guard against being critical if your child is shy also. Anything you obsess over will hold fascination for your child, whether it is by attraction or repulsion.

When a parent tries to control a child's feelings and desires and lives vicariously through his child, the child senses the emotional dependence of the parent and carries a heavy burden to keep that parent happy. It's a greater burden than any child should rightly bear. And if the parent's happiness is totally dependent on the child's actions, every failure will look like a threat to the family's well-being. Yet that well-being is your responsibility, not your child's. So take care to know yourself well enough to guard against living your life through your child.

Of course you want to and should rejoice in your child's accomplishments and share in her disappointments, but check frequently to see that the accomplishments and disappointments are really hers, not your own. Too often we adults feel at a loss to know what our life's passion is. We did one thing for mother, another for dad, and another for a teacher, and by adulthood we no longer knew what we ourselves wanted. A child feels lost if she comes to rely on a parent's pride and sense of defeat to gauge her progress instead of on her own sense of direction and passion.

So let your child have his own feelings, goals, dreams, and wishes. These may be like yours or different, but they are his. Let your child pursue interests and discover for himself whether it will become more than merely an interest. Affirming a child's feelings and interests is the most effective way to help him learn more about himself.

The more clearly you grasp, accept, acknowledge, and count upon your child's growing independence as a separate being, the more successful you will feel. With this kind of supportive letting go, you can get a wonderful, warm feeling envisioning you and your child in a maturing relationship of love and trust and mutual appreciation.

Respect gods before demi-gods, heroes before men, and first among men your parents; but respect yourself most of all.

PYTHAGORAS

If a child lives with acceptance and friendship,
He learns to find love in the world.

DOROTHY L. NOLTE

You can't get spoiled if you do your own ironing.

MERYL STREEP

"I have a life too, and I share it with my child."

❖ Modeling ❖

USA Today recently reported a 35-year study that demonstrated how parents are the "main support anchors in a child's life." This doesn't sound very revolutionary, except that the study showed some unexpected effects of a child's knowing that his parents care. The study followed 87 men from initial written assessments as students at Harvard College through their mature years. The researchers found that, independent of other factors like family health histories and smoking, men who at 20 felt that their parents were very caring and acted justly had significantly lower rates of heart disease, hypertension, and other stress-related disorders in their 50s than did the men who were not so sure of their parents.

I know you wouldn't be reading this book unless you cared a great deal about your child. But the key point in this study is that the child must know it. The child's perception is what counts.

Linda Russek, coauthor of the study, concluded: "The take-home message is to talk to your child and find out if he does feel loved. This is not about buying them stuff. It's about accepting the child's perception of their relationship with you as the truth [and acting in a way] that your child may experience you as just and loving." Coauthor Gary Schwartz explains, "When a kid feels cared about, it reduces the moment-to-moment stress in his life," setting the stage for a healthier adulthood.

The message is loud and clear that to do your best in preparing a child for a healthy adulthood, you will want to act in ways that let your child know that you are both loving and fair.

As you were experimenting with secret 4 from the last chapter and noticing how useful it can be to remember "It's my child's life, not mine, after all," you may have noticed also that, to do that successfully, it helps for you to be well grounded in your own life. If your own life is full and your identity secure, then it's easier to respect and adjust to your child's emerging identity and independence.

Secret 5 focuses directly on the important parental responsibility to be centered in your own life, so that you can share your true self with your child. The fifth of the seven secrets of successful parents is this: "I have a life too, and I share it with my child." This important secret is not about being selfish. It's about modeling a good life for your child and letting him learn in the easiest and most natural way possible: by your example. Your child learns best by observing and imitating the most important person in his life: you. You are his chief model.

Here are some key ideas to keep in mind as you explore the stories, examples, exercises, and insights you will find in this chapter on modeling life for your child.

- Your child learns mainly by your example, even in the later years.

- You create a working model of life for your child through showing him how you live.

- You can share almost any part of your life with your child at any age if you are honest and clear with yourself about it and then keep the discussion with your child clear and simple and age appropriate.

• The best way to introduce your child gradually to the skills of handling life's ups and downs is not to preach about how she is doing it but to model your own skills for her.

• If it feels like your child's lifestyle and yours are in conflict, you probably will not be content until you can resolve the conflict and discover how your lives can mesh and enrich one another.

• Know that the tones and attitudes you create in your home will be the familiar ones your child will try to re-create in later life. So as much as possible, create the same atmosphere that you will want your child to create for himself.

• Sharing your life is the best way to show you care.

Sharing Your Life

Your child assumes your life is important or you wouldn't be living it. If you share it, the child is honored and feels important too. Having a life and sharing it with your child affirms that life as an adult is worth living and that you have faith in your child to have a life of his own.

You might think that you can best give the message of caring by your generosity, or by your declarations of love, or by your efforts to give advice, or by your obvious worry when things go wrong, or by your pride when things go well. All of these help. But the best way your child will know that you care deeply for him is when you demonstrate daily that he is a welcome and important part of your own life.

Think how important good models and inspiring examples may have been in your life. Just recently a young mother reminded me how much harder it is for a parent to know how to be close and nurturing to a child when her own parents weren't close and nurturing. Here's how she put it: "No one's childhood is perfect, but I'm glad I had the experience of a caring family. I knew my parents cared about me, and that has made it easier to know how to be there for my son."

Your Own Parenting Models

Parenting is easier if you had a good model. Without it, you may not even know what options exist for building a loving, satisfying bond. With the seven secrets and the support of friends and family, you can have a successful parenting experience, regardless of your background. But you can see how parenting could be harder if you didn't have admirable models.

It's the same for your child. If like most parents you want desperately to make life easier for your child, *show* him how to live.

Reach into your heart and rely on your faith in your child and in yourself as a parent. Pay diligent attention to basic needs and listen intently and look for appropriate opportunities to let go. You will find the motivation you need to pursue your own life with gusto and find ways of sharing it with your child.

Family Versus Career

In the last few decades there has been a great deal of controversy and confusion about how much of your own life you should have while raising children. Women particularly have felt that life must involve more than changing diapers, running washloads, wiping messy chins, making doctor's appointments, checking homework, and driving kids around. And this has led to an exodus from the home.

The '60s generation of women wanted a voice in the political arena, in the marketplace, and in the civic center. They felt that women weren't being allowed to be whole people and that their point of view was being ignored in the decision-making processes of the wider community.

What these women, I among them, didn't realize at the time was that we were part of a larger historical process that began with the nation's mobilization for World War II. Before that, middle-class women thought they were free to choose to be mothers or teachers or nurses or writers or philanthropists. Women in the poorer classes had always worked of necessity; many also managed a family as best they could. The preferred choice then was to stay home—to *not* have to work. Americans were moving up the ladder, and fathers were proud they could support their families solo.

Then, with the war and the men in the field, even middle-class women were put to work outside the home. After the war, when society said proper women should get back to the kitchen, the women realized they were not free and decided to make a change. The same thing happened after World War I. (Unfortunately this is the kind of history we don't learn much about in school.) That time around, what women had learned during the war led to their getting the vote.

Women are still in the process of seizing their freedom to choose about how to participate in the life of the society outside the home. And good for us! But a side effect has been that the more conventional choice, that of being home manager and mother, has been demoted, disparaged, and even ridiculed. In the '40s, people assumed that a woman who had an economic choice would stay home during child-rearing years; by the '70s, people assumed she would go to work!

Now the pendulum is swinging back. Women are exhausted and burned out. Children are neglected. Men who share in home management and child rearing are now also feeling totally overworked, and men who don't do these things are maligned and ridiculed. One of my children's baby-sitters in the '80s told me that her mother had always worked and that, even though she knew her mother loved her and tried to be there for her, she was going to do her darnedest to be home with her own children.

There's still another reason things are changing again. Women are finding, as men had already found, that satisfaction in the workplace isn't all it's supposed to be, and jobs—let alone meaningful jobs or jobs that pay a living wage—are very hard to find. And of course, many parents are deciding that the stress on themselves and their children created by the long daily sep-aration, let alone the mediocre conditions in so many childcare environments, is too high a price to pay for an uninterrupted employment career.

While experts debate, parents must follow their gut feelings. With the pendulum swinging back, perhaps more parents will think more openly about their full range of options for what their life should consist of. Getting a life according to secret 5 doesn't necessarily mean getting a job. It may mean quitting a job!

Getting a Life

What does it mean to get a life? How much of a life must a mother have to avoid being too wrapped up, too obsessed, with her kids? How much of a life must a father have outside the family, especially if most of his time is spent doing things he can't share with his child?

I hope you will feel liberated to do whatever is right for you and your family. The point is to have a life that is your own, based on whatever your beliefs and goals are, and then to share that life with your child. Life is indeed more than all the child-care tasks listed earlier. But it includes hundreds of possibilities besides a career.

Parenting takes about 20 years. For some parents, the heavi-est duty lasts only until a child goes to school. For those choos-ing home education, the round-the-clock attention lasts a bit longer. But your options before and after this period are wide open, and you have options for what your life is to be during that period too, based on exactly who you are right now.

You will be able to most successfully apply secret 5 to your life when you realize that its core purpose is to let your child know, by your own example, that life is worth living and to show him how to do it.

He needs to know that life is not just a case of one genera-tion raising the next. Certainly child rearing is one of the most rewarding—if not the most rewarding—of all life's gifts and enterprises. A parent's example of dedicated and joyful parenting is the beginning of the seed of the next generation. But it's too much of a burden on your child to think that his life is the be-all and end-all in your life.

Would you want to have believed, at the age of 6, or 10, or 16, that growing up meant only that you would spend your life taking care of someone like yourself? I don't think many of us would have been so eager to grow up if we thought that was all there was to life.

Instead a child wants to know you as a whole person. He wants to know you as a loving and caring parent, mentor, protector, and admirer. But he also wants *and needs* to know you as a spiritual being, a community being, a friendly being, a busy being, a being at play, a creative being, a builder, a thinker, an outdoor person, a celebrant of life. He wants to know how you cope with loss, for instance, or success, disease, pain, celebration, time, growth, learning, challenges, friends, admirers, adversaries, success, mistakes, or weeds in your garden. It's your job to show him the whole of life through your life.

Let Your Child Know the Whole Person

Too often I hear parents expressing this litany to their child: "If only you could get your act together, I'd have time to do what I want to do." Really, who should get their act together here?

No child wants the burden of feeling he is depriving a parent of his desires. Our children are deeply programmed to want to please us; that's why a wink or nod or an arched eyebrow is so effective. But if you were to hold a grudge about how much of your life the child takes, he could never succeed at pleasing you. Having never succeeded in this important task, the child can experience acute frustration that lasts long into adulthood, even for the rest of his life. Perhaps on his own or in therapy or in a self-help group, he will realize that it was not he who failed but his parent, by not having a life purely his own that he could offer and share with his child.

Let your child know you had a life before kids, will love your life after kids, and are loving your life right now. Make the choices that keep you whole and healthy even as you dedicate yourself to your child as your first priority.

The Quality and Quantity of Time

When you share only a tiny bit of your life, your child feels small and unimportant. Every minute feels more intense, more critical, more powerful in her memory. It's the same for the parent. If you only can be together for an hour at the park this week and the hour turns out to be a disaster, neither you nor your child will forget it for weeks, if ever. And you both may feel that you have failed and let the other down.

In contrast, a bad trip to the park isn't so bad when you had lunch together and will follow it by supper and a video. The problem is time. If time is too short, the pressure is just too great, and the desire by both child and parent to have everything go perfectly can make both feel stressed and artificial. The child comes away knowing nothing more about the parent than that Mom or Dad is eager to please; the parent comes away recalling all the little things that could have been better.

Quantity time allows the child to learn from you what life is all about and how you cope with it. If you cope with it by feeling resentful, by yelling, by feeling trapped and overwhelmed, the child surely will learn that and might be better off just seeing you for a tense hour in the park. (Even that is still open to question. A parent who chooses to be around, even if she yells a bit too much, shows more caring than a parent who is rarely available.)

Those aren't the only choices! In our complicated and sophisticated lives, we must make a special effort to be whole ourselves in whatever way suits us and at the same time ferret out ways to share that whole self with our child. Downsizing the demands on your income, finding moneymaking enterprises you can do from home, using baby-sitting co-ops, working part-time, and sharing jobs are some of the options to help you increase your quantity time with your child.

"Whose Idea Was This Anyhow?"

Parents do one of the most ironically counterproductive things when they are trying to spend some very limited time with a child. They insist on doing something of the child's choosing. They feel this is one way to make sure the child will have a good time. And yet time and time again the child wants to do something of the parent's choice, something designed not to amuse the child but instead designed to reveal and share the parent's life. And the child doesn't even know how to ask for this because he doesn't know what he's missing.

Children don't seek entertainment from parents; they seek sharing and caring. Children are very good at entertaining themselves if given time to themselves *after* a good time with a parent. Your child wants the opportunity not to play more kiddy games but to see what life is all about and how you, his most adored mentor, experience it and deal with it.

When you are selecting activities for your time together, do some kid's stuff. And really do it. Get down on the floor, make up your own rules, throw stuff, and so on. But then also invite your child to do your kind of stuff, like collating reports, watching the news, talking about a magazine article, scrubbing a bathtub, dusting a bookshelf, decluttering the basement, playing chess, brushing your teeth, or chopping salad. Let him into your life, show him what it's all about, talk about it while you do it, and share how you feel about it and the choices you make every day. You may be amazed at the special pleasure your child shows.

Being a Better Role Model

When you are considering how you are modeling life for your child, and I hope you do so often, you might ask yourself some of these questions:

- Does your child see you when you have made a mistake at work? Or do you try to hide it or minimize it?

- Does your child see you when you are successful at your tasks? Or do you try to be modest and keep it to yourself?

- Do you try to include your child in your daily routine? Or do you connect with your child only when your chores are done?

- Do you exhibit a sense of control over your life—that what you do is by choice as a result of your life decisions as a whole? Or do you exhibit chronic frustration and lack of choice?

- Do you play as you work? Or will your child assume from your example that fun happens only at very rare times, ones specifically planned for?

- Do you take a moment before each task to imagine what part of it your child could do under your supervision? Or do you rush to finish your task and forget to include your child?

- Do you share a bit about your day before you seek to have her share about hers? Or do you sometimes launch into inquisitory questions that put her off?

- Do you plan some activities just for yourself, independent of your child, and encourage him to make his own plans too, just for his own enjoyment? Or do you feel guilty about doing things just for you and focus persistently on your child and his activities?

- Do you encourage creative play and flexibility in games? Or do you always enforce the proper rules when you play games with your child?

- Do you work well side by side, each trying out your own techniques as long as the options are safe? Or do you insist that your child do things the right way and the best way only?

- Do you try each day to share a bit about your feelings (about things other than the child and his doings) and a bit about your activities, your plans, your dreams, your past experiences, your insights, your philosophy of life? Or do you sometimes go for a whole day without sharing a bit of yourself with your child?

- Do you know that you are teaching your child not only how to behave and thrive but also how to carry the best of yourself, the best of your culture, and the best of all of human culture forward into the future? Or do you sometimes get stuck in a myopic vision of your role?

Once you realize you are part of this last, grand project, you can surely see that you will need to find opportunities for a lot of sharing in your everyday life!

How to Invite Constructive Imitation

As you ask yourself these questions, reviewing the ways you share with your child, and exploring new ways to do so, I hope you are beginning to appreciate your vast power as a model to your child. You might want to affirm for yourself right now how the key to setting a good example is "care and share."

Mary was growing more and more impatient every day with her son Pete's nagging for more junky gadgets and fancier, funkier clothes. She nagged him right back, complaining about his superficial friends and materialistic interests. Then she "hit bottom" one day, yelling at Pete that she didn't even have time to take him shopping because she had too much cleaning to do and he wouldn't ever help. She had to clean up the front porch, she said, where he had made a mess with his muddy boots, old bike tires, and so on.

Her outburst sounds pretty harmless, doesn't it? But she felt she had hit bottom, because she had sworn to herself she would never torment her children about housework. Her mother had done that and made her feel guilty and inadequate as a child. Now Mary was stunned to hear herself doing the same thing to Pete.

She needed to take secret 5 to heart. The next time her patience with Pete began to slip away, she began repeating to herself: "I have a life too, and I want to share it with you."

Mary thought hard about who she really was and what her life was about. She felt a lot better when she began to reexamine the picture that persisted in her mind: an always tired mother trying against all odds to keep a clean house and failing miserably at raising a boy who would be interested in more than teen fashion.

She realized, when she took some time to think about it, that she was an intelligent, caring, diligent woman with lots of ambition to make the world a better place, both through her family and other ways. She reviewed how she read a lot, shared with friends about public issues and health news, aggressively recycled any discarded things and consumed responsibly, and donated to groups championing a number of issues close to her heart. On top of that she worked hard on her marriage, at keeping a pleasant home, and on raising children who were honest, smart, caring people. And when she was finished raising children, she knew, she would expand her public efforts and feel good about the time she had spent on her family.

Knowing better who she was, Mary looked at her life now. She had stopped her career as a teen counselor to have children but kept her hand in by running a support group at the local shelter two hours a week. She had chosen to be home for her kids, even though in the heat of a stressful moment she often felt trapped. She was proud that she took the time to put good food on the table and to talk to her son about his taste in clothes rather than just ignore it. Her life was more full than she wanted, but there was nothing she wanted to drop. And it was only a stage of her life, and a very rewarding one at that.

Mary was ready to practice a little listening with Pete and then try to engage him in her life, now that she knew she had one. "You want to look good to your friends, don't you? Well, I want my front porch to look nice for my neighbors. I guess we aren't too far apart on that. In fact, if I don't want you to worry so much about what your friends think, I shouldn't let worrying about what the neighbors think make me yell at my son!"

Pete laughed.

"So, as you can see, we've let a lot of garbage accumulate on this porch. How about you and me trying to see how much we can get done here in 15 minutes. Shall we use your watch or mine?"

Mary couldn't believe it. Pete was a whirlwind and even seemed to enjoy it. When 15 minutes were up, he took another minute to bag the trash and take it to the trash can.

Mary's "Thank you" to Pete was more heartfelt than she could remember in a long time. Pete smiled and waved as he dashed down to the street on his way to meet his friends. "I'll wait on the new jacket until I can pay half. How's that, Mom?" he yelled back.

"Great!" said Mary. She had shared a bit of her life. Pete had loved it, and he had been empowered to make wiser, more generous decisions himself.

Your Ultimate, Irresistible Power

When I tell parents how powerful their example is, the most common reaction is fear. We each know too well how imperfect we are. We want our children to learn from our mistakes and avoid our shortcomings, not mimic or repeat them.

If you are afraid your child will be like you in the worst ways, she probably will be. On the other hand, if you actively cultivate your positive example, she probably will avoid your worst faults.

If you are fearful about a particular characteristic, it can become a self-fulfilling prophecy. Kids respond to the creative tension of a vision, whether it is good or bad. Whatever we are obsessed with becomes their obsession. Whatever worries us will preoccupy them, even if they have no conscious awareness of it.

Use Your Strengths to Crowd Out Your Weaknesses

Because your concerns can easily become your child's concerns, finding he is exactly like you or exactly opposite (without your even trying to pass on a trait) is not unusual, though it can be very disconcerting. For example, a parent who is poor at handling money and feels self-conscious about it never needs to say anything about it to his child. The child will still likely be fascinated by money. Such a child may be bad at handling it or good at it but will find it an issue.

No one can really say why this is true, except that children observe and imitate in ways that go far beyond any words or actions we can objectify and measure. They just sense the vibes when the parent speaks of money, or talks about rich people, or hears a report about campaign finances, or searches his pockets for change, or plans a modest vacation. The fact is, the child won't miss any cues; he's programmed to catch them all. Picking up cultural cues and parental attitudes, fears, dreams, and behaviors is a survival skill for the human child.

It may seem like bad news that there's no escaping the learning net of your child. But the good news is that your child does want to learn from you, to avoid your shortcomings and to build on your strengths. So you might as well be candid about both your weaknesses and strengths; don't make learning harder by denying your imperfections, trying to hide them, or worrying and obsessing about them.

The only way your powerful influence as a model can really go awry is if you deny your power and refuse to use it wisely. Then, instead of teaching and empowering your child, you leave him bereft of the guidance he needs from you.

Modeling Is Not a Choice

It's important to keep in mind that you are always setting an example. You can't pick and choose which actions your child will take as a model and which not. "Do as I say and not as I do" just doesn't carry any weight. For example, a parent might make an example to his son of being kind to others, but if he is not kind to his son in the process, the intended example is wasted.

Have you perhaps had the experience of finding yourself yelling, "Don't yell!"? Or how about "Say 'please'!" Shouldn't it be "Please say 'please'"?

Our actions speak louder than our words, and kids do as we do, not as we say. It's often more the medium than the message that touches our children the most. If things don't seem to be going well with your child, consider the example you are setting. If your child seems tired, alienated, depressed, disorganized, or overwhelmed, consider whether you are projecting any of these things yourself. Experience shows it's quite likely.

If your child is just the opposite of you, it may still be because your preoccupations are his, and he chooses to rebel. You may be familiar with someone who is a neatnik parent and bewails his bad luck in having a messy son. They may seem like opposites, but in fact they both choose to value themselves and express themselves by the way they treat their personal possessions. If the parent stops focusing so much attention on neatness, the child's tendency toward overt messiness will often subside.

How to Let Your Child In

In the classic movie *My Friend Flicka,* the son of a farm family asked for a colt of his own, but his father wanted to hold off until the son was more responsible and attentive to schoolwork. The mother suggested giving him the colt anyhow, because it would give him something to care for and feel good about. The father protested, "But I don't want to give him his reward before he has performed!"

Luckily Dad gave him the colt anyway. The child grew, and the father learned something about parenting. The father's life had been the farm and the horses. He had thought his son was a separate part of his life, one he had to squeeze in around the edges. But when he let his son into his life, by giving the boy a bit of the same kind of responsibility he had, his son felt trusted and empowered and had more of an atmosphere of caring and sharing in which to be open to learn from his father.

As this father learned, setting a good example means knowing what's important in your life and sharing it with your child. You don't have to have all the answers or be a perfect example.

Modeling Challenges

Often a parent will ask, "What should I be doing about my child's spiritual life? I believe in going to church, but I'm not even sure what I think of church, so how do I teach him?"

If your spiritual life is important to you, then talk about it. Share your questions, doubts, and inspirations. If you go to church, take your child with you a few times but don't force it. Have her come for you, not for her. Tell her you want her to come because you want to share your life with her, not because you think she needs to come or should be a regular churchgoer.

You can use your example to inspire many of your child's life choices and values, without knowing all the answers or what will be the right thing for your child in the long run. Sharing includes your interests and concerns and values, not just your activities and triumphs.

You instruct by sharing yourself and your example, not by putting artificial limits on your child's freedom or by judging his character or actions. Instead you set him free to learn from you in the most natural and empowering way possible. If you want the spiritual life to be important to him, simply *show* him how important it is to you. Or if you meet with resistance, simply present the spiritual life as a natural developmental option, saying something like, "Someday, when you are grown up enough, we'll *let* you go to church with us."

In every area of your life, share the parts you like best. Avoid implying that because you think something's good your child must also adopt it. Instead let good habits rub off onto her naturally, by virtue of your caring and the power of your example.

If you wish your child would pay more attention to some interest of yours, resist making an issue of it! Instead find or create opportunities to share your own feelings and to demonstrate exactly how you are involved and what gives you pleasure about your activity.

If you want your child to read more, for instance, resist complaining and setting impossible new goals. Instead have some good books and magazines around and let him see you reading.

Notice a good political cartoon or an amazing fact from a magazine and say, "Hey, did you hear about this?"

Tell your child about it just as you would a friend. Resist some moralistic tag line like, "That's why you should read more." Say instead, "I just love picking up these tidbits when I read." Before long you may notice your child thumbing through the literature strewn on your table.

Perhaps you love flowers and regret your child doesn't share this love. Have her do small things with you, like moving the pots around or tagging along to buy new seeds. Show her when a new blossom appears that gives you particular pleasure. Before long she will start asking questions and will get involved. Gardening may not become a passion, but she will absorb your example of enjoying something peaceful and beautiful and creative. It's the soft sell that works with kids.

Just as with a spiritual life, reading, or flowers, there are many other areas where parents often feel self-conscious and wonder why they are at a loss about how to instruct their child. They are at a loss because, instead of instructing, they need to share their life. Here is a short list of areas where your example is worth a thousand words:

Good eating habits. What does your child see about how you handle a snack attack?

Good sleep habits. What do you do when you are exhausted or sleepless?

Good grooming habits. Does your child get to see you do your morning or bedtime routine?

Good study habits. How do you prepare yourself for a project, like a flea market sale, a car repair, a homemade Christmas present, or a report at work?

Good social habits. Does your child overhear you making your own social plans on the phone?

Good exercise habits. Does your child know how important staying physically active is to you?

Your child needs to develop healthy and agreeable habits in so many areas. Small wonder that if you aren't demonstrating as well as instructing, she can get burned out from the accumulated instructions from both home and school! At home you have the luxury of a much more natural learning style, if only you know the power of your own modeling. Do put it to good use!

Modeling Beats Instruction

At home, teach your child, but not with lessons and instruction. That is necessary only when there are too many children to demonstrate for all at once. Moreover, it only really works for academic subjects where everyone can do exactly the same thing. The calculation 3 ×3 ×3 = 27 is the same no matter who does the thinking or who writes it down. But how do you chop lettuce for a salad? Would the next 19 people you meet do that the same way? Is one way better than another?

At home, use your example. Let your child see you and be around you and share with you in every area of your life that is important to you. You may not think something is important. In fact, if you spend any time doing it regularly it must be important. So share all of your life.

Let your child hang around when you are brushing your teeth. Let your child know when you are looking forward to some time alone with your spouse. Here are some more ideas:

- Let your child watch as you choose which jam has more fruit and less sugar in it.

- Let your child watch as you check the durability and price as well as the looks of your new sweater.

- Let your child see how you plan your next social event or how you do research to find out where to invest your $1,000 tax refund.

- Talk about what you are planning to say to a friend whose mother just died.

- Tell your child about how you regret that you forgot to return your uncle's phone call from last week.

- Tell your child when you are having a bad hair day!

- Let your child see how much you enjoy your favorite sit-com and how quickly you turn off trash that would pollute your sweet dreams at night.

There is little we need to actually teach our children if we create opportunities to share our lives with them.

Off to a Good Start

Good modeling can be done very easily as a natural part of your family life if you start out your parenting that way. Toddlers and preschoolers have no choice but to be with you until you decide to leave them somewhere else. They will pick up so much from just being around you.

How often have you or another parent noticed with amazement how a child imitates a parent's way of talking on the phone, or of saying good-bye as he is walking to the door, or of reading with one foot up on the other knee, or of addressing the dog or cat? This is the rule, not the exception. From the most superficial to the most deep, your child will imitate you. From the way you roll your eyes at a joke to your deepest source of anxiety, your child will not miss a thing. So make your example work for you every day.

Is your child already at a mobile age, either school age or beyond? Do you work outside your home after school hours or in the evening? Then it will be harder to start a program of really sharing your life, but it's always possible. Arrange your mornings so you and your child have some time to *live* together. Protect those evening hours during the week when you can share each other's lives. And do whatever you can to free up weekends to include your child in your weekend activities.

How to Get Unharried

With the pace of life today, you may be very proud that you do things efficiently and can crowd superhuman lists of things to do into one single day, every day. But if you want to share your life with your child, all this must slow down. You cannot share your life if you look or feel like an incredibly efficient automaton.

I have told many parents not to get frustrated when things take twice as long when you have a child's help. In fact, my own rule of thumb is that they will take four times as long. Making a salad, for example, might take you 5 minutes. If your six-year-old helps, it might take 20! But this isn't because she is so inept or because you will be too busy instructing her. It is because it takes time to do what you do, let her watch, let her ask questions, let her try her way, let her try your way, give answers, explain, modify and amplify, laugh, notice unrelated things, chat about something else, and then celebrate the job you've done together. Four times as long, 10 times as much fun, and 20 times more important!

With teens unaccustomed to sharing your life, hang around in their lives a little. Is your son installing a new stereo? Hang around, tell some funny stories, share memories, ask harmless questions. Then ask if you can get a little help with your car— checking the oil or brake fluid, taking it to the carwash. Anything!

Hang out at a CD store and notice what the kids are listening to. Watch MTV for 10 minutes a day. Ask your teen what she thinks of the hottest MTV star or what the best CDs are. Ask what the kids are wearing this spring that makes them really feel "with it." Tell her what you are looking forward to most about the approaching spring—some favorite shoes, a walk to the local park. Ask her if she would join you some Saturday afternoon on your walk.

Set Aside Your Agenda

You may be amazed at the good feelings that come for both you and your child when you do this kind of sharing, sharing of yourselves with no specific agenda in mind. Who you are right now has nothing to do with your plans and agenda. So too with your child. If you want to help your child cope in the world and build a life, let her glean all she can from how you are doing it just being you.

Times are hard right now, as American society reaches its maturity and the limits of unlimited growth. We have more products than we have time to use or money to buy or interest to learn about. For example, consumer researchers wonder if anyone will really care when we have 500 cable channels and have monitors in every room fully integrated with sound, television, film, and our latest family video. Will our lives be any better, less stressed, warmer, more meaningful?

Parents are bombarded with statistics on increasing cases of childhood attention disorders and distractibility, depression, chemical addiction, and suicide. Obviously our children are feeling the stresses of modern life, and that means the stresses of their parents' lives as well. It's a difficult task to share our lives appropriately. Many parents wonder how much they can share with a child about the real challenges in their lives. So let's look at this for a moment.

For example, the mother of a six-year-old girl in a troubled family wondered if the girl could or should be told that her father's a drunk and a wife rapist. Certainly not. But the truth can be told in an age-appropriate way that empowers and validates the child rather than frightening and debilitating her. She can be told that her father is allergic to drink and does nasty things he doesn't mean to do when he has been drinking.

Only if the mother sets this kind of context can this child interpret accurately what she sees and experiences. Remember, the mother is modeling all the time. If her mother is crying and reaches for the phone to call for help, the girl needs to know what is being modeled. If she knows her mother is feeling her own feelings and making difficult but intelligent choices, the modeling is helpful. But if she thinks she has done something wrong, the modeling will be misinterpreted and will be lost.

Children should never be forced to grasp more than they can handle in stressful family situations. Much less should they be cast in the role of confessor, counselor, or buddy to the parent. But even the most horrendous situations can be talked about in a way that both informs and protects the child, confirms her own intuitions, and supports her basic sense of self and right to hope for personal survival and safety.

Seeking Help Is a Sign of Strength

When protecting a child from stresses beyond her control or understanding is impossible, getting outside help and support becomes essential. To know when you need help with parenting is a sign of strength, not weakness.

If your family is in crisis, check the blue pages of your phone book for social services or call your church, doctor, or trusted friend. Ask for a recommendation for a counselor or support group or human services agency to help with your family's problem. Have faith that no situation is without a solution.

Applying the Secret of Modeling Through the Years

One of the most difficult decisions parents face on a regular basis is how much of the stresses of life they should allow to intrude in their child's life. None of our lives are ideal, and many parents want very much to protect children from the threats and unknowns of life as long as possible. But others believe that the sooner children find out how hard life is, the fewer illusions they'll have and the more experience they can build up before they are totally on their own.

Each family must find its own balance between these two extremes. I recommend erring on the side of protection, for two basic reasons. First, in view of our basic responsibility to protect our children from permanent damage while they're in our care, it's safer. And second, experience indicates that children who have a strong foundation of love and security from childhood have a wellspring of confidence and optimism that helps them when the going gets rough. They do better than children who have had to struggle with threats and insecurity from the start. The first group of children seem to have internalized a sense of self-confidence, hope, and control over their own lives that the second group often lacks.

It is up to the parent to run interference for the child until the child is fully capable of both understanding any threat and, at the same time, keeping it in perspective so that it doesn't overshadow his life.

In infancy, your baby needs you. Virtually no substitute will do. She must share your breath, your sounds, your heartbeat, your smell, your voice, your environment. It's best to take your baby everywhere and share your entire life. If a baby can't go somewhere, simply don't go there yourself. Even if you are crying, don't neglect your baby. She knows what crying is about, and it's OK that mothers and fathers cry too.

If, as for many parents today, your baby is not going to be with you all the time, even within weeks of his birth, do your best to leave the baby with someone who has a direct familial link to the child. That way, relationships that will inevitably develop will not be abruptly terminated. And do whatever you can to get the support you need to allow you to spend as much time as you can directly with your baby when you are at home.

In toddlerhood, your child knows if things aren't OK. You will have to explain in simple language. But instead of saying, "Your dad's lost his job, and I don't know where our next meal is coming from," you would do better to say, "Your dad's having some problems at his work." A toddler knows what problems are, and he knows his parents can take care of problems. But he also now knows why you are crying and that it's not his fault. And that's very important.

You can have more of a separate life now with a toddler, just as your toddler is beginning to have a separate life from you. He may want you to stay out of the room while he makes a surprise for you. And you may be leaving from time to time to do things he wouldn't know or care about. But if you are having a good day, share it with him, and describe your successes in terms that relate to successes he has experienced. And if you're counting money at the bank or the store, let him see how you do it. If you are cleaning, cooking, sealing envelopes, dialing a phone, or working on a car, find ways he can help. Conversely, if you find him at a task, ask what you can do to give him a hand.

In the exploratory stage, roughly age four to seven, you may get all kinds of questions. Resist getting impatient or blurting out clichés and witticisms that aren't responsive. If you don't know an answer, say so; then explore the issue together. If you say you'll check on it and get back to your child the next day, be sure you do.

Already in this stage you may find sharing your life harder than you thought it would be. Even if you make the time, your child may be eager to explore unfamiliar territory, especially with friends. But draw your child into your life at this stage, because he still needs your close supervision. His adventuresomeness can outreach his knowledge and caution.

In the growth stage, age 7 to 14, your example of how to deal with all kinds of issues becomes very important. If you are not modeling these things, someone else will. Try not to be preachy but rather exercise a leadership role. One description of leadership is the ability to make people feel good enough about themselves that they strive always to be moving toward a worthwhile goal. Ask your child to sample your workday activities, your leisure activities, your favorite entertainments, and so on. Then ask to sample his interests, old and new, from time to time.

With issues like money, competition, aggression, courtesy, planning, ecological responsibility, sexual responsibility, household work, and parenting, share your thoughts and use a recent headline to bring up new issues. Tune the car radio to public radio or another talk channel and chat lightly about the topics. Give a capsule description of your own experience when you were your child's age and ask what's going on for her that might be similar.

With the maturation years, age 14 to 21, sharing your life gets even more difficult because your child now has his own life. You will have done well to establish traditions of spending together certain times of day or certain days of the week or certain holidays during the year. It's very hard to initiate these events in this stage if the tradition is not well established, because friends seem much more important than family. But you don't have to let these events go by the wayside. And if you see your child less often casually, then it's perfectly reasonable to request a few new institutionalized interactions.

Keep birthdays and religious and other holidays fun and adventurous. Focus on the joy of being together and catching up and sharing favorite interests and activities. These will be the basis for your family get-togethers for the rest of your life, so make them worthwhile and attractive now. Best of all, you will most likely be modeling parenting for the person who will one day be parenting your grandchild!

Know How Much to Share

Even if your family is not suffering the worst kinds of stresses, there are still lots of temporary stresses that must be screened before they are shared with your child. You may sometimes find knowing what and how much to share difficult, so here's a way to think about it that has been helpful to other parents.

If what is going on affects the way you relate to your child, then you need to share something. If you don't, the child may blame herself for your change of mood. This is a child's most common reaction and the most devastating. If you are unhappy, you must be sure the child knows it is not her fault.

Share only enough so that it will make sense to the child why you are affected as you are. Avoid having the conversation in the heat of a crisis; you are likely to say more than you need to and more than is helpful to the child. Simply say, "I'll tell you all about it later," and then be sure to do so.

When you are a bit calmer and have a clearer view of the situation, you can simplify it to three or four simple sentences. Name the problem simply, reassure your child that you are taking care of things, make clear that it has nothing to do with her and is not her fault, and assure her that you are getting help if you need it. If you are afraid you will overwhelm your child, consult a trustworthy outside person to help you know how to express what needs to be expressed.

Children can understand a good deal, often more than we think they can. But always avoid the ultradramatic version and the gory details. The important thing is to acknowledge problems that are troubling you, give them a name, respect your own feelings, let your child off the hook, reassure the child that you will protect her, hear out her feelings, and do the best you can. Work hard to muster the faith you need for a change and a better future, for your sake as well as the child's.

Remember that even in a crisis the most important gift you can give your child is not a total understanding of the crisis, which no one can be expected to have, but your example of how to cope. Stay as calm and constructive as you can, get the help you need, make the changes you must, and keep your priorities clear. Safety and peace of mind for you and your child must always come first.

Parents' Bad Habits

A few pages ago, you were hopefully considering all the good habits you want to have brush off on your child and how best to let that happen. What about any bad habits you don't want your child to pick up?

Honesty is best here. What don't we like about ourselves? Are we willing to admit it to our children? And if so, what can we say we are doing about it? Are we content to give up on ourselves and not try to change, or do we want to set an example of persistent personal growth and self-empowerment?

Some of the greatest frustrations of children come from parents who insist that a child should avoid something like smoking because it is bad for health, although the parents continue with the dangerous behavior. Should the parent try to hide the behavior? Deny that it is as frequent or addictive as it is? Make a big distinction between adults and children that doesn't really make sense to the child? Enforce a double standard?

On one *Gordon Elliott* show, I appeared as guest therapist to a parent who was snooping on her children to catch them smoking. She suspected they were smoking but thought she had to catch them at it so that she could punish them justly. Their punishment was smoking a whole pack of cigarettes, which made them green in the face and very uncomfortable. But why did the mother suspect her sons were smoking? asked the host. "My cigarettes kept disappearing," answered the mother, "and it had to be them taking them."

The host was taken aback. "You yourself smoke!" he said.

"I've been trying to stop for years so I know how awful a habit it is once you get started!"

Perhaps all that energy, sneaking around to catch her kids sneaking around, would have been better spent at a clinic to stop smoking, herself.

Punishing a child for doing what you do yourself is going to feel pretty bad to most parents and utterly unfair to most kids. Instead, do your best to clean up your own act. Get a life you can be proud of.

Of course quitting smoking is one of the hardest things in the world to do. You don't have to raise smokers just because you smoke. But telling them off, catching them being bad, and punishing them won't stop them from imitating you. Instead, set an example of what to do when you have a habit you regret. Let them learn from your self-honesty, your candor about your problem, your efforts to stop, your willingness to seek help, and your struggles to improve your life in other ways and live according to what you believe.

If smoking, overeating, a messy house, too much wine, or anything else is a source of shame for you, your child will be fascinated by it. Here is something more powerful than my parent, the child will feel. It has to be fascinating. But even if you don't intend to quit your habit right away, you can take the thunder and lightning, the fascination, out of it by being honest and clear about it.

You can say something like: "Right now, I just don't feel I have the determination to conquer this bad habit. I wish I had never started it. But it has hold of me right now, and I have not made the commitment to change yet. I am working on myself in other areas now, and I hope I get to making this change before I suffer any serious consequences."

You will not be able to make your child's fear for your safety go away if she knows how dangerous your habit is, but your example of self-honesty will go a long way toward demystifying the bad habit for your child. If you call it as you see it, honestly and without self-defense or justification, your child will most likely be happy to oblige you by avoiding imitating you in your habit, instead imitating you in your desire to do what you know is right and healthy.

It's not uncommon to find parents who seemed content with their favorite addiction, only to decide to begin an abstinence and recovery program when they have the powerful extra incentive of knowing their child is holding them up as a model.

How to Share Anger

Before you come to the close of your exploration of the secret of sharing your life and setting an example, I want to focus on the emotion of anger. How to handle a child's anger comes up often when parents seek help; it seems to cause more fear in parents than almost anything else. What do you do when your child is angry, or even threatening to break things or hurt someone as a result of anger? Isn't this a time for specific instruction? How can modeling help here? And what if the parent has always modeled self-control and calm deliberation and still has an angry child?

Actually, an angry child presents a great opportunity to practice modeling. Some parents think they never feel anger or never show it; often they are afraid of anger because they know it can lead to violent and disruptive behavior. Perhaps they remember firsthand how their own parents got out of control when angry. Or their parents did not tolerate any childhood anger. They can be stunned by the intensity of a child's anger, especially when they have been doing their darnedest to have a happy, peaceful home.

The kind of candor and acceptance we've been discussing here, as you build awareness of your own life and how to share it, requires that you get in touch with all your feelings and be able to share them meaningfully with your child. All of us feel anger sometimes, whether we admit it or not. As one wise mentor of mine said, anger is simply what you feel when things don't go your way. The issue is what you do with it. If your child doesn't know that you get angry and doesn't see how you handle it, he has no model to help him deal with his own natural feelings when they arise.

When your child is angry, imagine times you have felt anger and lead your child gently toward understanding and accepting the feeling and then deciding how to handle it and what action or expression is necessary.

Here are some dos and don'ts to help you explore your many options in dealing with an angry child. As you read them, consider how important it is for you to be in touch with your own life of feelings, to let go of any fear of feelings, and to model how you deal with your own feelings as they arise.

When your child is angry at you,

Don't say:

"Well, you deserved what I did after the way you behaved." That's retribution.

"I don't know what to do with you." That's shaming.

"Don't you get angry at me!" That's a threat.

"You think *you're* angry!" Another threat.

"Don't make those faces at me or use that tone, or I'll show you what real anger is." Another threat—a feeling as a threat!

"Get out of my sight." That's abandonment.

"Keep it to yourself." That's dangerous suppression.

"You're lucky I'm not like my mother. I'd be grounded for a week for back talk like that." That's holier-than-thou self-pity.

"If you can't stop this, I could get really mad." That reinforces the fear of feelings.

"@#$%^&*+." That models desperation.

Do say:

"I understand you're angry with me because of what I said (did)." That's understanding.

"It's natural to be angry when I interfere with what you want. Let's talk more about what it is you want and see if we can find another way we can both be satisfied." That's acknowledgment and validation of the child's humanity.

"It makes me uncomfortable to see you so angry. Obviously one of us has missed something here. Please help me figure it out." That's willingness to problem solve, help, and cooperate.

"What have I failed to understand about your feelings, or what have you not understood in my words or actions?" That's good listening.

"I'd be angry too if someone messed up my plans like I did yours." That's empathy.

"I hear you. Right now you're furious at me." That's reflective listening.

"I'm sorry I spoke so harshly. I know I overreacted. I still must say no. Can we talk about it for a minute? I would like you to understand." That's candor and trust.

"I understand you're angry at me, but the way you've shown it is completely unacceptable to me. It just makes me angry too. If you think I'm not understanding you or am being unfair or oppressive, say so and put your feelings into acceptable words so I can hear them." That's clarity and firmness.

"I can tell by your behavior that you think you're not getting through to me. How can I help here?" That's validation and openness.

"OK. What are our options here?" That's faith in solutions.

"You feel very strongly about this. Perhaps I need to reconsider. Please tell me more about how you feel. If I don't change my mind, I hope you'll try to understand. It's because I am making a choice based on my knowledge and experience as an adult, and not to get on your nerves or rain on your parade." That's honesty and clarity.

Having thought about all these options in dealing with your child's anger, you may see how you can be empowered to tackle situations that might in the past have made you feel uneasy and even trapped in a no-win situation. Now, being aware of the model you present will enable you to deal lovingly and constructively with all your child's feelings and reactions.

Your most important area for sharing your life and setting a really useful example for your child is in the area of your own human freedom and dignity. Any time a parent behaves as if she is not in control of her own personal choices, she is diminishing her child's chances of responding to life with a positive, self-actualizing attitude.

The Process of Processing

As you consider the great value of this last technique you may ask, as other parents have, how you can say these things so calmly when you feel rightfully angry or upset.

Processing your own feelings can be the most important modeling you do. Parents are often more concerned with overt behavior than with interior processes, especially when they realize it's best not to try to control a child's thoughts or feelings. But just as your own feelings can get in the way of behaving the way you want, your child's feelings can do the same. While you are guiding overt behavior it's good to be modeling a healthy interior process.

Whenever you are uncomfortable with your child for any reason, resist the temptation to tell him immediately what he should do so you don't feel that way. Instead ask yourself exactly what it is you are feeling, using the feeling grid to be very specific. Then feel and explore that feeling. Know you are allowed to feel that way, without explanation or justification, as long as you want. Once you accept your right to have a feeling, it's a wonderful fact that a new one, more manageable and serene, will tend to replace it. And you avoid the resentment, guilt, and depression that can follow suppressed feelings. Once a difficult feeling is processed, you can hear and respond to your child without your feelings sabotaging your efforts. Meanwhile, you have modeled a healthy interior life.

Enlightenment Is a Two-Way Street

Knowing the power of your modeling can help you to be your best as a parent and as a person. If any of us were perfect we would be heavenly beings of light already, not parents. Perhaps you are already feeling like many successful parents do, that part of the reason we receive the special gift of becoming parents is to give us new opportunities to grow, each toward our own perfection, with new incentives, new perspectives, new strength, and new joys.

Think of your efforts to set an example as an ongoing process of your learning and then passing it on to your child. I would like to end this chapter with a vision from my great-uncle, Scott Nearing, who lived to the age of 100 and left more than 50 published books and pamphlets behind, mostly about how to live a sane life and help others do the same.

He said that each person is climbing a face of the same great mountain, each starting at a different place, you on your own path. As you come closer to the top of the mountain, you begin to see that you can't really see the mountaintop, high in the clouds. But it begins to matter less and less to you. You begin to realize that the path you have made is helping the younger ones coming up behind you, and this gives you more than enough satisfaction.

If you keep your sights on the mountain's heights, your path will be true, and your children will thank you. Your greatest gift to your child is to be authentically yourself, a whole human being using your mind, body, and spirit to make the best of what life brings and to give love to yourself and all who enter your life.

If you live authentically, dedicating every day to being true to your best self, then you can rest assured that your child will imitate that model. You can't know what will be your child's own strengths and weaknesses as he grows, nor what life will bring to him to challenge and propel him forward. Don't try to assess your parenting or the example you've set by making minute observations and judgments of your child's life. Instead set your sights on the innate goodness of your child and on her own intrinsic urge to be her own authentic self. Give her all the help you can by having a real life and sharing it with your child.

Where love rules, there is no will to power; and where power predominates, there love is lacking. The one is the shadow of the other.

CARL JUNG

The absurd duty, too often inculcated, of obeying a parent only on account of his being a parent, shackles the mind, and prepares it for a slavish submission to any power but reason.

MARY WOLLSTONECRAFT

Likely as not, the child you can do least with will do the most to make you proud.

MIGNON MCLAUGHLIN

Oh, to be only half as wonderful as my child thought I was when he was small, and only half as stupid as my teenager now thinks I am.

REBECCA RICHARDS

"I speak my mind, and I know
when to stop."

❖ Expression ❖

At the end of a workshop with the parents of high schoolers in a section of Philadelphia, I asked which of the ideas we had shared had been most useful. More than half said the communication skills. Time and again their questions began with a description of a setup with their teenager and ended with the question "So what do I say then?"

The sixth secret of successful parents is "I speak my mind, and I know when to stop." It's the secret of expression. Once you have taken in the ideas, stories, examples, and tips in this chapter, you will be well on your way to having just what good communication takes: courage, confidence, concentration, presence of mind in emotional crisis, knowledge of ways to express difficult thoughts and feelings, practical experience with what works and what doesn't, and—on top of it all—a kind of lightheartedness. No failed conversation is the end of the world, and you will always get a second chance with your child.

Here are a few key points to keep in mind:

- Effective self-expression is one of your most powerful tools as a parent.

- Good communication skills can be a natural gift, but they can also be learned.

- How you say it is just as important as what you say.

- There's no advantage in quick responses in conversation. Take your time.

- Careful listening comes first, before you decide to speak your own mind.

- The gentle silence at the end of your sentence or paragraph is just as important as your words.

Before you read some powerful ways to speak your mind and to have a positive impact in your child's life, I would like you to consider all the ways of communicating that don't really work. As I review these, I hope you will recall any times you may have tried one or another and consider whether you found them wanting.

Less-than-Successful Modes of Expression

The Authoritarian Stance

First there's the aggressive, authoritarian approach. An extreme example would be, "I know what's best for you, so just shut up and do as I say." Your child hopes you know what is best for her. But if you are impatient with her, if you are not interested in listening to her or not willing to explain your thoughts, and if you dig in your heels, standing on your parental authority alone, then her faith in you will easily waver.

The older she is, the more her faith can waver, because she knows she could understand you if only you would give her a chance, and she knows she could articulate her thoughts and deliberate with you if only you would let her.

The Parental Plea

The next mode is the pleading, martyrish approach: "Can't you do this one thing for me? After all I've given and done for you? Don't you know how much I love you? Can't you just trust me and help me out here?"

This approach fails, primarily because you're acting weak. Children know from millions of years of evolutionary history that their life depends on having a parent who is strong enough to support, protect, and provide for them. Few things are as scary to a child as when his parent seems vulnerable and weak. If a parent must beg, the child may feel powerful for an instant, but deep down he will feel bewildered and alone.

Pleading invites your child to test you by calling you on any seeming bluff of weakness or ineptitude on your part. Your child must test and test, hoping always to recapture that parental strength he knows must be there and cherishes and craves with all his heart.

Calling a parent's bluff often works. For example, Jerry, father of 12-year-old Fred, tried the pleading approach: "Give me a break here! I've been working hard all week for this family, and now you won't even rake the leaves out back? What am I working so hard for? You don't care . . ."

Fred then said, "Yeah, Dad. I don't care about how hard you work. You're working all the time."

Jerry's bluff was called. He switched right to aggression: "Well, I don't care either. Get out there and do the leaves—or else!" He came on strong instead of weak. In fact, Jerry ended with a bit of the next strategy, the threat.

Down with Threats

Obviously the threatening stance is not one you would choose to adopt. But it pops up anyhow when a parent is feeling desperate.

Don't even think of it as a last straw, though, because it doesn't work. It may get the immediate result you want, but the price is too high. Fred may do the leaves, but Jerry will pay for that with a major wound to the relationship. Healing may take much time, energy, and skill.

Any threat a parent makes amounts to a threat to withhold love and protection, which for a child feels like the threat of abandonment. Because a child is totally dependent on you, the threat of abandonment is ultimately the threat of death. Indeed, for the first millennia of human existence, parental rejection did mean death. This is deeply ingrained in our childhood psyches, so a parental threat creates the ultimate fear. It shouldn't be used lightly, if at all.

What about threats of physical punishment? Some parents assume that physical punishment is a form of communication. You are telling the child that pain follows upon performing any unwanted behavior. Parents who don't know of any other way to discipline a child may convince themselves that when they inflict physical pain they are doing it out of love, "for your own good," to teach an important lesson the child needs to learn.

I have yet to find a child who is really comfortable with the classic explanation, "This hurts me more than it does you." And I have yet to see a child who didn't know just as well before the punishment as after that something he did was wrong. The learning has already happened. The punishment is really designed to instill fear—fear of loss of parental love and support.

Do we want our children to make their choices based on fear? Perhaps in our parental desperation we do. Yet it's hardly the way to create confident, competent, content, and contributing adults. A child who is physically punished may one day grow up and physically punish her own child, the victim becoming the perpetrator. Few parents really want their own desperate moves perpetuated in this way.

Physical punishment moves down the generations only because that is the family model and each parent lacks any other model. Studies have shown that children who were not disciplined physically don't use this method with their own children.

They never find the need. They have other options. Likewise with any other threats of emotional or physical attack or abandonment. It's the fear that works on the child. Can the child ever trust you completely if she fears that you may be willing to abandon her for what may be a relatively minor infraction?

If threats and punishment don't work, then, what if you just say yes?

Out with Permissiveness

Why not just say nothing, some parents might wonder? At least it keeps the peace. A parent can just roll over and play dead and pretend nothing bothers him. If a child confronts him, he just backs down. It seems easy.

The yes approach doesn't work either. If you want to parent, you must be actively doing the parenting process—which is nothing unless it is involvement, making tough choices, getting your hands dirty.

Permissiveness doesn't work because your child has a parent exactly for the reason that he needs one. The child left to himself may feel very powerful for a time, but deep down he craves the guidance, support, and security only a parent can give. So if you back down from giving the kind of guidance your child needs, he will feel abandoned, just as with the threats above.

The most frequent outcome of the permissive, indulgent approach is a child who keeps testing the limits, often with total disregard for his own better judgment and personal safety. If his parent doesn't care, then he's not worth caring about, his sneaky subconscious will be telling him. He just tries more dramatic things to test the parent's apparent unconcern, to get the parent to notice. The daredevil child is a hurt one.

If permissiveness doesn't work, what about appeal to higher authority?

Appeals to Higher Authority

Invoking higher authority is a common strategy for parents with regard to activities—driving, smoking, alcohol use—that are forbidden by law for certain age groups. If a child is showing an interest in these things, or her peers are getting into them, it seems easy for a parent to say simply, "OK, but the police will take care of you!" or more commonly, "Don't you know that it's illegal? You'll get in with the wrong crowd. Wait until you're old enough to do it legally. That will be soon enough for us both."

For a child, however, there is no higher authority than a parent. Until a child feels that the laws of society are basically rational and fair, she has little reason to obey them except out of abject fear. If you want a child to respect the law, the best way is to see that your own rules and enforcements are rational and fair and that you model your own respect for the law.

Fear of the law is not much of a motivator for children, because what's to fear from the law if your own parents are abdicating their responsibility to guide you? If you can get away with things with your parents, why wouldn't skirting the law be even easier? Parental neglect is the worst scenario for a child. The possibility of a bout with the law seems minor compared with being let down by a parent.

Appeals to higher authority do not add to your own authority in the eyes of a child. Your authority must be unquestionable in your own mind to give your child the sense of confidence and security she needs. That society's authority agrees with you can certainly bolster you in your own conclusions, but it will carry little weight with your child. From your child's point of view, either you are sure of yourself or you are not.

If you need outside authority to feel confident in your own position, by all means use it that way in the privacy of your own thoughts. But when you share with your child, don't fall back on the law. Instead be sure in your heart exactly what you feel is right and healthy, and express that. You won't get the results you want if you abdicate your authority to some outside voice.

Just as with the law, appeals to any other outside authority are equally ineffective. Forget appealing to the other parent, the latest talk show advice (even if it's mine!), or the latest book— even this one! Use these to support your own confidence but not to impress your child. She won't be impressed. She wants *you* to be her parent, not a book, an outside expert, or a law.

Even appeals to God will not have much effect. Like trusting the law, children learn from their parents' behavior whether God or other authorities can be trusted. The earthly parent is the model for understanding the heavenly parent.

Rewards and Negotiations

How about bargaining? I know parents who spend all their time designing elaborate bargains. "If you do your homework now, I'll make your favorite icebox cookies. And if you do it well, I'll let you go to Jim's house Saturday, but you have to promise me to not swim in the creek over there and I'll promise you not to sort through your junk drawer again without asking."

Bargaining gets exhausting, and who can remember it all? It sounds like back-room caucuses before an election primary. Who's taking the notes, and who's going to enforce all this stuff? I think you'll agree that the child will remember all the promises you made a lot more clearly than you will, and much more clearly than he remembers the promises he made.

No, bargaining only wraps the parent around the child's little finger. You'll always be a step behind, renegotiating something you thought was long finished. And what's more, no child really wants to have this much control over a parent's thinking or obligations or time, nor does he want to think more than a day in advance, especially when something that feels perfectly complete in itself today could tie up his freedom tomorrow. And why should you the parent tie up your freedom tomorrow in the vain hope of having something happen more easily today, something that should happen simply for its own sake?

These six approaches to communication with your child—aggressive, pleading, threatening, permissive, appealing to outside authority, and bargaining—that most parents have tried at one time or another just don't work very well. Are there any other options? What's going to work better?

Where Failed Strategies Come From

Before I take you on a tour of some exciting strategies that will work—often beyond your wildest dreams—let me make a curious observation. These six unsuccessful approaches can be matched up with the four stages of the mourning process described by grief expert Elisabeth Kübler-Ross. This comparison can perhaps shed some light on why we do these things when they really don't work.

Permissiveness corresponds to Kübler-Ross's first stage, the stage of denial. Aggression and outside appeals are like the next stage, anger. Pleading and bargaining are aspects of the bargaining stage, and threats represent the stage of desperation. These four stages are all natural responses to a particular kind of situation: grieving. Could we be mourning something when we go through these vain efforts to communicate with our child? What might we be mourning?

We might be mourning the letting go of parenting. We mourn that we can't *make* our kids do anything. We're mourning the death of our false expectation that we can control our child. We feel the pain of realizing our child is a person unto himself. But in that realization, our true strength as parents begins, not ends, as I hope you are coming to grasp. We give up false power to claim our real power. And that power is truly awesome.

When a grieving person allows herself to progress through the stages of mourning as Kübler-Ross has described, she arrives at a place of acceptance and serenity. Here life begins anew. The object of the loss becomes the subject of the future. There is healing and new power. So it is with parenting. From your work with secret 4, letting go, I hope you achieved a refreshing sense of empowerment by knowing each day the limits of your control and the unlimited reach of your influence over your child.

Now I want you to take that achievement one step further and exercise your new power through good communication. As you give up illusory control, you assume your true moral authority as a parent, an authority on which your child desires totally to rely. In this chapter you will find out how to communicate better every day with your child in light of your new knowledge.

An End to the Illusion of the Need to Control

You may find to your delight that you not only don't need to control your child but also don't even need to pretend you do. The worthless strategies described earlier don't work because they are based on an illusion, a false premise, an imagined reality, not the real one. Once you have abandoned the false premise that you own or control your child, along with all the trappings of possession and control, you can ground your communications in reality. Suddenly things will go as they should, because your premises correspond with the actual state of affairs between parent and child.

That's why I always come back to what the basic parenting bond is about. And perhaps you will make this a habit yourself.

Applying the Secret of Expression Through the Years

Even in the infancy stage, it's important that parents be candid and genuine in their expression to their child. A healthy baby misses nothing when it comes to the parent's tone and facial expression and level of anxiety or contentment. Already she is tuning in on what gives you pleasure, what makes you adore her, and what rubs you the wrong way. The subtlest of signals, if they are honest, will begin a powerful bond of understanding between you that will continue to inform you both throughout the childhood years and beyond.

Sometimes we are tempted to treat children as sensorily impaired just because they don't give us the same verbal or overt physical feedback we may be used to from adults or older children. We might tend to speak too loud or slowly or exaggerate our actions and emotions. None of this is necessary. It's better to tone down your behavior and get yourself minutely attuned to the subtle but real signals your baby projects to you in response to your behavior.

We don't need to treat babies as intellectually impaired either. We should not speak to them as if they were "dumb" pets, in non-syntactical sentences, sentence fragments, one-word commands, exaggerated emotional outbursts, or excessively high-pitched diminutive tones.

The more normally you express yourself to your child, always gently and with love, the more quickly she will feel comfortable and masterful with your common language and culture and the more useful will be your mutual communications.

In toddlerhood, the terrible twos become such most often only because the parent feels uncertain and awkward with a dependent who nevertheless has a definite mind of her own. Again, there is no need to exaggerate your feelings or desires or proscriptions. Simply state them gently and firmly and clearly and exhibit total confidence that your child will eventually oblige as you wish. Give your toddler room to hone her skills of expression and provide lots of opportunities for modeling good expression for her.

In the exploratory stage, your expressions evolve into genuine discussions, with your child coming up with his own independent ideas. Let it happen and enjoy it. Know when not to jump in with judgments, qualifiers, cautions, and other detractors. Once you have expressed yourself, it's his turn and he knows it.

In the growth stage, offer your opinion on whatever you want but don't expect it to go unchallenged. I see this as a great opportunity to rethink a lot of things you might have taken for granted since your own childhood. You will need to have at least one good reason for every point you make. Distinguish your thoughts and opinions from your feelings. No one needs to explain or justify feelings. Just share them, help your child understand them, and trust her to give them appropriate weight—if not now, eventually.

In the maturation stage, your child will expect honesty and clarity, and he may well call you on anything that sounds disingenuous, inconsistent, hypocritical, or distrustful. Let him have his feelings. Practice noticing when to speak and when to shut up. If your child grows impatient, wind up your point quickly and ask what he thinks. If he has no opinion, that's OK. Simply acknowledge that the issue must not be that important to him or he may simply need more time or information. Express your feeling or opinion and then let go. The respect and trust this demonstrates will come back to you sooner or later. And you have set an example of honest expression that will enable your child to develop other valuable relationships in the future.

Communication: The Energy That Maintains the Parent-Child Bond

Parenting is the process by which a fully grown, experienced, and independent being who is coping with life with ever increasing maturity tries to guide a still growing, less experienced, and still dependent being who has been given into the parent's care with insoluble strings of love. It's actually a love that sets you both free. In parenting we share in the paradox of creation: bonds that set us free.

Communication is not the way you control your child. Instead it is the energy that maintains the natural bond between the two of you that gives you influence without control and invites your child to cooperate without compulsion. At each stage of your child's life, you will have some control because of your superior size, knowledge, and control over the environment of your child, but you will have less each day. And you will need to know exactly how much control you have and be developing all along your other skills for inviting cooperation and mutual trust so that your influence can be helpful and good.

So, how do you do this?

Why Communicate?

In the chapter about secret 3, you learned some new ways to improve your listening skills. At that time I also asked you to consider why your child communicates at all. Now the shoe is on the other foot. Why are you communicating with your child?

I hope that, with some practice in listening, you have grasped the two main reasons to open your mouth: to share with another and to request another to change. That is, you speak to feel more alive yourself by sharing yourself with another and to become more comfortable yourself by bringing about a change in another. Now, in addition to thinking about your child's sharing or requesting, you can be thinking about your own sharing or requesting.

To be completely honest with yourself and at ease with your impending conversation with your child, ask yourself "What do I want out of this conversation?"

To have fun?

To make a point?

To find out about my child's activities?

To find out if my child is OK?

To check on basic needs?

To judge?

To get it over with fast?

To stall or save face?

Think of other motives that you feel in your conversations and acknowledge them. Get rid of guilt and confusion about motives. You're entitled to feel any feeling for a moment. Just be honest with yourself and deal with it appropriately, and it will not poison your conversations with your child.

Next, decide what your principal motive is—to share or to request? Once you know your motive, be as clear as you can up front. Mixed motives cause a great deal of trouble. Here's an example.

The Dangers of Cross-Purposes

Marie was unpacking groceries when her 11-year-old daughter, Jan, slid quietly through the door, just back from her afternoon soccer practice. Marie was glad Jan had come home on time, because she wanted a little help with the groceries. She had a tight schedule to keep because she soon had to drive her son to his reading tutorial session.

Jan looked a little down. Perhaps she was disappointed with herself from soccer practice. Marie said, "What's the matter?"

Jan said, "Oh, nothing. I just got chewed out by Coach, because I hogged the ball—he said."

"That's too bad." Marie said, then continued, "can you help me unpack these things?"

Jan teared up and said, "Not now, Mom!" And she ran upstairs to her room.

It seems a fairly innocent exchange, but ended with a minor disaster. One side effect was that instead of saving time, as Marie had hoped, it would cost more time! As the caring parent she was, she dropped what she was doing and followed Jan upstairs to try to remedy the situation with some good listening.

Had Marie known exactly why she was asking about Jan's moping face and been forthright with her motives, Jan would not have felt suddenly abandoned and overwhelmed. Marie's approach had come across as one of unconcern. Let's reconstruct the conversation with a different approach.

The Language of Clarity and Caring

In our replay, Marie had all the same feelings as before. But when she saw the mope on Jan's face, she allowed herself to feel consciously her own mixed feelings, including disappointment that Jan might not want to be helpful right away and also distress that Jan was troubled about something.

Marie began slowly, knowing that "a stitch in time saves nine," as Ben Franklin said. She began first with acknowledging Jan and then acknowledging her own situation. "Hi, Jan, how was practice?" Marie resisted reading too much into Jan's facial expression right off, preferring to give Jan time to collect her thoughts in order to interact with her mother and share if she wanted to.

"OK, I guess." Jan's face didn't change.

"I'm in a squeeze trying to get stuff put away before I take Jake to his tutor. I thought you might help, but it looks like you need some time to recover from practice. Am I right?"

"Yeah, Coach said I was hogging the ball, but I didn't think so—I mean, I didn't realize it." Jan picked up a head of lettuce and put it in its bin in the refrigerator. "I didn't like him saying it so loud so everyone could hear."

"That must have been embarrassing," Marie said, stopping to look into Jan's face and then carrying a stack of breakfast cereal boxes to the cupboard.

"Yeah, it was. I was just trying to make a goal. I guess sometimes I try too hard!"

"I know. You have to rely on other people, too, to make things come out right, I guess," offered Marie.

Marie had stayed in touch with her own feelings and been honest about them. She wanted a change from Jan. She wanted Jan to get busy helping her. She was honest about her desire but also honest about her observation that it might not happen. She gave Jan the room Jan needed to share about the trouble at soccer practice. And when this was done, Jan was comfortable making the change Marie sought. She did help. And Marie fulfilled her parental desire of helping Jan interpret and work through and even learn something from an unpleasant experience.

Where Verbal Conflicts Come From

The biggest conflicts, as well as the littlest ones, come when motives are at odds. Marie wanted a change from Jan; Jan wanted to share. In the first scenario, Marie appeared to be open to sharing, so Jan felt betrayed when it turned out Marie only wanted her to unpack groceries. At that moment her mother looked selfish, uncaring, and even hypocritical because she had seemed caring at first.

In the second scenario, Marie was in touch with her own double motives—to listen and to get help—and so was able to express these and then be open to Jan's desires. For Jan, her mother's candor gave her choices and avoided betrayal and hypocrisy. She could do her sharing and also give a little help.

Urgency Is Parental Enemy Number One

In all the years I've worked with parents, urgency is the most dangerous factor in a modern family's life. We met it earlier, in our discussion about listening. It gets in the way of our speaking, too: "Not now. Let's talk about it tomorrow. Can't you see I'm busy?"

If you really want to guide your child so that she can think for herself as a mature adult one day, you need to take the time to guide her when she is actually in her thought processes and reaching out to you. Tomorrow may be way too late to guide a particular course of deliberation. Take the time to communicate. Chat and chat some more.

Don't think your conversation has to be about anything important. It helps to think of much of your conversation as chat. It will come out better that way. Even gossip isn't all bad. A fascinating university study on gossip revealed that gossip is not so much about criticizing others as about finding common ground and values with a trusted friend. Don't be afraid to compare notes on the latest news, the weather, the MTV star's outfit, the talk show host's favorite turns of phrase, a neighbor's accent. As long as no malice is intended, you can find common ground and values and a working trust on which to base more conversation.

Parents are often astounded to discover how easily their children begin to share when they take a moment to engage in this kind of chat. And it's fun! It's a great compliment to your child too, because he senses that you are really enjoying talking with him, as you would with a social friend of your own age or stature.

Invest Energy in Chitchat

Cultivate your light chitchat. Notice what interests your child in his leisure time and make an effort to learn to chat about it. I've never known or cared much about cars on my own account. But I ask my 18-year-old son interested and encouraging questions about cars to have him know I am interested in his life and share his values and enthusiasm for participating in his favorite interests.

If you do more chatting, you will be doing more sharing. Kids need a balance between requests and sharing. Too often all they get are the requests. Learn to share yourself often.

Responsive Parenting

Now that you have reviewed your motives for talking to your child, let's explore the conversational approach that works best with children. Unlike the six approaches we looked at earlier, which are based on false premises about you and your child, this responsive approach has unlimited potential because it is grounded in reality. The responsive approach relies on the solid premise that the parent's job is not to control but to protect, guide, and empower the child, one day at a time.

With the responsive, conversational approach you can

- Respond to the needs and desires of your child

- Respond to your own needs and desires

- Respond to the needs and desires of your relationship within the moment

This kind of responsiveness is not about just reacting to what's presented to you, because a big part of it is responding to your own needs. When you are genuinely responding to your own needs, you will tend also to become a more energetic and effective initiator.

Responsive parenting empowers you to know where you stand and to find out in the most efficient, comfortable, and trusting way where your child stands. Then, with the help of all the seven secrets, you will know exactly what to do by way of protection, guidance, or letting go.

Here are some other useful ideas for making your responsive communication get great results.

The "Three Nice Things" Technique

First, the three nice things. This technique requires you to say three nice things about your child or his ideas whenever you get the chance. It is especially helpful when your child has made a request or when you want something from your child. It's mandatory if you must say no.

When you find that you must turn down a child's request, you may be tempted, like so many parents, to convince the child that her proposal is a bad idea and can't be done. It feels like you are just building more disappointment if you admit it's not a bad idea but you have to turn it down for your own reasons. We all hate to disappoint our children. But it would be a mistake to belittle their ideas and not own up to our own motives in a vain attempt to prevent their disappointment.

A child whose ideas are shot down instead of respectfully declined will be more and more fearful of initiating anything. And since you have treated disappointment as a thing to be avoided at all costs, your child is likely to do likewise, operating well below her full potential for participation in life.

Before giving an answer, name three good things about your child's idea. This technique was best described by Peter Bergson, alternative preschool director and creativity consultant to business corporations, in his book *The Other Basics*. If your seven-year-old child wants to go out and dance in the rain just before a trip to Grandma's, you might say, "What a bad idea. Don't you know you'll be a mess for Grandma? And I went to so much trouble to get you looking nice!" Those are three bad things.

Instead you could say three nice things: "You would love to go out in the rain, wouldn't you? I'm so glad you love nature (1), and the cold rain would feel so refreshing (2). And it would be a good idea, because you haven't been outside since yesterday (3)! I wish we could do it. But you see, you would get very wet and feel pretty icky sitting on Grandma's couch the whole afternoon. What do you think?"

Choose any aspect of the idea that suggests your child is creative, rational, loving toward life, passionate, principled, thoughtful, energetic, observant, original, or any other quality you hope she will have throughout her life. No matter how crazy an idea is, three things are bound to apply. Take your time. Kids love to make you think.

Why three? The first says you're listening. The second says you are really considering your child's request. The third tells her you really appreciate her—it's a direct, personal compliment. By then, she feels good enough about herself to be able to be generous and to allow you the freedom to turn her down.

It works, and it feels good for both of you! Even if it seems artificial at first, go ahead and do it. It will become second nature with practice, and it will help you implement the other secrets by bolstering your positive image of your child and your faith in yourselves as an effective, loving parent-child pair.

Give One Good Reason

Another magical technique is the "one good reason." While you are finding your three nice things to say, work on finding one good reason for your final response. Kids aren't impressed with a long list of half-reasons. They can shoot each one down just like a negative-minded CEO. You need to do yourself the favor of taking a little time and coming up with your real reason for saying yes or no.

If you give a false reason, you will pay for it later, even if your child doesn't call you on it right then. Kids are trying to figure out the world. Any cause and effect you tell them will pop up later in similar situations. A false reason given months ago can confuse a child when the situation recurs and can even trip you up if your child confronts you: "But you said last year that you didn't like circuses!"

You will feel much more genuine and keep your and your child's lives simple and comprehensible if you come up with one good reason in each situation. If you really have two good reasons, each of which alone wouldn't be enough but together are decisive, just say so. This amounts to one good composite reason.

For example, if your 15-year-old daughter wants to go to a concert with some boys from school, you may want to rely on the fact that you've seen them dealing drugs on the corner. That's one good reason. If you're sure of it, then that's the one to give.

If you don't know anything for sure, you can still give one good composite reason. Perhaps you've never seen them without dark glasses, even inside, and you've heard them curse in front of her and even at her, and you have a bad feeling about their supposed travel arrangements to the concert. Your child could shoot each single reason down, but together they add up for you. Make that clear.

If you have really thought through your reasons, you don't need to defend them. You are certain of them, and your child will see that they are persuasive for you. If they don't make sense to her, by all means explain them so that she can understand. But don't feel you need to defend or prove anything. She doesn't have to be convinced or to agree with you. A parent's reasons are sufficient if they are well thought out and clearly expressed. Such reasons will be satisfactory for your child.

Remember, no matter what the immediate temptations, your child wants to know that you are immovable when you are certain. She can feel protected and know also that one day she can look forward to that kind of confidence and certainty as a mature person herself.

Thinking through your reasons also gives you the chance to discover if you have in fact jumped too quickly to your conclusion. In that case, you can revise your response without losing parental face. Sure you don't want to be wishy-washy, like a reed in the wind, or vulnerable to your child's nagging or dogged persistence. But an honest rethinking, based on your desire to take your child seriously and to have well-thought-out reasons for what you do, need never embarrass you and won't put you at a disadvantage with your child. It is all right to change your mind if you do it for good reason. Your child will not respect you for avoiding your own embarrassment at her expense. But she will respect you for owning up to a need for change when you deem it necessary. And you will be setting a good example.

"I" Messages

Another powerful technique you can put to work right away is the "I" message. Talk about yourself. When I was growing up, everyone was told, "Never begin a letter with *I*," "Don't talk about yourself," "Don't be self-centered." But that advice was designed to remind a child to take an interest in others. As long as his parents take an interest in him, he will naturally take an interest in others, following their example.

In fact, almost everything we say is about ourselves. Even if we are asking after someone else's health, it is not only because we want to know they are well but because we want to communicate that we care about them. That message is about us: we want them to know how we feel.

Slipping into an all-about-you style is easiest with a child. "How are you?" "How were your classes?" "You should wash your hands before eating." "Your friends are too messy." "You should learn more about what's going on in the world." "You don't show me enough respect." And so on, indefinitely. But it takes only a few of these to get a child down, or for that matter to get anybody down.

Consider some alternatives that focus on the "I" message. Think about whether, if you were a child, these options might not feel a whole lot better and still get the message across. In fact, they might get the message across better, by leaving you empowered to respond positively.

- Instead of "How are you?" you might say, "I hope you had a nice day. Mine was pretty good."

- Instead of "How were your classes?" you might say, "I know you were worried about your science class. I would love to hear how it went."

- Instead of "You should wash your hands before eating," you might say, "I feel a whole lot better when your hands are washed, because then I know you aren't getting any extra germs in your food."

- Instead of "Your friends are too messy," you might say, "You know, I've noticed how your friends just drop things when they're here instead of finding the wastebasket. I don't understand them. Can we move the basket or something?"

- Instead of "You should learn more about what's going on in the world," you might say, "I get a lot of pleasure out of keeping up with the news, and I wish I could chat about it with you. I just heard today that the new batch of cars is going to be even more polluting than last year's. That bothers me. What do you think?"

- Instead of "You don't show me enough respect," you might say, "I like talking to you better when you speak with more respect. I'd like you to try harder. Would you, please?"

As you read these "I" messages, you may have noticed how much better they would feel to a child compared with the "you" messages used before. So keep these guidelines in mind:

- Talk about your own feelings and reactions to the situation.

- Describe the child's behavior as specifically as possible, without provocative words or judgments.

- Keep the focus on the specifics of the present situation. It won't help if you get your child defending his entire past or trying to rescue his entire future from distrust.

- Avoid generalizations that include "always," "never," "again," or things like, "You keep doing that."

- Give your child choices whenever you can, like, "Do you want to wash your hands now or in a few minutes?"

- Rather than focusing on the downside of your child's way,

draw that child into the benefits of doing things your way. Remember the way the parent drew the child into a chat about cars to demonstrate the fun and benefits of being up on the news?

- Formulate your communications with the chat factor in mind. If you share yourself first, your child will feel safer sharing himself.

- Don't be afraid to ask what your child thinks, even if you know that you can't leave the final choice to him. Give that information up front but show you are still interested in his take on things.

When you incorporate the "I" message into your communications, you are already a long way toward two other important techniques. One is respecting boundaries—your own and your child's—and the other is avoiding passing judgment. These work together. Let's take a closer look.

How to Notice and Respect Boundaries

Your boundaries as a person are defined by what you are comfortable with. On the one hand, if someone crosses your boundaries uninvited, you may feel uncomfortable, invaded, violated, hurt, and diminished. Toward the invader you are likely to feel angry, betrayed, unsafe, disappointed, alienated, and distant— sometimes even guilty, for you let yourself down by letting the invader in.

On the other hand, if someone respects your boundaries you will feel comfortable. You may feel happy, safe, powerful, respected, valued, loved, important, and appreciated. Toward the other you may feel close, loving, admiring, cheerful, giving, and grateful.

How do you know where your boundaries are as a parent? Isn't your child too close to worry about boundaries? These questions bring us back to some of the discussion on modeling (secret 5). You are a person first, then a parent. The interplay is delicate and evolves constantly, but knowing yourself as a person is essential to knowing your boundaries as a parent.

For example, if you know you can't function well as a loving parent for at least a half hour after you return home from work, you have a boundary here. It might not be the same as anyone else's, but it is your boundary. If it is impractical or unreasonable, you should undoubtedly work on it, but today it is a boundary others have a right to know about. It needs to be posted, so to speak, instead of letting people cross your boundary, get snapped at, and not know what was the cause. Children especially will blame themselves.

As Socrates said, know thyself. Know your boundaries. If you don't know them, read up on what normal boundaries are.

Many of us grew up in homes with no models for healthy boundaries. I've known some parents who have spent most of their childhood discovering their parents' boundaries. The ones they found—for example, you can only talk to Dad between 11 and 3 on Saturday if you want to avoid being criticized—were so wide and unreasonable that the children often decided they would have no boundaries. When these people became parents, they were headed for early burnout and the added frustration of kids who don't respect their parents' boundaries and don't know their own.

Find Your Own Comfort Zones. Gwen came to me very frustrated. "I love my kids, would do anything for them, and do! But when they bicker it drives me crazy! I try to remain calm and let them work it out for themselves, which I know they will eventually do, because they do seem to like each other. But when they start calling each other names, I can't stand it; I totally lose it! I run in yelling, push them apart, and sometimes even push them to the floor and impose some ridiculous penalty. Why do I do this? How do I stop?"

Gwen had to learn about boundaries—her kids' and hers. She needed to show more respect for her own right to feel comfortable in her own house. She knew it was best to let her boys work out their own conflicts, but she was putting her ambition for their life instruction above protecting her own boundaries. That's what made her lose control.

Why can a breach of your own boundaries make you lose control? Because once your boundaries are violated, you will act emotionally, in self-defense, rather than rationally to suit the situation with your child. Gwen had a boundary that excluded name-calling. Her father's verbal abuse of her mother had tormented her as a child, and her tolerance for name-calling was low. But she hadn't realized this. She thought it was fighting kids, not name-calling, that ticked her off.

Once Gwen was aware of this boundary, she could take steps to prevent its violation and could stay in control of the situation as a rational parent. She would calmly monitor her children's interactions, but when she began to hear the bad names, she would go right away to them and speak her mind.

Gwen resisted saying, "Stop calling each other names! You know better. You know that's wrong and mean. You're going to get in trouble if you keep this up." That would be a "you" message and unnecessarily judgmental. It would put the children on the defensive and just switch the fight from boy versus boy to boys versus mother. She also resisted pulling them apart or pushing into their faces and yelling at them to quit it. That would have violated their physical and psychological boundaries.

Instead Gwen went with an "I" message—clear, honest, and short. "When you call each other names it drives me crazy, because it belittles you both. I know you are caring, courteous young men, and I'd love to hear you solve your problems in a more friendly way. Can I count on you to try harder on this?"

The boys looked at each other and at her and said, "OK, Mom." Then they simply began playing as if the fight had never happened.

When you know your own boundaries and protect them rationally *before* you are feeling defensive, you will be automatically speaking your mind, as well as modeling self-control and responsible personal interactions. Social skills are learned best, like everything else, by example. As a caring, careful parent, one of the most important things you can do for yourself is to have faith that if you are uncomfortable with a particular behavior of your child, the next person would be too.

Attention to your boundaries is actually the best yardstick for what to allow and what to discourage. Rather than trying to invent a lot of rules for your child to learn one at a time like the alphabet, let him see social skills in action. Let yourself be his first encounter with what works socially and what does not.

The Time to Abdicate. Abdication can save you all kinds of effort to figure out what's right behavior and what's not, how to express it exactly for all situations, and how to judge and enforce it in every circumstance. No parent is supposed to be Hammurabi, the ancient Babylonian king who developed the first comprehensive code of law for his kingdom. We parents don't have to be legislative, executive, and judicial branches, all bound up in one.

The legal, governmental model doesn't work half as well in the home as the imitative, responsive model. In government by strangers, one needs laws to be fair and just at arm's length. In the home, where love is, interactions are best governed by each family member's being aware of her own boundaries and comfort zones while being sensitive to the comfort and boundaries of the others.

How to Resist Crossing Boundaries. Not crossing boundaries can be difficult when others are begging you to invade theirs. Here is where your boundaries and another's cross. Just because you are invited in doesn't mean you should go. Sometimes you must treat other people with more respect than they give themselves, or you may need to show more faith in them than they have in themselves. If you don't, you may resent them when you help them too much and put yourself out while they are ungrateful.

How do you say no? Suppose a child gets a third detention in school, and the parent has talked to the teacher both times before to explain the child's situation and lighten the penalty. Now she's starting to feel railroaded. Her child seems to be counting on her rescue operations. Can she decline to help this time, when the circumstances seem the same as before? Will this make her appear inconsistent or spiteful or lazy or uncaring?

The subtle shift from helping a child out a few times to letting him become dependent in an area where he should be becoming more independent is especially important for teenagers. Yet it happens throughout childhood. Pay attention to your boundaries and his.

You might look at it this way. The first time, his boundary of responsibility and self-respect may not have encompassed the particular rules and limits of behavior at school. The second time, his boundary gets wider; he knows the ropes. But your boundary is thin, so you are willing to help again.

By the third time, the child knows his responsibility, and he may well lose self-respect if you rescue him one more time. And you notice that you are beginning to resent his taking advantage of your willingness to go to bat for him. Yet he asks because asking seems easy and it worked before. But now your boundaries have broadened with time and experience. You want to feel safe knowing your child has taken responsibility for his own behavior at school. So how do you speak your mind?

One parent in this situation said: "Jake, I'm concerned about your having this trouble in school. I don't feel comfortable helping you out a third time. If I manage your life so you don't have to deal with the consequences of your behavior, I won't be doing you any favors. I was happy to help the first time, but now I feel like you are taking advantage of my efforts. I'm going to have to let you deal with this yourself this time. I've raised you right, and now you need to handle this for yourself."

It's best if possible to let your child know ahead of time when you have bailed him out for the last time in a particular situation. Perhaps it will make him think twice about repeating the behavior if he knows his safety net is gone, and you will feel less guilty when you draw the line next time the incident repeats itself. But even if you didn't know you would reach the end of your tolerance or didn't expect it to come up again, it's all right to refuse assistance and let your child take full responsibility for his actions.

Remember to find your own boundaries and let them evolve as you and your child grow. Meanwhile you will become more aware of and sensitive to your child's boundaries. You may even see your home transform from one of rules and judgments and walking on eggs to one of respect and good sense and real comfort and relaxation.

Parent-to-Child Exercise. In workshops for parents, I have a favorite exercise that gets parents thinking about how they communicate. Imagine your child has just broken a favorite picture frame. I ask the parents to pair up and face each other. Then I ask one to kneel and the other to read the first list below to the kneeling parent.

The kneeling posture replicates the physical relationship most children under the age of 14 have to their parents. The child listener is at a direct physical disadvantage, so that anything you say that is the least bit intimidating becomes more so.

I ask the parents to reverse positions so that each gets to play parent and child. Then they read the second list the same way. It's always the favorite exercise.

To do this at home, stand in front of a mirror and imagine you are looking at yourself as a child. Now read the first list below. Write down five adjectives that describe how these messages make you feel, as parent and as child.

The blaming tirade:

"I can't believe you broke that picture frame."

"What's gotten into you?"

"Haven't I told you to be careful?"

"I can't believe it!"

"What's wrong with you?"

"Don't you care?"

"Why don't you be more careful?"

"You're like a bull in a china shop!"

Now do the same with the second list. Again choose five adjectives that describe how these make you feel.

Respectful displeasure:

"I see you knocked over the picture frame."

"You must have been moving pretty fast."

"Were you unusually carried away?"

"I know you know this kind of roughhousing and horsing around can break things."

"Sometimes breakable things seem to be in the wrong places."

"I'm really sorry to see that picture frame broken. It was a favorite of mine, as you know."

"What do you think we can do to fix it?"

"What can we do to prevent this from happening again?"

"I would really like you to be more careful in this room."

"How do you feel about it?"

Compare your two sets of impressions. After you have looked at the feelings you would have as a child listening to these two approaches, consider which effects you want to have on your child. Are there any changes you need to make in your usual tone or style that will move you more in the direction of where you want to be. What changes do you want to make, starting today? Be modest in your plan so you can stick with it.

In my workshops, these are the favorite adjectives parents report as children hearing the first set of messages: angry, uncooperative, unloved, alienated, frustrated. Each sentence hurts and diminishes the child in a slightly different way.

The most common adjectives describing the child's response in the second instance are these: empowered, sorry, loved, trusted, more cooperative. Each sentence builds the child's sense of self-worth and his power to grow and change.

Interestingly, even if I forget to ask, the parents in my workshops always want to share how they felt being the parent in each case. They often mention that they frequently feel at home the way they felt after delivering the first tirade. Many say they didn't even know they could feel as good as they did after the second approach. Often they are as struck by how much better *they* can feel as a parent as they are by how much better the child feels with the second kind of message.

Parents using the first kind of message report feeling frustrated, mean, desperate, hopeless, angry. In contrast, parents using the second kind of message most often report feeling powerful, honest, effective, loving, nurturing.

This exercise has a special story attached to it for me. I used it once in a workshop I was giving in Moscow in 1990. Two Russian men who were government lawyers took my instructions through a translator. They were kneeling down saying nasty and nice parental things to each other. As I watched I wondered if trying this under these circumstances was such a good idea! But both men rose to their feet and thanked me with big smiles for the special insights they had received. They said they would take greater care now when speaking to their children.

Have Confidence in Your Native Authority. Parental authority is a funny thing. First of all, it is automatic. It's in the human genes. The one thing that we know comes to us by instinct is our mammalian tendency to attach ourselves to our biological parents and to look to them for protection, guidance, and empowerment—for at least a fifth of our lives.

Second, parental authority must also be earned. Once the cognitive, rational powers of the human mind become developed, probably around age two, we parents must justify our children's continued trust in our protection, guidance, and empowerment.

We must validate that trust in our authority by our everyday actions. If each day you apply the seven secrets you are learning in this book, you will have no trouble earning and keeping your child's continued trust and respect.

Third, the one thing that doesn't work for parental authority and that parents are constantly tempted to do is to insist on that authority. If you have to insist on your authority, then you've already lost it! Thankfully, it is retrievable. There is room for mistakes because of point number one, about instinctual tendencies.

If you think you have to insist on your authority, you have automatically put your authority in question, which puts your child in fear that you have lost it, even if you really haven't. You both lose the battle, you because you feel bereft of your authority and she because, as long as she is a child, she wants a parent who has a nice mix of that comforting natural authority the infant relies on and that earned authority that the maturing child wants to know is there.

If your conversation starts to sound like, "But I'm the parent," take a breather and remind yourself that if your authority has to be insisted upon, then it's put into doubt. You are the parent, and the child knows it. In such times, call a time-out. Get back to the basics. You love your child and want the best for him, and you're facing what is really a temporary problem of manageable size (no matter how big it may seem). Send urgency and fear packing. With this shift in your attitude, the battle of wills will end right there, falling dead of its own weight like a punctured balloon.

You don't have to know everything or do everything right or say everything clearly and correctly the first time to earn respect and preserve your parental authority. Be quick to clarify, rethink, explain. Don't give up your mature prerogatives to make a mistake, to own up, to be assertive, to stick to your convictions, to take time to think, to do what you believe is right, to grow, to change your mind, to share yourself, to ask for the changes you want in your child, and to say what you feel and think and believe.

Short and Sweet

One more important technique is the "three or four sentences" technique. Try to keep any request, explanation, sharing, information, or command to three or four simple sentences. If you can't do that, then chances are good that you are not really sure yourself of what you want to say. Albert Einstein said that if a physicist couldn't explain a physics concept to a nonphysicist, then she didn't really understand it herself yet.

It's the same with parents. If you can't state it simply, then you probably don't understand it yourself and aren't ready to communicate it to your child. So take the time to get your thoughts down to three or four clear sentences that say what you mean in a kind, loving way. Here is a good way to organize the ideas you want to express:

- Identify the subject and where you and your child fit in the picture.

- Give any essential background about the subject clearly and simply.

- Then make your statement of request or sharing.

For example: "Cindy, I need to talk to you about something. Remember when you said your friend Rachel was getting into smoking pot with her boyfriend and you didn't know what to do? I came across a nice little book about peer pressure and helping your friends and stuff like that, and I thought it could be useful to you. Would you like to read it, or shall I, and then I'll talk to you about it?"

The mother could have said something like this. See if you think Cindy would have had a better or worse reaction. "Hey, Cindy. I want you to read this book. Harriet gave it to me because she said it helped her with her nephew, who was driving her sister crazy running around with the wrong crowd and getting arrested for hanging out in the park. She said she thought all the teenagers should read it. Your friends are starting to get into trouble—you said what's-her-name was going bad—so I think you really should read this. But don't bend it up because I want your brother to read it after you do. By the way, Mandy isn't trying anything bad, is she? You and she hang out together so much, and you don't tell me much about what you guys do. Anyhow, maybe you don't think you feel any peer pressure, but I think you do. Everybody does, I think. At least I did. I remember . . ."

She has failed at the three-or-four-simple-sentences technique. Her daughter has gone through so many feelings by the time Mom has finished that she feels numb and neglected. She can't register half of what was said.

Once you have finished your three or four sentences, let your child respond. Then listen carefully, and you will know what your next three sentences should be about.

You may hear complaints about the sound-bite mentality. But it's a psychological fact that we can't process more than about 100 words at a time as an integrated thought, especially if it's someone else's thought and we aren't even sure if we're interested in it. One hundred words is about 30 seconds' worth. Just about any important thought can be expressed in 30 seconds. A more expanded explanation is often indicated, but it will be wasted if the listener has not grasped the main thought in the first 100 words. So if you know you must say more, let the first 30 seconds sink in and then wait to see if there is more interest.

Even on public television or radio, with in-depth coverage of major issues, the reporters seldom speak for more than 30 seconds without switching to another voice or sound, be it a reporter on the scene, an interview subject, or a pertinent visual or sound effect.

Of course reducing everything to a simplistic catchword is going too far; most important ideas have at least two parts. But this does not mean that your child owes you unending attention. It may well be that at least half the children labeled as having attention deficits are just bored by adults who don't know the secrets you are learning now. Don't teachers often tend to go on and on without taking the risk of determining if their students are really interested in the subject?

What's in a Word? The psychological effects of the three-or-four-sentences technique may have far-reaching implications. They may indeed explain why we use paragraphs in writing. Think about what you say to your child in your ordinary conversation. Consider your words, sentences, and paragraphs. A word is a sound that evokes a mental idea. Its natural limit is how much you can say with one continuous movement of your mouth.

A simple sentence is a sequence of words that links ideas meaningfully into a thought. Its natural limit is a comfortable breath.

A paragraph is a sequence of sentences that develops a series of thoughts into a relevant sharing or request. Its natural limit is the attention span of the speaker and the listener. Can you remember a book or a passage you've read that tended toward long sentences or paragraphs? Do you remember sighing to yourself that you wished the writer would let you breathe or take a break, even when you knew you were interested in the material? I know I have. In fact, I've written more than a few of those passages myself—and imposed a few on my children!

In a course on clear writing I taught some years ago, I came across this tidbit. A formula had been developed to examine the average length of words and sentences in a passage and to compare it with the grade level of a person who could read and comprehend the passage comfortably. Some college textbooks proved to require 33 years of education!

If your child's eyes glaze over after the fourth sentence, don't blame her for inattention or yourself for not being clear or for not saying enough or being interesting enough. Just stop and shorten your paragraph!

Here's a short outline for almost any conversation with your child. Use it to help you recall and apply the techniques revealed here for expressing yourself—by way of either request or sharing—to your child. You can review it if an interchange didn't go well and you want to find out what happened. Or better yet, glance at it before any conversation you expect will be a bit challenging. It can help you frame your thoughts and leave room for your child's contributions.

Guidelines for Parent-Child Conversation

1. *Set the stage:*

  • Note where your child is. Acknowledge whatever task, activity, or state of mind you find your child in.

  • Note where you are. Acknowledge what task, activity, or state of mind you are in at the moment.

  • Say three positive things. Try to note three nice things about your child's current wish, thought, feeling, or activity, as the case may be.

2. *Take one of these actions:*

  • Make your request. State clearly and simply what you want from your child and why.

  • Share your thoughts or feelings. State clearly and simply what you want to share and why.

  • Respond thoughtfully. In the case of a request or sharing by your child, state clearly and simply what your response is and why.

3. *Solve any problem together:*

  • Offer help. Note that you are willing to participate in getting your wishes fulfilled, helping your child understand what you have shared, or getting his wishes fulfilled or his sharings understood.

  • Solicit options. If your wishes or responses or those of your child are not yet well formed, brainstorm creatively without judging either the expression or the merits of each suggestion.

- Wait. Avoid rushing the thinking process, since it can only shame the child and demean the importance of thought.

- Offer supplemental options. Make your own suggestions only after you have heard out the ones your child wants to make.

4. *Close:*

- Restate. State clearly the gist of a sharing or any commitment you or your child has made in response to a request.

- Commit. Wait for an acknowledgment of any commitment, including the how, when, and where and each person's role in implementing any action to be taken.

- Follow up. Plan a time and place to resume the topic and carry through with it, whether with reminders, adjustments, and reconsiderations or praise, appreciation, and thank-yous.

Know When to Stop

The three-or-four-sentences technique brings us to the second half of this sixth secret ("I speak my mind, and I know when to stop"). When you have completed your opening paragraph of three or four sentences, then what?

If you are like most parents, you may feel a good deal of apprehension about deciding when to stop talking. You may even keep going to forestall the bad news. You can never be sure of the response you will get from your child.

Your pause at the end of your thought is an invitation to your child to speak. You can soon appreciate its power.

Don't think of this space, though, as a blank blackboard that your poor child must cover while the impatient teacher stands behind him holding a yardstick and watching to see if he gets it right. That picture is enough to frighten any child into total silence in the hope that you will fill the space. And it's also a picture that most parents hate to impose on their child, so they often avoid creating the space at all.

Instead think of that space as a warm, sun-drenched meadow of wildflowers where you have invited your child to express himself freely in handsprings, spinning, running, or yelling. It's his big chance to share himself with you and the universe. That's more inviting, isn't it?

Silence Is Golden: Not Your Child's, but Yours!

Silence is golden. It gives everyone a chance to get a grip on emotions, needs, and wants and to think of the other guy. It gives you time to relax your brow and your shoulders and remember who you are and who you're dealing with. It gives you a moment to ground yourself in nature and in life's natural rhythms, so you can let go of urgency and impatience. It lets you synchronize with your child's vibrations, and vice versa. It lets your child listen, hear, absorb, cogitate, and decide how best to respond to what you've said. It allows you to make a little reality check, so you can keep your perspective clear, stay in touch with your priorities, and recognize all your options and opportunities. It lets you listen to the silence and, to paraphrase Deepak Chopra, to explore the spaces between the particles of matter, where our real power lies.

Beware. Long gone is the idea that children should be seen and not heard! The most important silences are yours, not your child's. Once you've spoken your mind, the hardest thing in the world can be to stop and to wait, and wait, and wait.

Any parent will be tempted to add one more great reason for her request, or one more great fact about her shared idea, or one more clarifying restatement, or one more thought of encouragement to the child. But once you have said your piece, it is the child's turn. Even if you have told him what to do and there is to be no negotiation, you still should wait for your child's acknowledgment and acquiescence. Only that way can you affirm your child's sense of self as he brings himself to accept the edict you have imposed.

Often a parent is so afraid of resistance that he will look away after issuing a demand, or will dismiss the child abruptly, or will move away abruptly. This gives the child an uncomfortable feeling about his own lack of power or importance or even his very identity and place in the relationship. If you want cooperation, you must treat your child with the respect he deserves as a small but whole person.

Dismiss Fears of Resistance

Fears of resistance can be a self-fulfilling prophecy. Your self-doubt about the effects of your talk will come through in your tone and body language. You can help dismiss any fears of your child's resistance by asking yourself these questions:

• "Am I afraid that if he resists I will back down?" Then affirm that you are sure of your demand and can be loving and firm at the same time. He wants a decisive, secure parent.

• "Am I afraid that if he resists I will be discovered for not really having thought this matter through or for not having given him a choice when I could have?" Then admit you didn't need to insist and you want to reconsider the matter, or simply accept that your child already knows you're imperfect and still loves you. You will lose nothing by having your humanity "discovered," as long as you admit to being human.

• "Am I afraid that if he resists we will get into an argument?" If you can see it coming, you can avoid it now that you have almost all of the seven secrets in your pocket. Affirm that you will have both the patience and the confidence to hear your child out about his reservations, and also the natural authority to gain voluntary cooperation in the end.

• "Am I afraid that if he resists it will take too much time to gain his cooperation nicely?" Then remind yourself that a stitch in time saves nine. Two minutes now may spare you the extra time it takes the rest of the day or the week to deal with a recalcitrant, moody, or depressed child. If you are chronically in a hurry when you are making demands, accept that your child is a higher priority than you have been showing and set aside a bit more time for each interaction. Just five more minutes will allow you to ride out the beautiful silence between you.

• Finally, "Am I afraid that if he resists I can't stand the rejection?" This is at the bottom of parental impatience more often than parents usually realize. We love our kids too much to take rejection by them lightly. It will be painful, and we may take it personally as a sign we have failed and can't succeed. We want acceptance by our children. Remind yourself that your child can reject everything you say without meaning to reject you. You needn't take any rejection personally.

Clean Out the Closet of Your Mind

If a fear of rejection by your child persists, so that you fear the silences and act impatient or verbose, try doing a meditation on your past history. Some past impression is likely to be making you take the rejection personally. Try to remember back to some event or person in your past that made you feel rejected when you were also in a helpless or abandoned state.

Consider how that situation is different from the present one, in which you are in charge and your child totally adores you. Remind yourself that your child's resistance to a demand is his way of asserting his own personhood and making choices before he acts. You've taught him to do that, which is to your credit! Like any mature adult, he must decide, even when commanded, whether to act or not, in order to preserve his sense of human freedom.

Once you have looked over your own stumbling blocks and rolled any troublesome ones aside, you can now wait out any silence at the end of your sentence and prepare yourself to enjoy whatever it is your child wants to say.

If your child is not used to these gifts of silence, she may not know what to do with them at first. Perhaps she hasn't been able to get a word in edgewise for quite a while, modern family life being as fast as it is. But if you know how impressive your parental power really is, you can exert your influence over the silence and even play with it.

The Grand Conductor

Just as an orchestra conductor has complete control over the silences between the notes in a symphonic piece—even though no one shows any signs of doing anything at that moment—so can you orchestrate the silences in your conversations with your child. Feel the energy in the silence and breathe even more energy into it, wafting it in the direction you wish. Smile, release your breath, rest your eyes lovingly on your child. Relax your arms, hands, and face into an open, welcoming state. In your mind's eye, form a vision of love and light enveloping you both.

After about three tries, your child won't be able to resist opening up. The success can be beyond your wildest dreams. For some, it's enough to make you believe in miracles!

Families! I hate you! Shut-in homes, closed doors, jealous possessors of happiness.

ANDRÉ GIDE

My 10-year-old daughter is my number-one power source.

HANAN MIKHAIL ASHRAWI

Cleaning your house while your kids are still growing is like shoveling the walk before it stops snowing.

PHYLLIS DILLER

There would have to be something wrong with someone who could throw out a child's first Valentine card saying, "I love you, Mommy."

GINGER HUTTON

"*I really get a kick out of my child.*"

❖ Celebration ❖

Now that you know six of the seven secrets of successful parents, you are surely on your way to expressing yourself better, listening better, letting go better, modeling better, paying better attention to basic needs, and having more faith in your child. You have probably already seen some gratifying results, even if you haven't tried very hard. Now you are ready to reap the unlimited rewards of successful parenting. This chapter will give you some new ways to really enjoy being a parent.

The seventh and last secret of successful parents is celebration: "I really get a kick out of my child." It's about having fun being a parent and letting your child know it. It's about joy, satisfaction, mirth, humor, pleasure, frolic, hanging out, and happiness.

When you really get a kick out of your child, you are celebrating your child's life, her contribution to your own life, and the glory of the bond between you and your child. You may feel filled up with love and pleasure, knowing all the while that you are also doing one of the most important and powerful things you can do for your child. You are showing her the depth and breadth and power of your love for her. And you are modeling that life is meant to be joyful.

This in turn empowers her to be the best she can be.

By showing your full enjoyment of your child, you prove beyond the shadow of a doubt that she is valuable and lovable just as she is, just for being her true self. Far from making her feel complacent, this plenitude of love empowers her to move forward to manifest and fulfill her whole being.

Here are a few key thoughts to hold on to as you explore with me the outer limits of parental pleasure.

- Children, like life, are meant to bring pleasure. Otherwise, why parent?

- Humor is an ally. Use it often and capitalize pleasurably on every instance in which your child uses humor.

- It takes effort to make time and room in your life for gratitude, connectedness, joy, fun, and laughs. It's not automatic, given today's lifestyles.

- Negative, exploitative, or put-down humor is risky at best and is better avoided. You don't ever need it to get a laugh.

The Virtue of Being Yourself

Chris Largent and Denise Breton are two philosophy professors who have worked to develop a model for a new, healthier paradigm for American society. They assert that the most disastrous thing that can happen to a child is to get the message that to be loved she must behave other than herself. This, they say, leads to alienation and suppression of the inner self, so that the child becomes more and more outwardly focused. She then can lose touch with her own inner voice and, as a result, limit her potential for developing her true identity and her own unique contribution to creation, thereby denying herself her greatest pleasure in life and her best chance to have a truly fulfilling, free, satisfying life.

After searching many disciplines to discover a line of thinking that would lead away from that destructive parental and societal message that says you must be someone other than who you really are, Largent and Breton found two helpful precedents. They rely, first, on the spiritual worldviews of traditional agrarian communities around the world and, second, on the thinking that has emerged as a result of the 12-step recovery movement.

You may remember the wisdom Jean Liedloff and others have described ensconced in the cultures of nature-based societies. These societies treat their children with honor and make them feel worthy and welcome as useful members of the community from the very start. At the same time, they allow them lots of leisure to play and experiment with each other and life.

From the recovery movement, authors like John Bradshaw, Melodie Beattie, and Anne Wilson Shaef have offered concrete ways to escape the hellish message of personal unlovability and unimportance. Their original impetus was to help themselves and others avoid the spiritual trap of addictive and codependent habits and behavior. But their strategies will work for anyone who is interested in getting more in touch with his true self and more free to achieve a fuller, more authentic life.

In my own book *Adult Children Raising Children*, I applied these ideas preventively for parenting. I showed how, even if you were raised with destructive messages of your unworthiness, you can raise your own children free of this burden, full of the joy of being loved and guided by your own example of loving freely in joy.

The recovery authors can show you how to reclaim your childhood and how to understand where your parents were coming from if they gave you any hints that you were not valuable just for being you. You can learn how to forgive your parents for their shortcomings and how to let go of your past. You can then make choices in freedom and joy each day, based on your best efforts to be ever more truly you and never less or other than your best self.

Lightening the Burden

Besides the insights from traditional and natural peoples and from the recovery movement, you can make good use of insights from the current movement toward a new spirituality. This movement proclaims new hope for humanity in an atmosphere of cooperation and understanding rather than competition and control. It attempts to reclaim the integrated worldview of traditional peoples and the wisdom of the early stages of today's great religions. This new spirituality has even touched scientific medicine with its call to attend to mind, body, and spirit as one in the healing process.

This new spiritual awareness calls upon you once again to lighten your burden from the past so that you can act more freely, honestly, and creatively in the present. It asks you to weed out last year's garden and plant anew, with fresh thoughts and more joyful efforts. Marianne Williamson, Deepak Chopra, Peter McWilliams, Thomas More, and Louise Hay have been leaders in this area.

In addition, you might consider the work of Norman Cousins, Patch Adams, and others who champion the central importance of fun and laughter for good health and a happy life. Their points apply especially well to parents. The challenges of modern parenting can contribute to any number of anxiety and stress-related disorders. An active, conscious cultivation of the fun side of life, the positive energies around you, the humor of it all, is essential to successful parents.

Now as you read these pages, I hope you will consider carefully how all these threads of insight and wisdom can be directly applied to help you really enjoy your child. By the end of the chapter, you can be well on your way to demonstrating openly the delight you feel in your child. Also you can begin to feel more delight deep within, ever more deeply and consistently.

I am saddened when I see the tremendous effort so many parents put into their child rearing only to forget this last of the seven secrets. They often feel unsuccessful, even when their children are doing just fine, because they feel so poorly rewarded for their efforts. Exhaustion and fatigue can be overwhelming to parents if they don't make opportunities to really enjoy the parenting process.

You can do everything "right," but if you are not cultivating and manifesting your joy in the very being and presence of your child, you are handicapping your parenting and passing up your greatest rewards. Making secret 7 your own can save you from this trap.

When you use the celebration secret with skill, you will be fully receptive to the positive feedback that is built into the parent-child relationship. Your energy level and motivation not only will stay high but will continue to grow.

What Is Love?

In my first book *You Can Postpone Anything but Love*, I defined love as a process of enjoying your loved one. That was a bold move when I look back on it. It seemed to me that you really need to know exactly what you mean by love before you can make it manifest in your everyday life. I had developed the definition by examining my own life and the lives of all the parents I had known. Having defined love in the context of parenting, I found the definition applied just as well to other relationships.

Now, after 12 more years of counseling parents and 12 more years of experience being a parent myself, I am even more convinced that this definition can really help you be the most successful parent you can possibly be. Here's my definition.

Love is about enjoyment. Love is looking for the good in another, finding it, enjoying it, and celebrating it with the other whenever possible.

I spell love this way:

Letting go

Observation

Validation

Enthusiasm

It's not enough simply to believe in the ultimate goodness of your child nor simply to encourage and praise good deeds. As a parent you must always be practical. You can't get inside your child's head. So what words and deeds of your own will best bring out your child's inner goodness?

You need to observe compassionately every day and look for all the specific little signs of the good in your child. You need to find them. Never give up. Look until you find them. They are always there. If you have the goodness in your own heart to care enough to be reading this book, then you can believe that your child has enough goodness in his nature to reveal and radiate that goodness as a beloved human being every single day. So seek and you'll find.

Every time you find some lovable little thing, take note of it, validate it in words and smiles, and celebrate it with your child. Show real enthusiasm for your child, even when his behavior is bothering you no end. Even when you are wondering why you had a kid in the first place. Even when you are longing for the days before baby or the days to come after the teen years. Look inside your heart and find your joy; find your sense of humor. Celebrate your child. Enjoy being a parent—right here, right now.

Cultivate Your Parental Sense of Humor

Let's look for a moment at what it means to have a sense of humor about parenting. Consider with me whether the essence of humor is not the ability to move freely between the general and the particular, the important and the trivial, the eternal and the instantaneous, the self and the other.

Isn't that exactly what parenting is all about? One minute you're looking at the world's hope for the future lodged in the heart of your child, and the next minute you are trying to find a misplaced sock. One minute your eyes can well up with tears of awe when your son sweetly helps your daughter onto a swing, and the next minute you're hunting for a postage stamp to pay your electric bill.

Isn't this kind of flip from high to low, cosmic to mundane, what makes a thing truly funny? And isn't it the essence of a parent's day? If you don't let the humor emerge, you can literally go crazy; the flip-flops become progressively more confusing and less meaningful. Without the ability to laugh, every little thing becomes a big deal; and the big things, the big, beautiful, affirming things, get missed entirely.

Real humor may reside exactly in that sudden flip in the mind from one extreme to another. Humor is a roller-coaster ride of the mind or, even better, the soul. During the instant of the flip, you can feel out of control and maybe even a little scared, but you also feel liberated and light.

A good joke has the same kind of catch that a roller-coaster has. It sends you first in one direction and then, as it whips you around a sharp turn, catches you in midflight on your trajectory outward and yanks you in another direction. It's a thrill. Ask any child. Take a roller-coaster ride yourself.

Roller-Coaster of the Soul

I'm not one for being out of control, or for trusting tall, skinny, erector-set-looking structures, or for wanting to have my stomach in my throat. I avoided roller-coasters for years. But to be able to share my son's exhilaration with the rides, I decided to give them a try. Roller-coasters still aren't my favorite thing, but I know now what the attraction is. It's that wonderful freedom that fills you with awe, even fear, but also hilarity and relief.

Humor does this. It is our mental, soulful joyride. Your thoughts are led one way by the setup and flipped another way by the punchline. We are thinking one way, and suddenly there's a new way of thinking superimposed on the first.

In the best jokes, the superimposition illuminates both thoughts. You feel enriched and enlivened by the experience and the result. The feeling of being caught, being tricked into thinking one way when the jokester is going to flip you in another way, can feel downright uncomfortable with a bad joke. It's only fun and funny and worth the trick if the two superimposed thoughts tell you something a little profound and exciting and positive about both.

You probably know people who seem just too serious to really laugh, even at a good joke. They may take life or themselves too seriously. Maybe they feel they can't afford the momentary surrender of control or the dangerous risk of letting go and finding a new direction to think in. They may be afraid of feeling wrong. They may fear looking stupid.

Rigidity: The Enemy of Humor

You may have noticed how rigidity in parenting can cause a lot of extra pain. Kids know we are not always right. They know we can easily look stupid at times. They know we are human, not always in control. They even appreciate our humanity, our imperfection, because it gives them permission to be human—lovable and imperfect at the same time.

Especially in parenting, you need flexibility. You can miss wonderful subtle moments with your child unless you stay open and spontaneous and ready to switch gears at the slightest hint of an opportunity to laugh, to be silly, to share joy. Flexibility is a parental asset worth your investment. Flexibility of mind is essential for finding the humor in life.

To cultivate your humor, you may want to look for like qualities in things that are not alike. Does your child's hair remind you of sunlight? Is your child's angry face reminiscent of an old, withered oak tree? Is your own tone of voice sounding like a first-time violin lesson?

Aristotle said that the true mark of genius is the ability to see similarities in disparate things, to see analogies rather than distinctions. He said that we tend to think recognizing differences shows how smart we are. But we learn more, he asserted, by noticing what different things have in common. By doing this, we learn more about the innate qualities of things and the patterns of their being and behavior.

So it is with humor. If you look for patterns of similarity in the disorder and chaos of family life, you will be open to the humorous flip that shows you a new pattern. That new way of looking at things can give you new insights and new ways of understanding your world and your child. And human beings like that opening-up feeling. It's fun and pleasurable. It's creative.

Albert Einstein said that for creative thinking you must immerse yourself in a thing, learn all about it, and then set it aside and work on something else. Only then, he said, is the big picture most likely to emerge and your original subject most likely to appear in a new light.

Humor does exactly this, in the flash of an eye. Human beings enjoy the creative process, and humor ignites that process within. So sudden is it sometimes that it can make your diaphragm suddenly contract in a full release of the body musculature. In other words, it can make you laugh!

Cultivate Your Laughter

It may seem odd to explore theories of humor here. But I hope you are beginning to see how very important your sense of humor can be to your daily parenting success. If your child is giggling, find something to giggle about yourself!

Your day as a parent can be filled with humor, little jokes, insights, little tricks, and realizations of profundity, if only you know how to detect and appreciate them. With these you can be constantly replenishing your parental energy and faith, even in the midst of everyday challenges both big and small.

Again and again I tell parents that parenting is meant to be fun. "If it's not fun, why do it?" opines Ben Cohen, guru of what he calls "caring capitalism"—that is, business with a social conscience. His phenomenal success with Ben and Jerry's ice cream has shown that fun and generosity and caring can go together well and are good for business. They're good for parenting too.

252 ❖ THE 7 SECRETS OF SUCCESSFUL PARENTS

Most parents assume they will one day have grandchildren. But you might ask yourself this question: If your child can't see from your example that parenting is a pleasure, why would he want to have kids himself? If he's not driven to parent for the fun and pleasure of it, then he will end up doing it out of either accident or duty, if at all. Of course parents want to avoid accidental parenting by their children. Let's take a moment to look at duty.

Fun and Duty

Duty could be considered another word for doing what *doesn't* come naturally to you, what *others* think you should. That kind of motivation brings back the ghost of that troublesome message you heard about before: having always to be other than yourself. As Largent and Breton explain, when you try to be other than yourself in order to please others or to feel more valuable or lovable, you turn away from your inner self. You become outer-focused and alienated from the spiritual forces that are there to guide you.

When duty is your driving motive, you are at the beck and call of whoever can convince you his request is more important than your own inner pilot. If duty drives your child, he gives up his inner guidance system for outside standards about what to do. He is then more vulnerable to peer pressure, extremist groups, and any other outside standard that purports to make him feel wanted and valuable.

A child who knows from his own parents that he is valuable and lovable, just as he is, is far less vulnerable. If his parents take pleasure in him, then he will take pleasure in himself, as self, and he will reach out to know more of himself and to express himself more authentically. The joy of being more fully himself is a far truer guide than any duty imposed from outside, whether by school, friends, law, gang, or parent.

Certainly some great thinkers like Immanuel Kant have defined duty as the highest goal. But I think you will agree, if you explore their arguments, that they speak of an internal sense of duty. I suggest this comes down to something very close to what I am talking about here. When you obey this inner call to duty, you find this kind of duty gives you a deep pleasure. You will feel more real, alive, good, and whole if you follow that inner sense of duty.

Consider the words of Mother Theresa and Albert Schweitzer, whose names are synonymous with selfless altruism. Both at different times have been asked why they do what they do. Where do they get their motivation to help others so unceasingly? Both have answered that they do it because it pleases them. They feel good because of what they do. It's not duty, some outside standard of what they should do, that sustains their efforts, but pleasure, an abiding awareness of what makes them feel most alive and happy and useful.

So it's not selfish to do what gives you pleasure. In fact it's the truest of guides. The trick is to know what really gives you pleasure, down to your very bones, deep into your heart, into and through your soul, for the long haul. That's an enviable state to be in, to know what gives you the greatest pleasure of life. If you model using your own pleasure in being a parent as your most reliable source of real motivation, your child will know how to go after the deeper pleasures of his life, even if these require the kind of dedication and commitment and full-time attention that parenting does!

"Follow Your Bliss"

Joseph Campbell is known as one of the world's authorities on the myths and symbols that motivate thoughts, words, and actions around the world. He summed up his learning with this injunction: "Follow your bliss!" That's your real duty as a human being and parent. Follow your bliss as a parent, and you empower your child to follow hers.

If you want your child to think and act in ways that reflect his true potential, and if you want him to take real, deep pleasure in life, and if you want him perhaps to someday raise your grandchildren so that the world may continue to enjoy the fruits of your parenting labor, then the most powerful thing you can do is to let him know how he gives you pleasure just by being in your life.

A successful parent named Brenda told me she had recently said these words to her older son: "I really love you, and I know you're the greatest. But after what you just did, right now I'm going to have to kill you!" She was laughing and so did he. She broke the tension of the moment with her humor and made him feel more relaxed and able to hear her distress over a bad choice he had made. She was talking his language, and he could hear her.

As she told me her story, Brenda added that it's impossible to show a child too much love, as long as your demonstrations of love coexist with meaningful guidance and firmness when needed. Brenda finished by saying, "Just tell all the parents it's OK to be cheesy in the '90s."

Let your child see the pleasure you take in him. Once you begin to show more of your pleasure and your joy and your bliss in parenting, you may soon see how your child places greater stock in his own inner judgment. You will have demonstrated that your child's very being is valuable and important and welcome. And you will see how he will take more time to determine what will really give him pleasure, rather than seeking instant gratification with mere promises of pleasure that will inevitably extract too high a price. And you may notice how he will be more resistant to shadows of pleasure, temptations like a smoke, junk food binges, betting, fighting, alcohol, or other mind-altering habit.

As you reach for new opportunities to really enjoy your child, you may discover that this is also the quickest way you can empower your child. If your child knows his very presence in your life gives you pleasure, then he has the best evidence that he is valuable just for himself.

He knows he's worth looking out for, and he will take a natural interest in learning how to function, how to cope, and how to live most sanely and productively for himself and others.

Your own joy will only grow. Before long, you will notice how he will actually give you more and more pleasure. A new comfort can invade your home, a new atmosphere of acceptance and unconditional love, a new pleasure in each other's presence, interests, and personality. You may even start to get a special feeling for what a pleasure it will be in the future to know this person when he is all grown up and your child rearing is over!

The Positive Feedback Loop

When you get a kick out of your child and let her know it, you're setting up the very opposite of the vicious cycle of negativity that plagues many well-meaning households. Instead you create a spiraling ascension of positivity.

Simply surrender to the wonder of the creative parenting process! Celebrate its surprise enlightenments and its abiding mysteries. Your enjoyment makes you feel good about yourself as a parent and empowers you to go forward. Your enjoyment makes your child feel good about himself too and empowers him to become more truly himself. It's a win-win situation all the way.

Some in the public eye have recently criticized the emphasis on self-esteem in child rearing. They express concern that the child is getting something for nothing. They urge that parental admiration should come only for good deeds. These critics think we may spoil the child by letting him know we love him just as he is.

Such concern is misplaced. Ask any parent who works hard on self-esteem, using the tools outlined in this book, and he will assure you that what he does works exactly opposite to spoiling or rewarding prematurely. Without self-esteem, children can't even begin to internalize positive motivation for their actions. Without self-esteem, they will become trapped in the attempt to be other than themselves. They will become ever more outwardly focused. They may be fearful to take initiative because they have no solid internal guide. They may try too hard to please and not hard enough to develop their own special talents and contributions.

These commentators also say that some schools have gone overboard by nurturing self-esteem to the exclusion of any real guidance about what is acceptable and laudable behavior and what is not. Of course this kind of instruction won't work. Self-esteem can only be nurtured in an environment in which the adult models are clear about what behaviors are proper and what are not and act accordingly. Neither parents nor school boards will tolerate a school that sets no standards of achievement. So lowering standards to pamper children's self-esteem is a red herring. Within commonsense boundaries, as explored in the last chapter about expressing what you think and standing firm when necessary, children must feel free to be themselves, and they cannot do this without knowing, profoundly, that they themselves are OK just as they are.

Loving your child just as she is, just for who she is, does not take away your power to guide and instruct that child's behavior. In fact, it gives you the motivation and capability to exercise that power more successfully. If your child knows she's OK, "worthy and welcome," then she can know that she starts with something to work with when you give her guidance and instruction. She has the raw materials to do what you suggest and to take constructive steps to imitate, obey, and please you even more. It's easy to respect a parent who respects you.

Applying the Secret of Celebration Through the Years

I regularly urge parents never to be shy about celebrating special family moments. Kids may think it's hokey and embarrassing or may pretend so before their friends, but I have yet to meet a child who regretted any celebration that was a sincere expression of the family's joy in each other.

Bring your baby to any celebrations you can. Just watch out for too much noise or loud music. Laugh and cuddle and smile and sing as much as you are able. Play games that make you feel silly, and don't mind if your family members laugh; playfulness is a wonderful gift that helps us get through life. And don't assume that babies shouldn't participate in events they don't understand. They don't know what a first birthday is, but they know for sure when a parent and family are having a good time. So have those birthday parties from the start, and include whoever seems appropriate to you each year.

When your child is all of a sudden walking around and reaching for things, there's a great tendency for parents to turn serious. Now, we think, we have to teach them how to behave. But not so. They teach themselves with the right parental exposure, stimulation, encouragement, and modeling. So keep your sense of humor, your sense of wonder, your sense of play and celebration. Take care to avoid too many people or activities at holidays because it's easy for this age group to get overstimulated and overtired and irritable before the day is over.

Your child in the exploratory stage, age four to seven, will begin to really understand holidays and eagerly look forward to them. In fact you may have to guard against too much anticipation at this age, because often these children can get overexcited and hit their peak long before the celebration day. At this stage, it's especially important to let your child know what an integral part he is of any family celebration. Find out what his favorite activities or sights or sounds are around each holiday and take care to make these a part of the family tradition. Find simple ways, as described in this chapter, to celebrate any special event in the lives of family members.

To your child in the growth stage, 7 to 14, family celebrations may seem old hat and boring, but keep them up anyhow. These may be the memories he remembers best when he has his own family. If you dismiss celebrations now, he will never know what he missed.

In the maturation stage, whether you are ready or not, your child may want to include others in your family celebrations or join in others' celebrations. Let go and let it happen. But be sure to let your child know that she is always welcome if she changes her mind and that your thoughts and wishes are with her wherever she is.

You needn't be surprised if your child one day wants to share these holidays with you again. By letting her have a choice about how to celebrate, you are giving her the freedom to seek you out again later and to bring new energy and excitement to your family's special occasions. Even with a maturing child, don't worry about being corny or silly or traditional. If you enjoy some activity or event and have a good time, it will have special positive meaning for your child, more than she may realize right now. And you will have modeled the value of real pleasure in life.

The Fun Begins with You

The hardest thing about really getting a kick out of your child and sharing your joy in his being is that taking pleasure must begin with you. Don't wait until your child does something noticeably good, or changes her attitude to something more tolerable, or starts treating you with more respect, or does something funny or offers something amusing. Then indeed your child may be easy to praise and enjoy, unless you live in fear that it cannot last (refer to secret 1!). But your real test comes when your child is being obnoxious, mischievous, careless, or disrespectful.

Can you still love her then? And show it? If you can, that's when she knows you really love her. That's when healthy shame, embarrassment, and constructive guilt feelings can kick in to guide your child and help you out as a parent. If she knows you love her in spite of her transgressions, then she will be more apt to want to please you again as soon as she can do so without losing face. If, in contrast, you withhold your love and enjoyment until she meets certain standards, her conscience can take a holiday under the cover of resentment and rage at undeserved loss of parental love.

So show your enjoyment in these difficult moments. Find something to love and celebrate it. After you've practiced this skill, the other signs of pleasure will come easily, and you will be almost finished with your life-changing initiation into the seven secrets of successful parents.

Look for the Goodness

If you really believe in the goodness of your child, you can find something to celebrate no matter how tense the moment. Even if it's too tense for you to say anything, just thinking happy thoughts about your child will affect your face and body language and take the sting out of the air.

You may find this difficult to do at first. It might feel like putting the cart before the horse, or rewarding obnoxious behavior. For some parents, it can take years of frustration before they are ready to take the leap of faith necessary to jettison their fears and show their joy all the time. But you can soon see what happens when you truly embrace your child just as he is and for himself. He is then empowered to become more of his real self, which we know to be wonderful from secret 1, about faith.

You see, you have a profound choice to make. Luckily I think by this time you have already made it, consciously or not. On the one hand, you can think of your child as a stubborn mule to be coaxed with a carrot and nudged with a stick. On the other hand, you can think of your child as a powerful wellspring of love and spirit, just waiting for the love and trust a family can give to gush forth full of life.

The love and awe you feel as a parent plus the frustrations you meet when you take the first alternative should propel you toward the more courageous and successful second alternative.

In the first case, you would probably get just about what you would have visualized, a child whose faculties are marginally above a trained quadruped's, with love and devotion you can hope for but with little initiative, always focused only on meeting essential needs and avoiding unpleasant experiences, with no higher goals.

In the second case, you can get a being beyond your wildest dreams: freer, more powerful, more loving, more decisive, more giving, more intelligent, more productive, more radiant than you ever could have imagined.

Make Childhood Profoundly Pleasurable and Productive

It's not really so surprising that we have pulled away from the profound appreciation and daily celebration of children and parents that characterizes traditional peoples and preindustrial society. Civilization as we know it tells us building and owning material possessions are the greatest of achievements. In such a society, children remain unproductive throughout childhood. They are just another possession, with future potential. A child whose father didn't claim him as an heir to his possessions was a nonentity in ancient civilizations.

It has taken us centuries to acknowledge that children are not possessions, or lumps of clay that we must mold to suit our ambitions, or nasty little bundles of animal drives that we must civilize by force, against their will.

Luckily the new spirituality, a new understanding of language and communication, new perspectives on history and culture, and the new freedom of each family to discover what really feels right and good have led us to new appreciation of what our children are really here for. We must enjoy them for *who* they are, not *what* they are. As actor Drew Barrymore said in her movie role as a child seeking to divorce neglectful and warring parents in *Irreconcilable Differences*: "Children are people, not pets."

Once you accept the totality of the gift your child is to both you and the world, you can at last feel fully conscious and proactive in your powerful role as a parent. And you can appeal knowingly to the highest inspirations of your child to be all she can be—physically, mentally, emotionally, socially, and spiritually.

You help her discover her full human dimensions by celebrating these from the start, and you might want to make celebration an everyday thing in your home. Secretly enjoying your child's bright side gets rid of parental shame and guilt and hopelessness. It breeds patience, contentment, and good listening. But the celebration is what really gets the love across to your child.

Even if you fear there is more than meets the eye in a given situation and believe you should be worrying instead of celebrating, for the sake of the power of your love you can give your child the benefit of the doubt and never regret it.

Knowledge, Wisdom, and Joy

Seventeenth-century French poet Antoinette Deshoulieres said of religious faith, "Seeking to know is too frequently learning to doubt." The same is true of faith in your children. The only antidote is to have faith that you will learn what you need to know in good time, without violating your child's integrity and personal boundaries and without making your life miserable.

Time and time again, the parent who maintains trust and therefore remains close to her child will find out important things sooner than a parent who suspects and alienates her child. As a parent who trusts and celebrates your child, you will find out what you need to know in one of three important ways.

First, because you are close and attentive, you can learn important new information by easily noticing even the most subtle changes in your child's behavior. And you will have the trusting relationship there, so you can ask appropriate questions. Second, your child's own awareness of your trust and love and her guilt over deceiving you will make it impossible for her to keep a dangerous secret from you for long. Your child will spill the beans, either on purpose or by mistake, to get out of her discomfort. And third, if you lead your own life and share it with your child, important information will cross your path. If you're out there, you will be in the stream of data that you need to have.

Parents today seem more fearful than ever of not knowing. They may feel guilty because they supervise their children so much less than their parents supervised them. And the onslaught of media information makes many parents fearful that violence, disease, and death wait in ambush for their children, around every corner. But the reality is that you have the primary influence, by your attention to basic needs, your example, and your faith. A parent's insistence on knowing everything is likely to drive a child toward the dark side rather than to protect him from it.

Just as you cannot know everything about a friend, or know the whole inner life of your spouse, or even understand yourself totally, you cannot know your child completely. You aren't meant to. This is not a prerequisite for your total faith and enjoyment. You are in a relationship with your child; your bond is between spiritual equals, each with boundaries, a personal path, and a part in the collective destiny, each a mystery of intimacy and novelty for the other.

Especially with a child, things are changing every day. You can go mad thinking you should be able to anticipate and prevent every risk. Instead celebrate your child's gifts and skills, whatever they are, and cultivate your vocabulary and body language for lauding and honoring his being, just as I have urged you to honor your own.

Awe and Wonder

Awe and wonder are better attitudes than suspicion and inquisition when it comes to kids. They comprise a spiritual attitude, one that allows you to respond genuinely to each situation as it arises. After all, your child may be closer to God than you think. Jesus said of the children in the streets, "For of such is the kingdom of heaven."

No child wants to be bad. If it looks like she does, you can be sure she has decided, at some level of her psyche, that being good doesn't work. It doesn't make her feel alive, loved, valuable. It's not fun. All you have to do is slowly change that impression by daily, hourly manifestations of your joy and love. Since we teach by example, let the love you show for your child serve as his example of how to love himself.

As you put more joy and celebration into your life, you will be building up courage to take more lightly those things that are essentially unimportant and to be more steadfast on those things that really matter. Love is not a new toy, a go-ahead to act against your better judgment, a permission to depart from your well-thought-out bedtime policies, for example, or a call to lie on the child's behalf to a teacher, employer, doctor, or relative in exchange for a promise to change.

We might do any of these things under some circumstances for specific purposes, but they are not in themselves expressions of love. If they are not love, you can bet the child won't feel them as love. If a child gets what he wants against your better judgment or because you are tempted to take the easy way out in the name of love, the child will not feel loved.

Counselors' offices are filled with people who had parents who thought these things showed their love. That love is so confusing in our society is a sad thing. It's really quite simple. Love is a matter of your own spiritual core reaching out to the spiritual core of your child through connection and celebration.

Love is the one and only source of real parental power for good in your child's life. You may recall that the only real difference between you and your child is your size and your experience. Your child has all the same complex emotions, the same variety of stresses, and the same urges as you to grow, to heal, to connect, to eat, to sleep, to play, to learn, to celebrate, to revel. He also has the same task as you do: to make the best of each day, to fill up a human life.

With your only advantages being size and experience, you can see how you must rely heavily on your mutual, innate programs to want each other's love and respect. Your child's attachment and admiration for you come naturally to him, but you can probably appreciate that your only personal claim to your child's respect is the quality of your protection (by virtue of your size), the quality of your guidance (by virtue of the wisdom of your experience), and the respect you show for his innate being, or personhood (by virtue of your love).

No matter what daily frustrations come your way, then, or fears for the future, or guilts about what might have been, or confusion about how to proceed presently, it is love that is always at the ready and always appropriate to share. You can postpone anything but love!

264 ❖ THE 7 SECRETS OF SUCCESSFUL PARENTS

It takes practice to discover what little ways feel best to you and how best to reach your own child. But it only takes a bit of courage and faith to usher in greater success, and I guarantee you'll see and feel the results.

Never put off until tomorrow the love you can give today.

Here are some specific strategies for taking pleasure in your parenting and celebrating your child.

Smile Power

The easiest way to celebrate your child is with a smile. The power of the smile is severely underestimated in today's serious world. Often we see pictures of traditional peoples and think they look very serious. But when you were first told to stare into a box for no apparent reason, you didn't smile either. People who have spent some time with traditional peoples almost always remark on the ready ease of their smiles and laughter. They let it be known that they really enjoy life, especially their family and children.

The power of your smile is truly inestimable. When models train for beauty contests, they are told again and again that the way to win over a beauty judge is with a smile. Your smile tells your child you are secure within yourself and unthreatened by his behavior. It tells him you find him and life in general worth smiling about. Your genuine smile, seasoned with acceptance of your child as he is and drawing on your own serenity within yourself, celebrates the humanity of your child and your shared humanity.

At some level your child always sees your smile and feels it. He may resent it, be sarcastic about it, hate you for it, complain about it. But it may bother him precisely because it is not the reaction he sought, precisely because the smile gets to him. It calls his bluff of alienation. He wanted control; he wanted a reaction to put you off balance, to have you take on his problems. Instead your smile gives him a stable, loving, confident, powerful parent who knows her limits, boundaries, responsibilities, and joys. His parent takes him seriously for sure, but always with love and joy. He doesn't get what he wants but he gets what he needs.

Deep down, no child can resist the quiet celebration of love in your parental smile.

More Opportunities for Celebration

In the chapter on secret 2 (attention to basic needs), I gave you a list of specific ways to show your love—by body language, word, and deed. Review that list now and as often as you want. Here are a few more ways to show your pleasure in your child.

• Think of any anniversaries that come up during the year when you can celebrate your child's life or your life together. Whenever they come, mention them and think of something a little special to do, like a special lunch or dinner, a movie, a miniature golf game, a board game on the floor with popcorn and pretzels, a favorite video, home movies of the family, a party, a walk, a visit with friends, or a trip to the child's favorite park, museum, store, or sports event.

• Make or buy fun cards, pennants, button pins, trophies, stickers, ribbons, balloons, bumper stickers, flower bouquets, signs, certificates, posters, or other mementos for any little success or milestone in the child's life.

• Save any cartoons, magazine photos, or news clips you think would be fun to share with your child, and share them promptly and lightly.

• Praise any achievement, no matter how small. Hang around when your child is hard at a task and share your encouragement and delight.

• Arrange to have your child around positive-minded people whenever possible. Keep this in mind when choosing sitters, tutors, stores you frequent with your child, relatives, guests, and so on. Even in a restaurant, if your server seems grouchy, ask to sit at another table, near the window or closer to the bathroom or whatever. Keep your child's environment upbeat and supportive. Your child's childhood is an investment of good feelings that he can draw on the rest of his life.

• When bad things happen, model acceptance and hope and renewal. Accept feelings of despair, acknowledge them, and then share feelings of reassurance that nothing is the real end, though it can feel like it.

• Say things like this:

"I'm glad you're in my life."

"I love it when you laugh."

"You have such a wonderful sense of humor."

"Your take on life really refreshes my thinking."

"I love the way you can see the bright side of things."

"I love hearing your perspective."

"Is it time for a giggle fest?"

"You know just when to say something funny."

"I love to share little jokes with you."

"I need some time out. How about you?"

"Laughing is so therapeutic!"

• Watch a favorite sitcom together. Pick one everyone likes and make a weekly celebration out of it. Tape it for anyone who is missing and watch it again. Laugh together.

• Play music often. The more often you play it, the more humming and singing will fill the house. Find out what songs each of you likes and share them often. Listen to the lyrics and try not to be judgmental. Take turns with each other's favorite tapes in the car. I remember when my own mother couldn't believe I loved a song titled "I want to hold your hand." But thank goodness she just registered her mild exasperation and let me keep listening! Ask what any disagreeable lyrics mean to your child and practice secret 3 about listening. Then praise your child's love of music.

• Share love for a pet. Few things can match the sheer fun of watching a kitten play with some string, a puppy wrestle for a stick, a bird preen itself, or a ferret chase after your foot. Even a fish can find a voice if you let it: "Wow, food! I thought it would never come. Uh-oh, now wait a minute. Isn't that piece a bit too big for my tiny little mouth? I'm going to go hide!" Rent the video *Homeward Bound* or *Babe* or watch a few of the animal cartoons from your own childhood if you want instruction in animating your animals.

• Assemble a puppet collection. Make your own from socks or buy one or more that especially speak to or for each of you. We had a plywood theater for years that my children decorated. They held puppet shows for us parents, and we had lots of laughs.

• Have a dress-up party. Put on your old stuff, your fancy stuff, your bummed-out stuff, or all your stuff at once, layered high. Let everyone try on your stuff. Be as outrageous as you can. At every seasonal change or holiday, have some good laughs.

• Do the same with hairdos, shoes, makeup, face paint, jewelry, scarves, and belts. Consider nothing sacred—that is, nothing more sacred than your privilege to enjoy playing with your child!

• Do impressions of favorite people, entertainment stars, public figures, animals, professions.

• Sing while you're cleaning or fixing. Stop and do something crazy like rolling on the floor or mimicking an animal or plant, or even a desk or lamp. Stretch your imagination, and you'll stretch your child's.

• Find noncompetitive games that get you both working and laughing together—kiteflying, rocket building, collecting—or fun cooperative physical challenges like these:

> Lock elbows back-to-back while sitting on the floor and then try to stand up together, cooperating to find the best balance.

Lie on the floor with each person's head on the next person's stomach and let someone begin to laugh. (This takes at least three people.)

Sit opposite each other with feet wide apart and toes touching and roll a ball back and forth.

Sit side by side, legs outstretched, and try to keep a bouncing ball in the air with your knees.

I've listed some great books about these sorts of games in the resource section.

• Tell funny stories at bedtime. Read some aloud. Always appreciate your child's story even if it doesn't have much of a recognizable plot, purpose, beginning, or end. Ask interested questions but avoid judgment or criticism.

• Make up funny limericks about yourselves and each other.

• Play "20 questions," "animal, vegetable, or mineral," or the "My name is" game that follows the alphabet: "My name is Allen, I'm from Alabama, I'm an aviator, and I like avocados." Or play charades, *Pictionary*, or the fold-down story game where each player writes a line of a story without seeing what came before. If anyone gets stuck, don't chide or shame; simply help them out with lots of joy and encouragement. It's the striving and the surprises that are the most fun, not showing how smart or stupid anybody is.

• Compliment any little thing you notice; stay alert and pay attention so you will notice often:

"Thanks for picking up your shoes."

"I like the way you stacked your books."

"That's a great mountain you made with your potatoes!"

"Your hair is in a wonderful chaos this morning."

Enjoy everything about your child, and your child can give you more joy than you've ever imagined, for the rest of your life.

Joy and Freedom

You may recall that, at the beginning of this book, I suggested our job as parents is to fully operationalize our parental love— to make love real. Every day we need to channel the amazing power of parental love—the key to the success of the human family—for the benefit of parents and children alike. This love is the energy behind all of our efforts. If we take a little extra care each day we can save ourselves a lot of trouble, as I hope you have seen in your experiments with the first six secrets.

With the secret of celebration you can magnify and amplify the effects of your efforts. Sharing your satisfaction and joy makes love real and obvious for your child. We wouldn't keep doing this parenting thing, generation after generation, if it didn't bring joy. Just ask anyone with great-grandchildren if they have any regrets about becoming a parent. Their answer will ring loud and clear.

Don't wait until your child turns out right. Celebrate now. Your expressions of joy give your child the great gift of knowing her life has meaning and goodness for another—the other she cares most about. You add to her freedom by letting her know that your parenting is freely given with unconditional love. Her very life and being is full recompense for all your efforts. "It's my pleasure," you can say with your eyes. "I will always get a kick out of you."

We shall never understand one another until we reduce the language to seven words.

KAHLIL GIBRAN

The family is the nucleus of civilization.

ARIEL AND WILL DURANT

I'm going to stop punishing my children by saying, "Never mind! I'll do it myself."

ERMA BOMBECK

The very commonplaces of life are components of its eternal mystery.

GERTRUDE ATHERTON

Conclusion

Now that you have accompanied me on this adventure to discover the seven secrets of successful parents, I hope you have seized upon these secrets as treasures with which you can daily improve your life with your child. All that is left for me to do is to help you remember the seven secrets easily, so that they will pop into your head whenever you want them, which I hope you will find to be just about all the time!

When I'm giving lectures and seminars on the seven secrets, this is how I remember them: by the acronym FALLMEC. FALLMEC sounds like an ancient native ancestor, doesn't it? Think of this ancient ancestor reminding you of parenting wisdom that has sustained humanity through the ages. Here's how FALLMEC can remind you of the seven secrets and give you guidance in every situation.

F—Faith: Have faith in yourself as a parent and in your child as a child—show your unshakable faith.

A—Attention: Pay attention to the basic needs of your child. Give your unfailing attention to meeting your child's basic needs, so that your child's higher functions can develop naturally and optimally.

L—Listening: Listen to your child, hear your child out, and respond only with empathetic reflection and gentle guidance of your child's own thinking process.

L—Letting go: Let go a little each day, letting your child gradually assume the full responsibility for your child's own life.

M—Modeling: Model life for your child. Set an example by your attitude and by your thoughts, words, and deeds. Be aware of your own needs and boundaries as you respect those of your child.

E—Expression: Express yourself for yourself. Let your child know what you think, believe, intend, and feel in a gentle, loving way, and to the extent that is relevant to your child. Stop when that has been done.

C—Celebration: Celebrate and enjoy your child. Celebrate your bond and revel in your satisfaction and fun, no matter how small or large.

Whenever you feel the slightest hesitation about how to proceed in your parenting, you can remember FALLMEC and ask yourself: "Have I had faith, paid attention, listened, let go, modeled, expressed myself, and celebrated my child?"

You will know then exactly what to do.

And you can make it a daily habit to refresh yourself, find your balance, prepare for any difficult confrontation, renew your spirit, confirm your intuitions, test your inclinations, affirm your gifts and skills, forgive your imperfections, and pat yourself on the back by repeating these seven secrets, which I hope mean a great deal more to you now after you have read this book than they did when you first heard them:

"I would never give up on my child. I pay attention first to my child's basic needs. I always hear my child out. It's my child's life, not mine, after all. I have a life too, and I share it with my child. I speak my mind, and I know when to stop. And I really get a kick out of my child!"

Thank you for sharing this journey with me. I wish you the greatest satisfaction and success, all the days of your parenting!

> *What's the use of a new-born child? . . .*
> *To raise the dead heart?—to set wild*
> *The fettered hope?*
>
> WITTER BYNNER

Resource Guide

There are so many titles I wanted to include here! The resources I've listed, including books, film videos, and organizations, are included to give you a wide range of ideas for further exploration of topics mentioned in *The 7 Secrets of Successful Parents*. There's only room for a few of my favorites. They range from straightforward instruction in child rearing to ways parenting might fit into or be enriched by diverse cultures, ecological connections, or new concepts of body and mind. These titles can be particularly helpful to further enlighten your parenting. I hope that whatever you may read next, you will notice how almost any new insight in any realm of your life can increase your self-awareness, understanding, and success as a parent.

BOOKS

Pregnancy and Childbirth

These books can help you get off to a great start using the seven secrets of successful parents that you've discovered in this book. The thrust of these books on the birthing approach is to have faith in the natural processes of human procreation and to pay special attention to the basic physical, nutritional, and emotional needs of mother, child, and family.

Bradley, Robert. *Husband-Coached Childbirth*. 3rd ed. New York: Harper Collins, 1981.

Brewer, Gail. *What Every Pregnant Woman Should Know*. New York: Random House, 1977.

Dick-Read, Grantly. *Childbirth Without Fear*. New York: Harper & Row, 1984.

Hazell, Lester. *Commonsense Childbirth*. New York: Berkley, 1976.

Leboyer, Frederick. *Birth Without Violence*. New York: Knopf, 1975.

Sousa, Marion. *Childbirth at Home*. New York: Bantam, 1977.

Breastfeeding

These books can help give you support in enjoying the deeply rewarding relationship of breastfeeding in spite of some cultural or social resistance.

Breastfeeding is the easiest way I know to build a firm foundation of faith between parent and child, because it demonstrates so clearly that the natural system works. It also can form a comfortable basis for good listening and expression as well as lots of easy enjoyment of the parenting bond.

Kippley, Sheila. *Breastfeeding and Natural Child Spacing*. New York: Penguin, 1975.

Pryor, Karen. *Nursing Your Baby*. New York: Pocket Books, 1991.

Torgus, Judy, ed. *The Womanly Art of Breastfeeding*. Schaumburg, IL: La Leche League International, 1987.

Childcare

Though many books on childcare are by doctors, don't assume this means you need to be preoccupied with the health of your baby. Good health is a natural state of affairs if basic needs are met. Doctors have taken the childcare advice role simply because parents ask them the questions they would have once asked of the extended family, including grandparents, aunts, uncles, or others. Remember that many doctors see children only clinically, not every day doing their normal healthy living. If any advice goes against your best parental instincts and intuitions, find another solution.

Brazelton, T. Berry. *Touchpoints: Your Child's Emotional & Behavioral Development: The Essential Reference*. Reading, MA: Addison-Wesley, 1992.

Brazelton, T. Berry. *What Every Baby Knows*. New York: Ballantine, 1988.

Gesell, Arnold. *Infant and Child in the Culture of Today: The Guidelines of Development in Home and Nursery School*. Northvale, NJ: Jason Aronson, 1995.

Hymes, James. *The Child Under Six*. 2d ed. West Greenwich, RI: Consortium, 1994.

Spock, Benjamin. *Baby and Child Care*. New York: Pocket Books, 1951.

Parenting

I have tried to choose parenting books that will best support you in your efforts to build a responsive parenting style as described in this book. These books will bolster your faith and understanding about the wonderful, independent personhood of your child and about his bold, innate drive to unfold his best destiny. The authors' approaches emphasize a positive, nurturing, and spiritual style as opposed to a controlling, authoritarian, and instructional style.

Armstrong, Thomas. *The Radiant Child*. Wheaton, IL: Theosophical Publishing House, 1985.

Aronson, Linda. *Big Spirits, Little Bodies*. Virginia Beach, VA: A.R.E., 1995.

Bates, James. *Becoming a Complete Parent*. Sydney, Australia: Hampden Press, 1989.

Bettelheim, Bruno. *A Good Enough Parent: A Book on Child-Rearing*. New York: Vintage Books, 1987.

Bettelheim, Bruno. *Dialogues with Mothers*. New York: Free Press, 1962.

Brazelton, T. Berry. *To Listen to a Child*. Reading, MA: Addison-Wesley, 1986.

Briggs, Dorothy. *Your Child's Self-Esteem: The Key to His Life*. New York: Doubleday, 1975.

Campbell, Ross. *How to Really Love Your Child*. New York: NAL, 1982.

Caney, Steven. *Steven Caney's Kids' America*. New York: Workman, 1978.

Crary, Elizabeth. *Without Spanking or Spoiling*. Seattle: Parenting Press, 1979.

Daley, Eliot. *Father Feelings*. New York: Pocket Books, 1979.

Dodson, Fitzhugh. *How to Parent*. New York: NAL, 1973.

Dyer, Wayne. *What Do You Really Want for Your Children?* New York: Avon, 1986.

Faber, Adele, and Elaine Mazlish. *How to Talk So Kids Will Listen and Listen So Kids Will Talk*. New York: Avon, 1982.

Forbes, Malcolm. *What Happened to Their Kids? Children of the Rich and Famous*. New York: Simon & Schuster, 1990.

Fruett, Kyle. *The Nurturing Father*. New York: Warner Books, 1988.

Gesell, Arnold. *He Hit Me First: When Brothers and Sisters Fight*. New York: Warner Books, 1989.

Ginott, Haim. *Between Parent and Child.* New York: Avon, 1969.

Greenspan, Stanley and Nancy. *First Feelings.* New York: Penguin, 1986.

Leach, Penelope. *Your Growing Child: From Babyhood Through Adolescence.* New York: Knopf, 1986.

Leman, Kevin. *The Birth Order Book.* New York: Dell, 1987.

Pearce, Joseph Chilton. *Magical Child: Rediscovering Nature's Plan for Our Children.* New York: Bantam, 1977.

Pittman, Frank. *Man Enough: Fathers, Sons, and the Search for Masculinity.* New York: Berkley, 1993.

Rogers, Fred, and Barry Head. *Mister Rogers Talks with Parents.* New York: Berkley, 1986.

Rolfe, Randy. *You Can Postpone Anything but Love: A Guide to Enlightened, Spiritual Parenting—for an Enriching Bond Between You and Your Child.* New York: Warner Books, 1990.

Seligman, Martin. *The Optimistic Child.* New York: Houghton-Mifflin, 1995.

Stallibrass, Alison. *The Self-Respecting Child.* Reading, MA: Addison-Wesley, 1989.

Trelease, Jim. *The Read-Aloud Handbook.* 4th ed. New York: Viking, 1995.

van der Meer, Antonia. *Great Beginnings: An Illustrated Guide to You and Your Baby's First Year.* New York: Dell, 1994.

Wilford, Jane. *What to Do with the Kids This Year: 100 Family Vacation Places with Time Off for You.* Charlotte, NC: East Woods, 1986.

Education

The books listed here take modern educational policy to task and ask whether the typical educational experience is truly helpful in creating the confident, creative, contributing, and contented adult you seek to have your child become.

Ames, Louise Bates, and Joan Ames Chase. *Don't Push Your Preschooler*. New York: Harper & Row, 1980.

Dennison, George. *The Lives of Children: The Story of the First Street School*. New York: Random House, 1969.

Gatto, John Taylor. *Dumbing Us Down: The Hidden Curriculum of Compulsory Schooling*. Philadelphia: New Society, 1992.

Goleman, Daniel. *Emotional Intelligence: Why It Can Matter More Than IQ*. New York: Bantam, 1995.

Holt, John. *How Children Fail*. New York: Dell, 1983.

Holt, John. *How Children Learn*. New York: Dell, 1982.

Kiyosaki, Robert. *If You Want to Be Rich and Happy, Don't Go to School*. Lower Lake, CA: Aslan, 1993.

Kozol, Jonathan. *Death at an Early Age*. New York: NAL, 1986.

Kozol, Jonathan. *Illiterate America*. New York: NAL, 1986.

Miller, Alice. *For Your Own Good: Hidden Cruelty in Child-Rearing and the Roots of Violence*. New York: Farrar, Straus & Giroux, 1990.

Nabhan, Gary, and Stephen Trimble. *The Geography of Childhood*. Boston: Beacon Press, 1994.

Neill, A. S. *Summerhill: A Radical Approach to Child Rearing*. New York: Pocket Books, 1984.

Orr, David. *Earth in Mind: On Education, Environment, and the Human Prospect*. Washington, DC: Island Press, 1994.

Richman, Sheldon. *Separating School & State: How to Liberate America's Families.* Fairfax, VA: Future of Freedom Foundation, 1994.

Home Education

Home education is becoming a more popular option today, so I have listed here some of the most helpful books. The literature is rich and varied, so if you are interested, use these titles as just the beginning. For more about my own successful experience homeschooling my children through high school graduation, please turn to the appendix.

Colfax, David and Micki. *Homeschooling for Excellence.* Philo, CA: Mountain House, 1988.

Farris, Michael. *Home Schooling and the Law.* Paeonian Springs, VA: Home School Legal Defense Association, 1990.

Holt, John. *Teach Your Own: A New and Hopeful Path for Parents and Educators.* New York: Dell, 1982.

Llewellen, Grace. *The Teenage Liberation Handbook: How to Quit School and Get a Real Life and Education.* Eugene, OR: Lowry House, 1991.

Pride, Mary. *The Big Book of Home Learning.* Westchester, IL: Crossway Books, 1986.

Shilcock, Susan, and Peter Bergson. *Open Connections: The Other Basics.* Bryn Mawr, PA: Open Connections, 1980.

Family Life and Choices

These books address specific areas of concern, like setting and adjusting priorities for family and work; addressing histories of abuse; the political, cultural, and social setting of childhood; and public policy. Use these books to help expand your vision and options so that you can make the best choices for you and your family—and can get involved in policy if you are inclined.

Brazelton, T. Berry. *Working & Caring*. Reading, MA: Addison-Wesley, 1992.

Breton, Denise, and Christopher Largent. *The Paradigm Conspiracy: How Our Systems of Government, Church, School and Culture Violate Our Human Potential*. Center City, MN: Hazelden, 1996.

Cahill, Mary Ann. *The Heart Has Its Own Reasons*. New York: NAL, 1985.

Clinton, Hillary Rodham. *It Takes a Village: And Other Lessons Children Teach Us*. New York: Simon & Schuster, 1996.

Cornelius, Ruth. *All Together: A Manual of Cooperative Games*. Eureka, IL: Lentz Peace Research Laboratory, 1950.

Edelman, Marian. *The Measure of Our Success: A Letter to My Children and Yours*. New York: Harper Collins, 1993.

Elkind, David. *The Hurried Child: Growing Up Too Fast Too Soon*. Reading, MA: Addison-Wesley, 1981.

Fraiberg, Selma. "Every Child's Birthright." In *Selected Writings of Selma Fraiberg,* ed. Louis Fraiberg. Columbus: Ohio State University Press, 1987.

Judson, Stephanie. *A Manual on Nonviolence and Children*. Philadelphia: New Society, 1984.

Lappe, Frances. *What to Do After You Turn Off the TV*. New York: Ballantine, 1985.

Leach, Penelope. *Children First: What Our Society Must Do—And Is Doing for Our Children Today*. New York: Random House, 1994.

Lowman, Kaye. *Of Cradles and Careers: A Guide to Reshaping Your Job to Include a Baby in Your Life.* Schaumburg, IL: La Leche League International, 1984.

Moynihan, Daniel Patrick. *Family and Nation.* San Diego: Harcourt Brace Jovanovich, 1986.

Shilcock, Susan, and Peter Bergson. *Spaces for Children.* Bryn Mawr, PA: Open Connections, 1984.

Thevenin, Tine. *The Family Bed.* Garden City Park, NY: Avery, 1987.

Vanderkolk, Barbara, and Ardis Young. *The Work and Family Revolution.* New York: Facts on File, 1991.

Wilson Schaef, Ann. *Women's Reality: An Emerging Female System in a White Male Society.* New York: Harper San Francisco, 1992.

Child Nutrition and Health

The books listed here will help you understand and appreciate your child's basic needs in greater detail than could be contained in this book. They will show you exactly how best to support your child's physical and mental functions. The emphasis is on natural living, including nutritional solutions to troubling behavioral and emotional habits.

Armstrong, Thomas. *The Myth of the ADD Child: 50 Ways to Improve Your Child's Behavior & Attention Span Without Drugs.* New York: NAL-Dutton, 1995.

Chopra, Deepak. *Perfect Health: The Complete Mind/Body Guide.* New York: Harmony Books, 1990.

Crook, William. *Help for the Hyperactive Child.* Jackson, TN: Professional Books, 1991.

Crook, William, and Laura Stevens. *Solving the Puzzle of Your Hard-to-Raise Child.* New York: Random House, 1987.

Feingold, Benjamin. *Why Your Child Is Hyperactive.* New York: Random House, 1985.

For Tomorrow's Children: A Manual for Future Parents. Blooming Glen, PA: Preconception Care, 1990.

Randolph, Theron, and Ralph Moss. *An Alternative Approach to Allergies.* New York: Bantam, 1982.

Smith, Lendon. *Feed Your Kids Right.* New York: McGraw-Hill, 1979.

Children Around the World

I've included several titles here that deal specifically with careful anthropological observation in societies that are more traditional and less technological than our own. These books give added insight into the natural process of child rearing.

Kitzinger, Sheila. *Women as Mothers.* New York: Random House, 1979.

Liedloff, Jean. *The Continuum Concept.* Reading, MA: Addison-Wesley, 1985.

Mead, Margaret. *Cooperation and Competition Among Primitive Peoples.* Magnolia, MA: Peter Smith, 1937.

Montagu, Ashley. *Touching: The Human Significance of the Skin.* New York: Harper & Row, 1971.

Special Issues for the Family

These books address specific social issues and particular behavioral and health issues affecting children. If you have a problem or concern, please use these books as the beginning of your search and keep searching until you find your solution. They can also be a call to become more politically involved in creating a family-friendly world for your children.

Cook, David. *When Your Child Struggles: The Myths of 20/20 Vision.* Atlanta: Invision Press, 1992.

Edelman, Marian. *The State of America's Children Yearbook.* Washington, DC: Children's Defense Fund, 1996.

Levine, Katharine. *When Good Kids Do Bad Things: A Survival Guide for Parents of Teenagers.* New York: Pocket Books, 1991.

Males, Mike. *The Scapegoat Generation: America's War on Adolescents.* Monroe, ME: Common Courage Press, 1996.

Parents Anonymous. *I Am a Parents Anonymous Parent.* Los Angeles: Parents Anonymous, 1974.

Rhodes, Warren, and Kim Hoey. *Overcoming Childhood Misfortune: Children Who Beat the Odds.* Westport, CT: Greenwood Press, 1993.

Rolfe, Randy. *Adult Children Raising Children: Sparing Your Child from Co-dependency Without Being Perfect Yourself.* Deerfield Beach, FL: Health Communications, 1990.

Smith, Blaine. *Overcoming Shyness.* Downers Grove, IL: Intervarsity Press, 1993.

Somers, Leon and Barbara. *Talking to Your Children About Love & Sex.* New York: Penguin, 1989.

Visher, John and Emily. *Stepfamilies: Myths and Realities.* New York: Carol, 1980.

Westheimer, Ruth, and Nathan Kravetz. *First Love: A Young People's Guide to Sexual Information.* New York: Warner Books, 1985.

Zimbardo, Philip. *Shyness.* Reading, MA: Addison-Wesley, 1990.

CHILDREN'S BOOK CATALOGS

Several catalogs keep a lookout for helpful parenting books as well as for unique books and resources for kids.

Chinaberry Book Service, 3160 Ivy Street, San Diego, CA 92104.

Enlightened Environments, P.O. Box 1408, Durango, CO 81301.

Hearth Song, 2211 Blucher Valley Road, Sebastopol, CA 95472.

FILM VIDEOS

It's worth it to buy a video directory with a family section in it and make deliberate decisions about what videos to rent or to allow your kids to rent. Make the extra effort it takes to balance your reluctance to have your child watch undesirable stuff and your child's eagerness to try fringe material. A standoff just invites dishonesty. If you are careful and patient and express your thoughts and feelings skillfully according to what you have gleaned from this book, you will find common ground. The same goes for video games, Internet connections, magazines, and so on.

Also, chat with other parents about the impact of various films and other media. Get in the information stream and then make your own decisions according to what you have learned, your own sensibilities, and your unique perspective on your child's level of development, feelings, and interests.

When possible, watch each video with your child. With an older child, wander through and catch a scene you can chat about later.

ORGANIZATIONS
HELPFUL TO PARENTS

The organizations listed here range from various resources for personal help with family problems to groups through which you can push for positive change in the larger society, whether it be for better nutrition, a cleaner environment, peace, safer products, or a more sane and healthy society. Use these groups as information sources for tracking down other organizations or periodicals in your particular realm of interest. Addresses can change quickly for volunteer organizations, so don't give up if you have to do some detective work.

Also, be sure to check the local listings for human services in the blue pages of your phone book. This is the best place to start for finding local support services, whether church, government, educational, volunteer, or self-help.

Children's Defense Fund
Marian Wright Edelman
P.O. Box 96553
Washington, DC 20077-7187
Child advocacy

Educators for Social Responsibility
23 Garden Street
Cambridge, MA 02138-9990
Advocates for supportive social policies

Feingold Association of Washington
P.O. Box 18116
Washington, DC 20021
Nutritional support for child allergies and behavior

Food & Water
3 Whitman Drive
Denville, NJ 07834
Environmental safety

Foresight America
P.O. Box 357
Blooming Glen, PA 18911
Preconceptional care and family nutritional support

Growing Without Schooling
729 Boylston Street
Boston, MA 02116
Home education

Institute for Food and Development Policy
145 Ninth Street
San Francisco, CA 94103-2628
Advocates for family-friendly food and economic policies

Journal of Family Life
72 Philips Street
Albany, NY 12202
Family support

La Leche League International
1400 North Meacham Road
Schaumburg, IL 60173
Breastfeeding support

Lamaze Birthing Training
1200 19th Street NW, Suite 300
Washington, DC 20036
Natural birthing

MADD—Mothers Against Drunk Driving
511 East John Carpenter Freeway, Suite 700
Irving, TX 75062-8187
Parents against irresponsible drinking

Mothering Magazine
P.O. Box 15790
Santa Fe, NM 87506
Parenting support

Open Connections
312 Bryn Mawr Avenue
Bryn Mawr, PA 19010
Home education and natural learning

Tough Love International
Box 1069
Doylestown, PA 18901
Support for parents with kids in trouble

Women Strike for Peace
110 Maryland Avenue NE, Suite 302
Washington, DC 20002
Parents for peace

Worldwatch Institute
1776 Massachusetts Avenue NW
Washington, DC 20077-6628
Information on worldwide trends

Appendix

HOME EDUCATION

I am often asked about our wonderful experience homeschooling our two children through graduation. One reason we decided to home educate was what I learned from families I had counseled. I found that school was most often the primary cause of stress within many otherwise successful families. Getting up for a bus, settling down to homework, going to bed on time, and dealing with the stresses of the artificial social and academic environment of school caused the vast majority of persistent parenting problems.

Most parents curious about home education ask the same four questions. In case these also are your questions, I thought I'd take this opportunity to answer them.

Question 1. "How can you stand spending all that schooling time with your child?"

Answer: With the seven secrets, the answer to this is easy. It's a pleasure. And it's only a fifth of my life: 3 waking hours out of 15, 20 years out of 100.

Question 2. "It's hard enough being a parent. I'd never be able to be a teacher too. How do you do it?"

Answer: The only reason we need teachers for school-age children is to engage in that special activity of teaching—that is, instructing some 20 kids, all the same age, all doing more or less the same things when that's not what they want to be doing. A parent who just continues teaching the way she did before school age never has to change hats. Many caring parents today get deeply involved in their child's school activities. They can think of home education simply as "eliminating the middleman."

Question 3. "What about socialization?"

Answer: That's a 20-dollar word. I always wonder how the questioner would translate it. "Do they have friends? Aren't you isolating your child? Won't they be wimpy, unable to compete, if they haven't been toughened up in school?" Homeschoolers find friends in all different activities, much as adults do, and they go the extra mile to get together often. Experience shows they usually have more confidence socially, rather than less, having had more of that invaluable parental input that children need so much all the way through to adulthood and having voluntarily pursued their treasured friendships.

Question 4. "How do you assess your child's progress?"

Answer: This too strikes me as another euphemistic bit of lingo with a distinctly institutional flavor that needs a translation and has little to do with real kids. I think it translates this way: "How do you know you have taught them enough or the right things? Will they stack up against the competition for jobs? Aren't you afraid of experimenting on your kids?"

It's hard to do without objective measures when we are dominated by European scientific culture, in which everything is supposed to be objectively validated. Most homeschooling parents do worry about what and how much to teach. But it really is a non-issue. With a combination of stimulation and love, the vast majority of kids will learn on their own what they will need to know to succeed in life. Those that won't may do even worse in school.

Of course, you can throw in stimulating experiences that are in line with whatever subject you want most to have your child focus on. But my only regret about our homeschooling experience is that we were not more free to pursue exactly what the children would have chosen for themselves—always, of course, under our supervision and guidance. Pennsylvania required us to cover specific subjects each year, to have periodic standardized testing, and so on.

It's not hard to know if your child has functional skills or not or whether she is progressing. And there is nothing magic or definitive about what is taught and when in schools. Parents only worry about such things because they assume that particular skills must be acquired by specific ages and they feel they are competing with others. Yet even in school the prescribed lessons are seldom completed.

A mother who recently began to homeschool reported that her son's class had completed only the first chapter of a world history textbook by the middle of the year, and she easily completed the other half-dozen chapters in less than three months of homeschooling. When you want to get the job done, nothing works like personal attention together with the freedom to work.

A wise school principal once told me that in her school they didn't pressure kids to read in the early grades. It wasn't necessary, she said, because the school had found that if the children were surrounded by books, by exciting teachers, and by lots of love, they would all be reading fine by third grade.

As far as competing for jobs, most homeschoolers don't want to be a cog in a giant wheel and will never even *want* to be tabulated and pigeonholed based on a set of numbers and letters. If they do choose that route, they can build their record through work experience, something homeschoolers have much more flexibility to do, or they can take a course of formal study later that will achieve their own specific goals.

And as far as experimenting on our children, institutionalized school is the great experiment, not home education. Compulsory schooling, a mere 100 years old, was historically established precisely to develop a workforce for the industrial age. Industrialists sought to have workers with a reliable set of uniform but unimaginative skills, amenable to supervision and adaptable to the corporate industrial setting. Schools on the frontier were designed to allow for sharing the rare commodity of books. Except in the poorest areas, books are no longer hard to get.

We fault schools for not creating leaders; yet they were not designed for that. An amazing proportion of our leaders today have had unconventional schooling experiences, either joining schooling institutions late or leaving them early. I'll name just a few: Dave Thomas of Wendy's, Ted Turner, Bill Gates of Microsoft, and Jimmy Carter. Going back in history, consider Abe Lincoln, Eleanor Roosevelt, Beatrix Potter, Helen Keller, and Albert Einstein (who flunked high school math), all of whom benefited from home education.

The longer you homeschool your child, the more it can feel like the most natural continuation of the positive, responsive parenting you have been doing in the preschool years. It tends to make institutional schooling seem rather irrelevant to life. If home education is not an option for you, you can still keep in mind the limited role that school can play in your child's total education, and you can continue your central role as parent with vigor and confidence.

Index

About the Author

A family therapist since 1985, **Randy Rolfe** has a son and daughter, ages 19 and 17, respectively. She is known worldwide as a lecturer on parenting, family communication, and natural health. Her previous books include *You Can Postpone Anything but Love: Expanding Our Potential as Parents; Adult Children Raising Children: Sparing Your Child from Codependency Without Being Perfect Yourself;* and *The Affirmations Book for Sharing: Daily Meditations for Couples,* coauthored with her husband.

Randy grew up in suburban Philadelphia, traveling to a different part of the world each summer with her parents, brother, and sister. Inspired by what she saw, she studied international relations at the University of Pennsylvania and graduated Phi Beta Kappa, with social science honors. After study at the University of Virginia law school, she graduated with honors from Villanova Law School and joined a large Philadelphia law firm, one of its first two female lawyers.

Randy married her college sweetheart, also a lawyer, and in 1976 they declared independence from the dual-career yuppie track they were on. They bought a tumble-down homestead in the

Adirondack foothills, rebuilt it, raised their food, and fought for a clean environment, native rights, and natural health freedoms.

They gave birth and began parenting in their adopted, family-centered community. They were caught in a financial crunch as recession hit rural New York, and the family returned to rural Chester County, Pennsylvania. There Randy wrote and self-published her first parenting book. It was well received, and she founded the Institute for Creative Solutions to counsel parents. Meanwhile, she and her husband began homeschooling their children to have more time, influence, and fun with them.

Randy is a popular TV guest therapist, appearing over 40 times on national talk shows including *Sally Jessy Raphael, Montel Williams,* and *Geraldo Rivera,* as well as appearing on radio and in print. She has lectured in Canada and Russia, as well as nationwide.

Dr. Robert E. Kay (author of the foreword) graduated from Tufts University Medical School and had his psychiatric training at Walter Reed General Hospital. Following his military service, he served as Medical Director of The Center for Child Guidance and was a board member of The School in Rose Valley, Pennsylvania. Father of three, he works with children, adolescents, adults, and families. He has written numerous articles on interviewing techniques, child rearing, the American school system, and the teaching of reading. In recent years he has been greatly involved with the homeschooling and home education movements and has presented his ideas on radio and television as well as in court.